BLACK WOMEN IN
UNITED STATES HISTORY

Editor

DARLENE CLARK HINE

Associate Editors

ELSA BARKLEY BROWN

TIFFANY R. L. PATTERSON

LILLIAN S. WILLIAMS

Research Assistant

EARNESTINE JENKINS

A CARLSON PUBLISHING SERIES

See the end of this volume for a comprehensive
guide to this sixteen-volume set.

Jane Edna Hunter

A CASE STUDY OF BLACK
LEADERSHIP, 1910-1950

Adrienne Lash Jones

PREFACE BY DARLENE CLARK HINE

CARLSON
Publishing Inc

BROOKLYN, NEW YORK, 1990

See the end of this volume for a comprehensive guide to the sixteen-volume set of which this is Volume Twelve.

R00769 70689

Library of Congress Cataloging-in-Publication Data

Jones, Adrienne Lash.
    Jane Edna Hunter : a case study of Black leadership, 1910-1950 /
    Adrienne Lash Jones ; preface by Darlene Clark Hine.
        p.   cm. — (Black women in United States history ; v. 12)
    Includes bibliographical references.
    ISBN 0-926019-18-X
    1. Hunter, Jane Edna, 1882-1950. 2. Afro-Americans—Ohio–
    –Cleveland—Biography. 3. Afro-American women—Ohio—Cleveland–
    –Biography. 4. Afro-American leadership—Ohio—Cleveland–
    –History—20th century. 5. Social settlements—Ohio—Cleveland–
    –History—20th century. 6. Cleveland (Ohio)—Social Conditions.
    I. Title. II. Series
    E185.86.B543   vol. 12
    [F499.C69N4]
    973'.0496073 s—dc20
    [977.1'320049607302]
    [B]   90-1394

Typographic design: Julian Waters

Typeface: Bitstream ITC Galliard

The index to this book was created using NL Cindex, a scholarly indexing program from the Newberry Library.

Printed on acid-free, 250-year-life paper.

Manufactured in the United States of America.

It is with deep gratitude and love that I dedicate this work to my late mother, Thelma Clement Lash Spaulding, Ph.D., who taught me by example the joy of seeking knowledge; and to my father, Wiley I. Lash, who never ever let me consider blackness or femaleness to be a limitation.

Contents

List of Illustrations

All photographs are courtesy of the Phillis Wheatley Association, unless otherwise noted.

Preface

Adrienne Lash Jones's excellent biography of a remarkable Black woman leader, Jane Edna Hunter of Cleveland, Ohio is a model of precisely the kinds of studies that are needed in order for the field of Black Women's History to flourish. Grounded on meticulous research and written with stylistic grace, this book provides a penetrating glimpse into the process of Black institution building in a northern urban center over the course of the first half of the twentieth century.

Jones traces Hunter's rise from the South Carolina plantation where she was born in 1882 to her migration to Cleveland in 1905 and details the difficulties she encountered in trying to create and sustain the Phillis Wheatley Home and Association for working Black girls. While the broad contours of Hunter's life resemble the haunting example of Booker T. Washington's *Up From Slavery*, Jones has refused to make of Hunter a one-dimensional character or a Black female Horatio Alger. Instead Jones has painted a portrait of a complex, determined, ambitious, autonomy-seeking Black woman whose trek towards dignity and service in behalf of her community compels attention.

Although Hunter had completed nursing training at Charleston Hospital and Nursing School and at the Hampton Institute in Hampton, Virginia, the northern variety of racial discrimination erected almost insuperable barriers in her search for work and a place to live. Loneliness, rejection, and frustration punctuated her first few years in Cleveland. In 1911 Hunter called together a core of similarly disillusioned and dejected Black domestics to discuss the establishment of a Working Girls' Home Association. Eventually it was renamed the Phillis Wheatley Home Association.

The Phillis Wheatley Home was patterned after, with significant differences, the segregated Young Women's Christian Association. It provided shelter, recreation space, training in domestic arts, employment opportunities, and security for thousands of young migrating Black women. In 1927 the Association moved from an apartment building to a new eleven-story facility. It was one of the earliest and most successful social service agencies for Blacks in Cleveland. Indeed, the Phillis Wheatley Association became the largest independent facility of its kind in the country, and a model for many similar facilities and organizations established under the auspices of the National Association of Colored Women in a number of northern Communities.

The establishment of the Phillis Wheatley Home, it should be pointed out, did not meet with universal acclaim. As Jones documents, class tensions and internal group conflict quickly erupted in Cleveland's Black community. Some members of the Black middle class opposed the establishment of the Home on the grounds that it was an all-Black institution and thus threatened to retard racial integration. Hunter endured the criticisms from Blacks as she adroitly cultivated strong support from "the right white people." One of the many contributions this volume makes is its graphic depiction of the dilemmas faced by the Black leadership in northern urban communities.

Jones's history of the Phillis Wheatley Home and of the woman who created it enlarges our understanding of "women's institutions" and "women's culture," while shedding light on the impact of race and class in the construction of gender conventions within the Black community. Hunter's instrumental role in the preservation and survival of the Black community made her a significant agent for social change. As we view Black women through the lens of Hunter's life, we see them working to provide such basic community services as hospital care, relief for the poor and homeless, vocational education for young adults, pre-school facilities for children of working mothers, and homes for the aged.

This important book in Carlson Publishing's sixteen-volume series, *Black Women in United States History*, ably demonstrates the vitality of Black women's culture as reflected in the network of clubs, sororities, women's auxiliaries to fraternal orders, and church organizations. Jones uncovers the strategies Black women employed to deal with gender issues in a society devoted to preserving racial and class inequalities. In making this work accessible to scholars, students, and researchers Carlson Publishing has greatly facilitated the working out of the Black Women's History research agenda. I am delighted to be a part of this exciting and useful project.

Darlene Clark Hine
Michigan State University

Acknowledgments

The renaissance of interest in Black Studies and Women's Studies, with reinterpretations of American culture and history by the scholarly community, has significantly changed our perceptions of the importance of those experiences in the shaping of this country. However, black women have not shared in this renaissance. Perhaps it is because the methodologies for reinterpretation have not sufficiently changed to include the experiences of a group which has suffered the double oppression of blackness and femaleness, and thus does not fit neatly into either one of these categories. Thus, the study of black women presents a challenge to reexamine the black experience *and* the female experience in this country, and to attempt to create a different focus which can add a new depth to the study of American civilization. My belief in the importance of recording and reinterpreting this largely untapped reservoir of experiences provided the basic motivation for this study.

The decision to re-enter the academic sphere, after my child rearing years, was directly related to my desire to understand and to articulate the experiences of women, who, though neglected by traditional historians, had always played significant roles in the black community. Having grown up on several black college campuses, I was keenly aware of the enormous influence of women in the church, in the academic community, in social service institutions, and in the neighborhoods. Yet their contributions must be analyzed and interpreted if we are to truly understand either intra-racial or interracial relationships in cities and towns across the nation. Thus, what started as a hobby, the study of the black female experience, became a life-long pursuit.

There is no way that I can truly express my appreciation for the marvelous support which kept me on course during the time that I was preparing this manuscript. I was blessed with the encouragement and help of countless friends who patiently listened to my frustrations as I set about to "look" for

Jane Hunter, and ended up "finding" myself. These brothers and sisters were wonderful cheerleaders when the going got rough.

The American Studies faculty at Case Western Reserve University, including Gene Wise, Steven Brobeck, Park Goist, and Department Chairman Morrell Heald, were always encouraging, challenging, and understanding. I commend their commitment to interdisciplinary study, which allowed the flexibility I needed to pursue my goal. At the same time they kept me focused on the need to give thoughtful and serious consideration to materials which describe and analyze the American experience. Most of all, they helped me to understand the value of developing the skill to express myself in writing. Also to Professors Curtis Wilson and Butler Jones at Cleveland State University I owe a special debt for their willingness to share their expertise in black history and the sociology of the black community.

Among my community of academic support, fellow graduate students in the American Studies program were especially encouraging. Through them I learned to respect and celebrate the diversity of American culture, and to appreciate the worth of my own unique perspectives.

Most importantly, my interest in women's history was stimulated, nurtured and encouraged by a very special academic advisor and untiring friend, Linda K. Kirby. Her excellent instruction and advice, and her insightful critique of my work during six years made me keenly aware of the responsibility one must accept before challenging the validity of "traditional" methods, sources, and assumptions. Her open-mindedness was an invaluable model for my personal and academic development.

I would also like to acknowledge the excellent cooperation of the staff at the Western Reserve Historical Society, with special thanks to Olivia Martin, head of the Black History Archives. Also, the very gracious staff at the Phillis Wheatley Association, who were always helpful and accommodating, deserve special commendation. Mrs. Tommy Patty, executive director of the Wheatley Association, was very generous with resources, time and encouragement, and I am very grateful.

I have reserved the most important thank-you's for last, because they truly come from the bottom of my heart. To my three wonderful sons, Darryl, Derek, and Brian, I am eternally thankful. Their belief in me provides continuing inspiration. As the fathers of the next generation, they deserve to have a deep understanding of the history of their foremothers as well as forefathers, so that the race can continue to celebrate the value of each of its members.

And to my beloved husband, L. Morris Jones, M.D., whose flexibility, patience, kindness, understanding, and love have nurtured the wife, mother, student, and blossoming scholar, goes my deepest debt of gratitude.

Adrienne Lash Jones
January 16, 1990

ONE

Black Cleveland: Origins and Development of a Community

The period between 1877 and 1901 has been described by one author as the "Nadir" for black people in American history.[1] Following the weak presidencies of Rutherford B. Hayes, Chester Arthur, Benjamin Harrison, and William McKinley; the indifferent presidency of Grover Cleveland; a quarter century of compromise with white supremacist laws in Southern states; rampant violence against Southern blacks; and indifference to or justification for denial of the rights of blacks by the Northern power structure, the plight of blacks in America could have seemed overwhelmingly difficult at best.

In the face of these distractions, however, black Americans struggled to find their own solutions to questions of survival for the race. Their overwhelming resolution was to become equal citizens and to participate fully in the social, economic, and political systems. Strategies to achieve acceptance and equality varied with locality, personalities, population composition, and availability of economic resources. It is the variety of circumstances and people which provides numerous opportunities for study, leading to a better understanding of the history of urban America, in general, and the black community, specifically.

William E. B. Du Bois, prominent black scholar of American life, ushered in the twentieth century with a succinct warning to the nation:

> The problem of the Twentieth Century is the problem of the color line, the question as to how far differences of race, which show themselves chiefly in the color of the skin and the texture of the hair, are going to be made, hereafter, the basis of denying to over half the world the right of sharing to their utmost ability the opportunities and privileges of modern civilization.[2]

His accurate assessment of the depth of the nation's most pressing issue foretold the coming struggles, based on color, which would plague a society

1

undergoing tremendous and rapid change. As Americans moved from farm and village to industrial urban complexes, indeed the problem of color became an entrenched part of the nation's identity. Residential patterns in newly forming cities became racially delineated, resulting often in burgeoning black ghettos, in already-deteriorating city sectors. Employment opportunities in newly industrializing urban complexes followed ethnic and racial policies which excluded black workers from skilled occupations.[3] Poverty became identified as a part of the stereotype for blacks, as they struggled to survive in cities which were essentially inhospitable to their presence. The century opened with a difficult heritage in race relations, at best.

In sharp contrast to the national picture of nineteenth-century race relations, Cleveland, Ohio, sloppily sprawled along the shores of Lake Erie, was a city destined to become a near perfect example of the twentieth century's failure to successfully resolve the complex issues of race and racism. Unencumbered with many of the nineteenth century's residual effects of massive black migration to the cities of the Northeast, Cleveland entered the twentieth century with a heritage of New England liberal racial attitudes, which had fostered forceful activity during the abolitionist period before the Civil War, a reputation for fair treatment of blacks, liberal civil rights legislation (which was fairly enforced), and, most importantly, a minuscule black population of less than 6,000, or 1.6 percent of the city's total.[4]

Throughout the nineteenth century and into the twentieth, the city experienced exceptional growth, largely due to its strategic location at the northern terminus of the Erie Canal (completed in 1832), which connected the Ohio River and Lake Erie. This important waterway, along with the completion of railroad linkages to New York and Cincinnati, ensured Cleveland's commercial dominance of northern Ohio.[5] Total population of the city grew from 17,034 in 1850 to a phenomenal 381,768 by 1900.[6]

In contrast, the city's black population grew at a much slower rate. Blacks comprised under 2 percent of the total until the census of 1920, when they accounted for over 4 percent (3,035 in 1900 to 34,451 in 1920).[7] The small but growing black community ran counter to almost all stereotypes about black urban life. Contrary to sociological descriptions of black migrants before the 1940s as having a higher proportion of females to males and having female-dominated households, Cleveland migrants consistently maintained a larger number of males, with male-headed households. Also, large families were clearly the exception rather than the rule, with census statistics indicating that in 1880, for example, 68.4 percent of all black households in the county contained four persons or fewer.[8] Black families resided mainly on the city's east side near the Central Haymarket, but, prior to at least 1880, most lived in single-family dwellings, well integrated among the faster-growing ethnic populations. Cleveland newspapers often boasted of the lack of segregation in public facilities such as the schools, lecture halls, theaters, hotels, and restaurants.[9]

The economic status of blacks in nineteenth-century Cleveland was better than in any other Northern city, surpassed in the Southern states only by New Orleans. According to the 1870 census, the average value of the real estate owned by black property holders in Cuyahoga County was $2,350; the average wealth per person (real estate and personal property) for the entire black population was $198. While the average annual income was $500 for most workers, the income of blacks was impressive. Black citizens in Cleveland averaged, for example, approximately one-third more than blacks in the neighboring cities of Cincinnati and Pittsburgh.[10] Occupations ranged from 1.3 percent professionals, to 26.2 percent skilled workers, 16.8 percent semi-skilled, 25.9 percent unskilled, and 22.9 percent in domestic service. These occupational categories compare favorably with occupation statistics for foreign-born whites in the same period.[11]

Beginning with the city's first permanent black resident, George Peake, who settled in what is now Lakewood and owned a one-hundred-acre tract of land, there were many black success stories. Black businessmen and professionals offered their services to integrated clientele and seem to have been patronized with little note of their color. Especially lucrative were personal service businesses such as barbering, tailoring, and catering. To be sure, these occupations followed closely the domestic and personal services rendered by servants or slaves to masters, but nevertheless, blacks found these skills highly marketable. There were also examples of less traditional opportunities. One black college graduate, William Howard Day, who came to Cleveland in 1847 after graduation from Oberlin, became compositor and local editor of one of the city's newspapers, the *Cleveland Daily True Democrat* (1851–52).[12] Another, Madison Tilley, made a small fortune as an excavating contractor and land speculator.[13]

Black citizens also played an active role in Cleveland politics during the nineteenth century. The question of the black vote in the North was seriously debated prior to the Civil War, and Cleveland blacks were active in seeking the ballot. Ohio history records a Constitutional Convention in 1802 which denied blacks the privilege of the vote and the right to testify in court against white persons. It also declared them ineligible to hold public office or to serve in the state militia.[14] Further, a series of Black Codes excluded them from jury service and public education. However, the prevailing sentiment found in the Western Reserve seems parallel to that of the New England settlers who predominated in the early century: militant abolitionism and a tendency to berate the state codes against blacks.[15]

A well-organized northern Ohio underground railroad provided refuge and cover for thousands of fugitives making their way to Canada, even after passage of the Fugitive Slave Act of 1850.[16] Black participation in the anti-slavery movement in Cleveland was vigorous, including meetings, state and national conventions, and a Vigilante Committee. Much energy was directed from the small black community to lobbying for repeal of Ohio's Black Laws and attainment of full citizenship rights. Blacks successfully gained the support of many liberal whites in the area, working behind the scenes until finally Ohio ratified the nation's Fifteenth Amendment in 1867.

In 1881, the first black state legislator from Cleveland was elected. John Patterson Green, a lawyer, had first been nominated by the Republican County Convention in 1877, but he was defeated in that election by sixty-seven votes. He served two terms in the legislature (1881–83 and 1889–91) and was elevated to the state senate in 1892. In between Green's two terms in the legislature, another black man served two consecutive terms. Jere A. Brown, a lifetime Republican politician, served from 1886 to 1889. Two other blacks, Harry C. Smith, editor of the city's black newspaper, and William Clifford, lifetime Republican activist, were elected to serve in the state's 71st General Assembly (1894–95).

In all four cases, nomination and election resulted from a liberal white voting population, controlled by the Republican politics which dominated the area. The black voting population was much too small to have represented a significant voting bloc.[17] Election of four blacks to state offices probably best symbolized the extent of racial liberalism which prevailed among Cleveland voters in the nineteenth century.

However, the examples of race cooperation and white liberalism cited above cannot outweigh other important factors essential in maintaining racial harmony during the nineteenth century. Most obvious was the loyalty of the small black voting population to the Republican Party, and perhaps most obscure was the fact that the black community was highly organized during the century. An overview of both factors can help to illustrate the importance of each.

Republican politics in many ways reflected control of the city's economic and political affairs by the wealthy elite. For example, during the last decade of the nineteenth and the first decade of the twentieth centuries, millionaire Republican boss Marcus A. Hanna held tight control over the city's political machinery through a network of patronage in return for favors which effectively bought allegiance from Cleveland's voters. The loyalty of blacks to the Republican Party dated back to its inception as the party which favored the abolition of slavery and under whose administration this mission was fulfilled. Political activism on the part of Cleveland's black leadership sometimes was key to Hanna's influence at the state and national level, since the majority of black voters nationwide were loyal to the Republican Party. More specifically, it was the organizational skills of a black Cleveland barber, who was able to convince the black delegates at the National Republican Convention of 1892 to support the Hanna bid for party control, which eventually led to the election of Hanna's presidential candidate, William McKinley. George Myers, the barber, then became a key figure in national Republican politics among blacks and the dispenser of political patronage among local blacks. His influence, especially among the city's black elite, provided an important link between the upper echelons of both races.[18]

The city's nineteenth-century black population, while geographically dispersed, was a cohesive, organized group which on the one hand took an active role in the professional, business, social, and political life of the city, while at the same time participating in all-black social and civic organizations. Leadership was assumed by the more educated and affluent, who, through the black newspaper, political clubs, social organizations, and church activity, were visible to the majority of blacks and to the white leadership. This group also was often called upon by whites to articulate the sentiments and concerns of the entire black population.

There is no question of the strong integrationist orientation of the leadership group of that era. This was evidenced by their rhetoric demanding political and social inclusion in the life of the city, even though there was often an implied acceptance, on their part, of some of the prevailing Darwinist notions related to the lack of readiness of the majority of the race to participate. The notion of "racial uplift," which continued to be a dominant theme for blacks well into the twentieth century, suggested group unreadiness regardless of individual achievements. A strong, unavoidable identification of the elite with *all* race members seemed to have the positive result of making the community cohesive and manifested itself among blacks by a spirit of helping one another for the benefit of the whole race.

The first record of organization among black Clevelanders dates to 1830, when a small prayer group formed the foundation for the African Methodist Episcopal Church which became St. John's. Their first building was acquired in 1848, with a membership of fifteen. By 1878, membership had grown to 350.[19] This mission was followed by four others of different denominations after 1860. Records show that prior to the mid-1860s blacks were integrated and active in white churches. However, with the founding of a black Congregational Church in 1864, there was an exodus to all-black congregations. By the end of the century, only a few of the black elite still attended predominantly white churches.[20] Although it has been estimated that membership in the five black churches represented only approximately 40 percent of the black population, their mere existence indicated both the decline of institutional support for race integration as well as the trend toward black self-direction.

Civic organization among blacks outside of white-dominated anti-slavery and colonization societies began in 1832, when John Malvin, an ex-slave, called together a group of black women and men to organize a school.[21] Ohio's Black Laws at that time prohibited integrated public schools and did not provide money or means for the education of black children. Although support for the school seems to have been difficult for the tiny black population, the group succeeded in demonstrating a strong desire for education, and subsequently, after a change in the state's laws, blacks were fully integrated into the city's new public school system.

An outgrowth of the school organization appears to have been the Young Men's Union Society in 1839.[22] An advertisement in the *Herald and Gazette Newspaper* indicated that the society was formed "for the moral, mental, and political improvement of its membership."[23] Activities ranged from sponsorship of a public reading room, through a lyceum series for anti-slavery debate and discussion, to active participation in anti-slavery state and national conventions for blacks.[24]

As the black population increased, so did the number of organizations in the black community. Fraternal lodges began in 1855, with formation of the Mason's Eureka Lodge. Although two black men (both of very light complexion) belonged to white Masonic lodges, they were the exceptions.[25] By 1910, most national fraternal orders were well represented in the black community, including several chapters of the Masons, Odd Fellows, and Elks (all established before 1880), and the True Reformers, Mysterious Ten, Good Samaritans, and Knights of Pythias (established after 1890).[26] Some orders had white counterparts, but many were components of national black orders. They were sometimes complemented by female counterparts, with membership composed of wives, mothers, daughters, and sisters of members of the lodges.

Fraternal lodges, along with political organizations such as the Sixth Ward Union Republican Club (active before 1870), the East End Afro-American Club of the 21st Ward (organized in 1900), and the Attucks Republican Club (organized in 1907), provided social interaction among elite and middle-class blacks. They also represented opportunities for building leadership in the community, as well as a reliable support network for politicians and community activists. Considering the small black population, these organizations very likely included persons of many diverse backgrounds and levels of educational and financial achievement, and supplied a means for dispensing job opportunity information, political patronage, political support (for black and white candidates), and professional contacts. Thus, these formal organizations provided a valuable internal structure for the black community, as well as accessibility to the white political and social systems, for blacks, through formal and informal organizational ties.

A look at census statistics between 1890 and 1910 reveals the beginnings of a shift from a somewhat progressive liberal racial climate in Cleveland to an interesting preview of the problems which were to beset the city in the twentieth century. Between 1890 and 1900, the black population doubled from 2,989 to 5,988, maintaining a proportion of 1.5 percent of the total population. During this time, blacks lived in every one of the then forty-two wards.[27] Daily contacts between black professionals and businessmen, who were located in the city's downtown area, and the wealthy whites, who patronized their services, helped to maintain an atmosphere of congenial relationships for the most part, despite the noticeable acceleration of all-black organizations and all-black church membership. Blacks in every economic and social echelon understood the unspoken parameters inside which they were expected to remain. These boundaries confined them to a primarily black social life, with notable exceptions such as Charles Chesnutt's active membership in white literary and social clubs and John P. Green's friendship with the Rockefeller family. Also, job expectations revolved around personal service businesses such as catering, barber shops, dressmaking, and tailoring. A few doctors, lawyers, schoolteachers, personal service personnel for very wealthy whites, and entrepreneurs comprised the leadership of the black elite class, while the major portion of black workers were in domestic service and unskilled-labor jobs. At the turn of the century, there was only one black man, Walter C. Wright, secretary to the president of the Nickel Plate Railroad, in a bona fide white-collar job in industry.[28] Thus, the leadership class was almost entirely dependent upon white patronage and clientele for their livelihood.

The belief of the black elite in the inevitability of race integration was based on personal experiences which included a perception of acceptance by whites for those among them who most closely resembled the white middle-class life style which was held to be "traditional American." The unskilled and uneducated were constantly prodded, through race newspapers and in churches, to strive to become educated, to save their money, to purchase homes, to vote, and to lead good Christian lives as a means for individual as well as race progress.[29]

Throughout the nineteenth century, the city's most articulate blacks disparaged any hint of race separation.[30] They reinforced wholeheartedly the notion that the best could rise to the top and gain acceptance in an integrated society. Personal gains were touted as gains for the race, as leaders struggled to overcome the prevailing race stereotypes which abounded. In the period when blacks were being systematically moved to the position of "second-class citizenship" throughout the nation, black Clevelanders basked in the passage of a model Ohio anti-lynching law which was initiated by black Cleveland legislator Harry Smith.[31] Perhaps, however, there was some evidence of a crack in the facade of liberalism in the Western Reserve.

Notwithstanding Republican political control, which tended to be racially liberal, sentiment against Republicanism can also be traced throughout the century. The *Cleveland Plain Dealer*, for example, offered editorial commentary against racial equality and in favor of the Democratic Party's support of slavery and later racial conservatism.[32] This view, while generally unpopular during the nineteenth century, gained increasing favor in the early part of the twentieth century. It was the forewarning of a national trend to ostracize blacks from the country's social, economic, and political mainstream. This attitude was most certainly harbored by a minor, but nonetheless important, Cleveland core. Also, in the pages of the *Cleveland Gazette*, experiences of a disturbing nature were reported. Reports of segregation and general mistreatment of blacks in public facilities such as restaurants, department stores, pools, parks, and theaters became more frequent news. By

1900, for example, twelve civil rights suits against restaurant owners who discriminated against black customers were in the Cleveland courts.[33]

Concurrent with the shift in Cleveland's racial climate during the first decade of the century, a national articulation of a shift in focus for solutions to race relations came with the ascendancy of Booker T. Washington to prominence. Washington, ex-slave principal of Tuskegee Institute in Alabama, suggested in a major speech at the Atlanta Exposition in 1895 that blacks should discontinue their stress on political activism and social equality, and instead should strive for economic gains through hard work and struggle. He promised that blacks could gain eventual acceptance into the mainstream of American life, when they had achieved economic success and had earned the respect of whites. This differed from the ideology of prior black leaders. They had always tied hard work and Christian values to political activism and a demand for equality. Washington's shift in focus for race progress equated economic advancement with equality and represented acceptance of the current racial status until such time as the race had become ready to assume equal citizenship rights.[34]

Interpretations of Washington's blueprint for race success became guideposts in both the South and the North. For whites, he represented affirmation that blacks were not yet ready to assume equal participation in the economic, political, and social order of the country. Southern whites found his emphasis on the Southern agricultural experience as the perfect base for black economic achievement helpful to their need to retain black workers in an economically depressed industry dependent upon cheap labor. Whites in the North were relieved of their responsibility to live up to their professions of race acceptance, as Washington shifted the blame for lack of progress to blacks themselves, who were not ready for inclusion.

For blacks, Washington personally represented the ultimate example of race progress. His slave birth and gradual rise to power provided a black version of the currently popular Horatio Alger myth. His reinforcement of middle-class values, enhanced with economic platitudes, satisfied the need for a road map for success. His deemphasis of education also justified to the majority their inability to obtain an adequate education under the segregated systems of the South and their subsequent inability to fit into the Northern union and labor systems. His skillful manipulation of popular symbols and myths like the gospel of wealth and the doctrines of Social Darwinism enhanced his effectiveness among whites and blacks alike.[35] Exhortations encouraging pride and cooperation among blacks essentially removed blacks from the doors of white institutions (public and private) and discouraged insistence that they should be included. Traditional black leaders, who for the most part did not agree with Washington, found it virtually impossible to stem his wave of influence as the chosen black spokesman to the nation.

Despite opposition to Washington's platform by Cleveland's traditional black leadership, the new race ideology gradually intruded into the city because of three important concurrent circumstances. The first important change was a shift in the geographic origins of black migrants to Cleveland. The second change was a gradual move from the traditional leadership in the black community, who were dependent upon white patronage for economic survival, to a new group whose primary economic base was the black community itself. The third change was an increasingly hostile national and local racial climate. An examination of each of these circumstantial changes can help to re-create the scenario which in some ways helps to explain twentieth-century race relations in the city.

In 1900, of all non-white residents of the city, 38.4 percent had been born in Ohio and 35.6 percent had migrated from the upper South and border states, with most of those born in Virginia.[36] The high proportion born or raised in the North found it easier to be assimilated into the general life of the community. Their still-small numbers and their relative dispersal into predominantly white residential communities made their presence fairly inconspicuous, especially when compared with the much larger influx of the foreign-born.[37]

Leaders tended to have been educated in Northern (mostly Cleveland) schools. They were well known to the white establishment through their jobs, the services they provided to whites, and by virtue of their integrated education in schools in the area. They expected, and often demanded, full integration into Cleveland's economic, political, and institutional mainstream. Ohio's Civil Rights Bill of 1884, which prohibited discrimination in public facilities, was their insurance. During the nineteenth century, the courts almost always upheld the rights of black citizens in civil suits, often awarding monetary compensation for acts of discrimination.[38] Integration had been experienced by the leaders, and was seen to be inevitable for the majority of blacks who were willing to conform to traditional or conventional behavior and value standards.

The next decade witnessed an important shift in race relations. Even though their numbers held to 1.5 percent of the total, the black population increased to 8,448. By the 1910 census, 6,000 blacks lived west of East 55th

Street in a fairly confined strip bordered by Euclid Avenue to the north and Woodland Avenue to the south.[39] New job opportunities during the decade were confined to the unskilled level in the growing steel and manufacturing industries. Traditional service business opportunities dwindled as European immigrants flooded the city and became more favored to fill the jobs formerly relegated to black workers. Unionization of such skilled trades as carpentry, brick masonry, floor laying, painting, wallpaper hanging, waiting tables, and barbering increasingly shut black workers out. Blacks were also excluded from skilled factory jobs.[40] Rationalizations for exclusion of black workers ranged from protection of white clients who feared black workers in their homes to the refusal of white workers to socialize with blacks in union rituals and events.[41] This followed a national trend which viewed black workers as incapable of work more sophisticated than agriculture and increasingly tied blacks to crimes of sex and violence. Industry favored immigrant European labor, and Cleveland, a major immigrant host city, had no scarcity of new arrivals looking for work.

In a comparison of census statistics between 1870 and 1910, Kenneth Kusmer noted a decline of black male employment in the skilled trades, from 31.7 percent of all black males in Cleveland in 1870 to 11.1 percent by 1910. He cited three major explanations for the decline: first, a 4 percent decline in the proportion of all workers engaged in those trades during the decades preceding World War I; second, a sharp decline in the number of blacks among the older trades of the nineteenth century, such as blacksmiths, shoemakers, and trades related to carriage transportation; and third, complete exclusion of blacks from the newer specialized trades such as cabinetmaking, typesetting, electrical wiring, and plumbing.[42] While blacks fared better in federal and municipal jobs because of the use of standardized tests, the accompanying standard procedure of excluding black employment in areas such as the police and fire departments severely retarded the growth of a substantial middle class. With approximately three-tenths of the black force locked into low-paying service and unskilled labor jobs, a steady decline in skilled and semi-skilled jobs, and exclusion from white-collar and skilled municipal and industrial jobs, blacks in Cleveland experienced a sharp decline in percentage of property ownership and in residential mobility. Foreign-born immigrants quickly surpassed blacks in all categories of economic progress between 1870 and 1910.[43] The black position at the lowest rung of Cleveland's socio-economic ladder solidified.

Between 1910 and 1920, the proportion of blacks in Cleveland who had been born in Ohio fell from 35.7 percent to 16.9 percent. Migrants into the city from the upper South and border states represented 31.2 percent.[44] The new migration, which accelerated considerably during World War I, also accelerated the process of residential segregation. Black migrants faced substantial housing discrimination, and thus crowded into neighborhoods which already had enclaves of black families. In 1910, no census tract in the city was more than 25 percent black, but ten years later, two tracts had exceeded 50 percent.[45] Residential segregation also led to separate education in neighborhood schools, which were increasingly identifiable by racial composition. The Southern system of racial segregation by law had conditioned the newcomers to acceptance of separation by race as the norm. The Southern political system had by that time all but excluded blacks in most states, so that separation by race, while disappointing to blacks coming from the South, was a familiar condition.

As the black population became more visible in the old sixteenth ward, a business strip developed which was geared to meet the needs of the new residents. Black doctors, dentists, and lawyers began to locate in spaces convenient to their black clientele. Black barbers, forced out of their downtown locations as Europeans replaced them, began to open shops in the heart of the growing black community. New entrepreneurial businesses such as funeral homes, cafes, realty companies, and recreation outlets grew in direct proportion to the increase in black population. The new black professional and entrepreneur was likely to be relatively independent of white economic support. Race cooperation became redefined from cohesiveness to force whites to respond to the institutional needs of blacks, toward an urgency for blacks to support their own race's businesses and to find ways to provide needed institutional support.[46] Even Harry Smith, editor of the *Gazette* and a leader of the more traditional elite, began to urge blacks to "support your own."

Perhaps the best evidence of the shift in ideology was the organization in 1905 of the Cleveland Board of Trade, a group of black professionals and businessmen. Although, as stated earlier, the black community had been organized in various configurations since 1830, the groups had traditionally emphasized Republican politics, social activities, and church and fraternal membership; and, as in the instance of the Young Men's Union Society in 1832, organization had been a means of interacting with the white community as a cohesive body to seek support for issues relating to blacks.

Leadership in almost every case had come from the tradition of integration and usually represented the old elite families. The Board of Trade was definitely a break from the old tradition. Membership lists included only Jacob Reed, co-owner with a white man of a downtown market, from the old group. The two sons of John P. Green, former state senator, are the only others with recognizable connections to the old group. Newcomers to the business community, providing business and services to the growing black community, made up the membership roles. The group's stated purpose was "to promote the advancement of Negro business locally."[47] Their affiliation in 1906 with the National Business League, a Booker T. Washington–sponsored organization, indicated the race-solidarity movement among new black leaders. Membership in the Cleveland Board of Trade and its successor, the Cleveland Association of Colored Men (a somewhat broader-based club), also represented the changing racial climate in Cleveland, a climate which was increasingly hostile to its black population.

The newer leaders exhibited a stronger tendency to accept segregation and discrimination as at least a temporary condition to which blacks must adjust. Their support of Washington and his vision of eventual integration through demonstration of the race's economic success was best exemplified in the slogan on the masthead of a new, pro-Washington black weekly, the *Cleveland Journal*: "Labor Conquers All Things." Among regular features were articles about local blacks who had "pulled themselves up from poverty" through hard work and sacrifice and were now successful citizens, owning homes, and living in harmony with the middle-class standards of the time. Self-made leaders provided a model for a philosophy of self-help for the new black community.[48]

The shift in occupation and ideology of the leadership and upper class of the black community was representative of the change in race relations for the majority of the small black population in Cleveland in the late nineteenth and early twentieth centuries. While the leadership implored the working class to work hard, save, and live up to middle-class standards, the reality of the lives of the largest number of blacks increasingly seemed doomed to a narrow existence where mere survival, by necessity, was their ultimate goal.

Shifting racial ideologies, job opportunity gains and losses, and population expansion also made differences in the roles of the women in the black community. Expansion or contraction of the traditional role of black women in their own community can be compared with concurrently shifting roles of white women, especially the economically similar foreign-born, to illuminate the effects of change in the black community.

Previously discussed shifts in the attitudes of whites toward blacks had a profound impact on the socio-economic capabilities of black families. One result of the changes was a shift in status of large numbers of black women from homemakers to employed contributors to the families' resources. Although black women were not spared harsh treatment because of their sex during slavery, studies of blacks after slavery indicate that, where economically feasible, the women were likely to work in their homes, much like their white counterparts. Mass withdrawal of black women from the fields following slavery significantly undermined the labor pool which had been available in the South. In fact, following the emancipation of the slaves, it was considered dishonorable for a black man to let his wife and children work in the fields.[49] Black women and men were determined to establish stable homes after the ravages of slave life, with its history of broken families.

Education of black women and men was seen as the only real means for providing a better life for future generations. Most often the education of women in the black community was discussed in the context of their roles as nurturers of the family. Dr. Alexander Crummell, a well-known black minister of the nineteenth century, wrote in 1883, "A true civilization can only . . . be attained when the life of woman is reached."[50] Black women had their own contribution to make in uplifting the race.

Early records of Cleveland's black community give some indication of several different roles played by women in the nineteenth century. A letter dated November 20, 1857, from William Wells Brown, noted slave fugitive and author, to William Lloyd Garrison's abolitionist newspaper, the *Liberator*, described Cleveland's black population. He mentioned a Mr. Oliver, owner of a store on Erie Street (East 9th), whose daughters were "highly educated and would grace any drawing room in the land." This was true despite their origins in Richmond, Virginia, a slave state. A Mr. Morris from North Carolina was noted as a fine tailor. His wife "would do honor to any society in which she might appear." A Mrs. Parker was described as manager of her husband's provision store (at what is now Central Avenue and 30th Street), while he was employed on the Mississippi River. She was said to possess "goaheadativeness" to a far greater extent than most women, "and would be a fortune to any business man." Perhaps most interesting is the fact that the only two teachers mentioned were women. One, Miss Allston, was a teacher of music, being "very proficient on the guitar and piano." A Miss Stanley was a "teacher in one of the day schools, and her education places her in the front rank of her profession."[51]

The descriptions found in Brown's letter help illustrate that black women were accepted not only in the traditional home setting, but in business and teaching as well. Their education and accomplishments seem remarkable at a time when most blacks were still enslaved and few women, black or white, were being educated. Brown's comments do not indicate that he found them remarkable because they were women, but rather because they were black. The emphasis on race accomplishment rather than that they were exceptional women should be considered an authoritative commentary about black life. Brown was well-traveled, visiting practically every community in the North to promote the anti-slavery cause. One can surmise from this letter, as well as from similar evidence from the period, that women were functioning partners in the economic and social life of the black community. The women mentioned in the letter had counterparts in many cities in the Northern states.[52]

The earliest record of an all-female organization among the city's blacks was the announcement of the formation of an auxiliary to the Odd Fellows. Organized in 1868, the Ruth Degree was composed of wives, mothers, daughters, and sisters of lodge members.[53] Prior to this organization, female participation in mixed-sex groups did not appear to be extraordinary. For example, a vigilance committee to aid escaped slaves in the 1850s lists five men and four women as members.[54] Among the city's black elite, women participated actively in the Social Circle, an elitist mixed-sex organization which met for the ostensible purpose of literary and intellectual growth as well as social interaction among a select few. The women contributed regularly to the club's literary lyceums and internal publications.[55] Among the city's less affluent blacks there is no record of organizations and leisure activities in which women participated, except for church activities.

For the most part, until the last decade of the nineteenth century, the majority of the women in the black community confined their lives to home-centered activities. Those who worked outside their own homes were mainly employed as domestic or personal-service workers. The fact that work was available for black men and the limited range of jobs available to women, probably accounts for the fact that females comprised only 17.5 percent of the black work force, compared to 13.3 percent females in the total work force, according to the census of 1870.[56] Of women who worked outside of the home in that year, 65.7 percent were in domestic service, compared to 61.7 percent of all black women workers.[57] Family life seems not to have been significantly different, in structure at least, for black and white families. Men were, by far, the breadwinners in both.

By 1910, however, the occupation picture had changed noticeably, Statistics indicate that by 1900, 36.5 percent of all black females sixteen years of age and older were employed. This compared to only 16.8 percent of Cleveland's foreign-born women and 23.4 percent of all women in the city.[58] Kusmer's study of Cleveland's occupational trends indicates that there were two reasons for the significant difference between black and white female workers between 1890 and 1910. First, black women found it difficult to obtain positions outside of domestic service, while foreign-born white women moved into clerical work. Second, after marriage, most white women (especially immigrants) quit their jobs and devoted their time to raising children.[59] With the increasing occupational discrimination against their husbands, the incomes of black families required that the women seek employment outside of the home in order for the family to survive. This pattern has remained virtually unaltered throughout the twentieth century.

Another significant difference in the experience of white women from their black counterparts can be found in the history of the women's club movement. As the nineteenth century drew to a close, white American women's organizations had evolved and broadened from literary and social circles to activities which involved social responsibility. Especially among the middle class, women's clubs proliferated, and a new determination that they must heal the ills of society seems to have caught the imagination of women across the country. Formation of the General Federation of Women's Clubs, whose programs were educational in the broadest sense, with state federations and a wide diversity of interests, was only one indication of a growing sense of strength through increased membership. Interests as varied as upgrading school education, changing the labor laws to protect women and children workers, encouraging college attendance for women, and integrating women into denominational hierarchies led to descriptions of a "new woman."[60] A new sense of sisterhood seemed to transcend social divisions, except for race. Only in a significantly few instances were black women allowed to participate in the new movement.[61]

Among black women, the thrust for organized reform came from quite different circumstances. Their history as participants and spokespersons for the abolition of slavery, as organizers and sustainers of churches, and their never-ending struggle for changes in segregation laws and practices had accompanied their pursuit of literary and social uplift. In the North as well as in the South, racial discrimination barred them from all but the most menial jobs, so that unionization was not a concern. Obtaining and maintaining the vote was seen as a race issue, as terrorist activity increased in the South to take the vote away from black men. The right to serve on school boards and to gain admission to all-male colleges was entirely irrelevant, as racially divided school systems with wide discrepancies in expenditures of public money between black and white children became a practice all over the country. Black women had little time to be involved in personal growth and instead seemed more concerned with uplift of the race.[62]

The call for black women's groups to organize into a national federation separate from the white women's organization came in direct response to two important factors. First, the myth that black women lacked moral character, and second, the violence which threatened the lives of countless black women in the South.[63] Black women organized to confront their own particular position in society, and to address issues which they considered to be critical to the quality of life among their race. Their exclusion from white women's clubs was far less important a reason for the establishment of all-black women's clubs than the distinctly different nature of their circumstances as part of a subordinated race. Women's clubs in the black community tended to be organized around support for needy students, support of a church, care for the indigent, the sick and the aged, and were less likely than their white counterparts to have grown out of earlier literary and cultural societies.[64]

In Cleveland, organizations of black women followed the national pattern. The Cleveland Home for Aged Colored People is a good example of these local organizations. It was incorporated in 1896 in response to an appeal from one of the older black residents, Eliza Bryant, a respected woman in the community. The idea received enthusiastic support from a group of women. They were able to raise funds and purchase a home within three years. This organization provided Cleveland with its first secular institution established exclusively for blacks by their own community since a school for black children was begun before the war. It is interesting to note that the institution was fully supported by blacks, with no dissension from an otherwise integration-oriented leadership.[65]

In the year 1905, the black-oriented "race uplift" magazine the *Colored American* carried a glowing, illustrated article entitled "Cleveland and Its Colored People," which boasted of fine homes belonging to black citizens.

17

According to the article, the progress of blacks was "due to the slight amount of prejudice encountered . . . with a full and unlimited opportunity."[66] This statement is exemplary of the facade of race progress and liberalism perpetuated by a leadership group which was almost desperately holding on to a nineteenth-century memory of Cleveland. Their commitment to bourgeois values and their aspiration for order and security revolved around the credo of hard work, thrift, planning, and saving for the future to gain acceptance into the main social order. While espousing integration as inevitable and within the grasp of their own generation, they provided clues to their own paradoxical existence by supporting a much-needed facility for aged blacks. Their response to that need in their midst was only one example of community cohesiveness and awareness. Although rhetoric such as that found in the *Colored American* article denied acknowledgment of limitations on blacks solely because of race, the Home for Aged Colored People served as a reminder that the black community was not totally integrated into the social mainstream. Decreasing social and economic opportunities for the overwhelming numbers of Cleveland's growing black population would become a more popular issue during the coming decade.

TWO

Foundations for a Life of "Self-Help"

Late nineteenth-century life for blacks in the rural South provided a sharp contrast to the evolving sophisticated economic, social, and ideological problems of their brothers and sisters in the urban North. Faced with a large population of ex-slave blacks, freed from bondage without plan or compensation, and a white population temporarily shaken from a secure position of absolute political and social control, the South did not make the transition from the obsolete agrarian economic base of pre-war years to the more profitable and expanding industries which could absorb both skilled and unskilled labor. Former plantation owners, who formed a Southern bourgeois class, concentrated their efforts on regaining land and political domination. At the same time, blacks faced overwhelming problems of economic survival, access to education, civil rights, and the right to exercise the franchise. These issues continued to consume their attention on through the twentieth century.

The post-Reconstruction formulation of black codes, which restricted the social and political rights of black people, coupled with the failure of the federal government to provide protection for black rights or compensation for their centuries of involuntary servitude, virtually assured a new South scarcely different from the old. After only a few years of hope for equal access to the nation's social, political, and economic systems, especially in the South, blacks faced the harsh reality that the basic change the war had made for them was that their legal status as chattel had been overturned to the more positive category of "freedmen," which ended ownership by one man of another. However, as the newly freed men reluctantly returned to work on farms which did not belong to them, they resumed work under circumstances which fostered a new bondage, the share-cropping system. Under this arrangement, the freedman, instead of working for a wage, rented a plot of land and paid to the plantation owner a certain portion of the crop.[1] This kind of contract seemed an advantageous alternative where blacks were unable to purchase their own land because it gave them the opportunity to organize their own time and to raise their own food.

However, as the system evolved, it became one of debt peonage, whereby plantation owners took advantage of tenants' lack of education and manipulated them into a cycle of insolvency and dependency not unlike their former circumstances.[2] Blacks once again provided the white South with cheap labor, as white landowners regained control of the economic and political systems. Lack of capital, lack of education, repressive laws, and racial animosity can be counted as the chief reasons for deteriorating conditions, after an all-too-brief federal reconstruction period.

Although migration to Northern urban centers provided blacks with a means of escaping the harsh realities of Southern life, their ties to family and the land remained strong. At the end of the Civil War, just over 90 percent of the total black population lived in the South, much as it had since 1790, and this situation did not change until the 1920s.[3]

Prior to 1910, black migrants tended to move short distances and to stay within the South. At a time when the American population was shifting from rural predominance to urban centers where jobs and opportunity were present, blacks followed the pattern, but more slowly. There was a general shifting of population from "field to factory," with blacks moving in search of employment and wealth, first in areas closest in proximity to their roots, and later to larger Northern centers where opportunities were more plentiful and a life free of racial oppression seemed an irresistible promise. This migration pattern, precipitated by the black search for a sanctuary from racism, resulted not in the finding of a haven but in the nationalization of racism.[4] While Northern blacks struggled with the philosophical and ideological implications of racial exclusion, Southern blacks were frequently involved in a struggle for physical and emotional survival. Hunger, harassment, and sometimes violence were frequent manifestations of the racism of Southern life. Economic hardships and difficult social conditions were a way of life for the average black family. Another part of that life style, however, though frequently overlooked, was the network of support from extended families, the strong ties to church communities, and the simple pleasures children found in life on a farm (even though it might not be owned by one's family).

Many families struggled to remain together, with determination that each generation would make strides toward a better way of life. It was possibly optimism that there was a place for them somewhere in America which provided motivation and impetus as families moved from one geographic location to another, from farm to town, and from South to North.

The family of Jane Edna Harris Hunter, the subject of this study, provides an interesting example of post-Reconstruction black life. While this is not a study of an average or typical situation, the family relationships, geographic movement, aspirations, and interactions with other blacks and with whites offer some insights into life in the upper South prior to 1905, when Hunter migrated to Cleveland, Ohio. Her family illustrates three generations of Southern experience, which can be documented through her own recollections in an autobiography written in 1940, *A Nickel and a Prayer*.[5]

Jane Edna Harris was born into the family of Edward and Harriet Harris on December 13, 1882, on the Woodburn Plantation near Pendleton, South Carolina. She was the second of four siblings and the first daughter of the union. Her older brother, Winston, was born on the Hankel Plantation several miles away, where the young couple had moved when first married, before returning to the farm where they had first met and where Jane was born.[6] Two additional daughters, Rosa and Rebecca, completed the family.

Edward Harris, Jane's father, was born in slavery, the son of an English plantation overseer and a "full-blooded Negro woman."[7] His mixed parentage was not unusual.[8] He was hardworking and protective of his family. He tried to hold the family together, even though they faced a seemingly unending cycle of poverty, taking seriously his position as head of the household and chief breadwinner. His wife worked only occasionally, when they were nearly destitute. Harris did not own land, and thus he followed the work pattern of the majority of black farmers who moved from plantation to plantation, seeking fair treatment and better wages. Although the family was extremely poor, they were evidently not bound by debt to one farm. Perhaps his strongest values were his strict regard for morality and a high valuation of education. He was extremely influential in raising the children, and, although he was not educated himself, he intended that his children would not suffer the handicap of illiteracy.

Edward Harris named his first daughter after his English grandmother, Jane McCrary. Jane Harris described her father as Anglo-Saxon in complexion and features, and commented that his "English blood ruled his thoughts and actions."[9] Harris was considered a very desirable marriage partner because of his mixed parentage.[10] When he courted Harriet Milliner and asked for her hand, her family was elated. Harriet also had been courted by a darker man of "mixed blood," and Harris was considered by far the more desirable

Birthplace of Jane Edna Hunter, Woodburn Plantation, Pendelton, S.C.

choice. The bride's father happily supplied a wedding supper with turkeys, pigs, and chickens to celebrate the union.[11]

Although Harris was a devoted father and family guardian, he was also a very volatile and jealous husband. Hunter remembered several occasions when his outbursts were precipitated by jealousy of the man who had been courting his wife when he first met her. Although there was no indication of unfaithfulness on the part of the mother, the mere presence of the other man at a social occasion could spark an outburst from Harris. His fits of violence made family life stressful.

Jane's mother, on the other hand, was an extremely generous and cheerful woman. She was remembered as almost childlike in her enthusiasm for work and play. She was quite a contrast to her fair-skinned husband, with a rich dark complexion and more Negroid features. Harriet Milliner was born on the day Abraham Lincoln signed the Emancipation Proclamation, thus escaping slavery by only hours.[12]

Harriet's parents gained the distinction of land ownership shortly after the war with the purchase of sixteen acres adjacent to the Woodburn Farm. Thus, they were not subject to the financial harassment which accompanied sharecropping and were able to live better than their neighbors. Hunter fondly remembered the Milliners' farm as having "touches of beauty and comforts unknown to [her] parents."[13] Grandma Milliner was remembered as a cultured and refined mulatto. The couple had nineteen children. In addition to caring for her own family and farming, Grandma Milliner served as a midwife for the community, having been trained as a practical nurse by her former master, Dr. Thomas Pickens. Grandfather Milliner farmed his land and supported the family in much better style than his son-in-law, and Hunter remembered taking refuge with her grandparents when things became difficult between her parents at home.

In addition to all the children of the Milliner family, they also shared their home with Grandma Milliner's mother, "Great-grandmother Cumber," a woman who lived to the age of 111 years.[14] Hunter described her great-grandmother as a hearty woman who ruled the Milliner kitchen with stern discipline. She kept the children in line with switches worn tied to her waist, which she would use whenever any chore was slighted. She was also remembered for her cunning selfishness. As an example, the great-grandmother liked fresh hickory nuts and would send the children out to pick them just after they fell from the tree. When they presented her with baskets full of fresh nuts, she would reward them with stale nuts from the previous year's harvest, rather than give them a few from the new crop. Jane quickly learned to make her own reward for the chore by tip-toeing past her great-grandmother as she dozed after a meal and filling her pockets with some of the freshly picked nuts.[15] Perhaps such lessons learned from Jane's association with her ex-slave great-grandmother became part of her adult personality, for she manifested a talent for always finding a way to get around obstacles in order to achieve her own goal.

Hunter's memories of Great-grandmother Cumber are consistent with descriptions of women and men who survived slavery.[16] Her cunning and guile can be viewed as part of a repertoire of survival tactics which sometimes included a combination of the art of deceit and coercive power. When given a goal (or job), this combination helped to facilitate its accomplishment.[17] The older woman not only knew how to get her own way, but she also inadvertently transmitted the lesson to the young child by challenging her to learn how to satisfy her own desires while accomplishing the task set before her.

Great-grandmother Cumber's position in the family was also an accurate portrayal of the prestige of the elder woman in black nineteenth-century life. She had a specific assignment in the family (to cook the meals and keep the kitchen) and carried it out scrupulously. Her authority over the children was also very typical for her status as the eldest woman.[18] The large Milliner clan provided a four-generation extended relationship, which was prevalent among black families. The authority of each generation over the next provided security and protection for the entire group. In-laws became an integral part of the family so that they were scarcely distinguishable from the blood relatives.[19] This large assemblage of relatives served as influences and aggravations throughout Hunter's life.

Harriet Milliner Harris and her husband never achieved the economic standard of living set by her land-owning parents. However, Hunter remembered that even the worst living quarters were always spotlessly clean under her mother's care. Harriet attempted to create a homelike atmosphere in every little cabin which the family occupied, planting fragrant wildflowers and a garden at each place. She kept the children clean and well disciplined, and seemed to fill the traditional female role of nurturer and homemaker. Her occasional employment was strictly supplemental to her husband's earnings. She and her oldest daughter shared a respect for beautiful and orderly surroundings and a capacity for the hard work required to maintain the desired environment.

The Harris family was deeply religious. Their social life revolved around the Methodist Episcopal Church. Prayer meetings and revivals were times for church members to gather, sharing gossip and meals. When the children of the family were old enough to go to school, the family moved into the town of Pendleton, where Silver Spring Baptist Church conducted a school. The family transferred their membership to the Baptist church and Edward Harris submitted to baptism by immersion.[20] As a teenager, Jane belonged to the African Methodist denomination at Woodburn Farm and later, in Cleveland, she joined the Presbyterian Church which provided her "college" experience. Presbyterian women subsequently provided a base of support for Hunter's Phillis Wheatley Association.[21]

Reflecting back on her childhood in her autobiography, Hunter made several observations which bear examination. Her perception of family roles and relationships played a significant part in her adult choices and behavior, especially in her feelings about color and race. For example, because of her father's volatile temperament, there were frequent quarrels between her parents. The trouble was duly noted by the small community and the Harris's problems became common gossip. Through eavesdropping, Jane discerned that most of the talkers sided with her mother, indicting her father for his unreasonable jealousy and behavior. The child, therefore, became the silent, unyielding champion of her father.[22]

In analyzing her choice to side with her father, Hunter pointed out the cultural conditions which most likely contributed. Of all four children, she was the one with color and features which most closely resembled her mulatto father. She described her own complexion as light and her features as fine (Anglo). She had soft, wavy hair like her father.[23] Her mother, a woman of much darker complexion, seemed in the child's mind to have a less compatible identity to which she could relate. Hunter conveyed the feeling that she and her father shared an alienation from the mother because of their white physical characteristics and their more cerebral approach to life situations. Her explanation for the rift in the family revolved around her perception of the conflict between white and black experiences during slavery, which she felt created an internal conflict for her father.

In her autobiography, Hunter spoke of "the happier circumstance of slavery [where] there had been a trustful dependence on the part of the Negro, and affectionate protection on the part of the Master." However, she further elaborated, "there was always the possibility of cruelty in the dominion of the owner, and beneath the trust and dependence of the slave smoldered resentment that might readily kindle into flame."[24] Hunter rationalized her father's volatile nature as a manifestation of his confused reactions to people of his own race as well as to those of the white race. It can be speculated that Hunter felt that he lashed out at his darker wife as master would lash out at slave.

Hunter explained her mother's retaliation against her father as "the resentment bred of slavery that made [her] seek to thwart father's will."[25] One could interpret this as a kind of response of the mother to the father's Anglo characteristics, which made her view him as slave viewed master.

Jane thought of herself as one caught between the two. As she said:

> To mother, I was the living expression of this difference which made happy family life impossible. She disliked and feared the characteristics of the white race in me, as she disliked and feared them in Father, but with no power to explain or rationalize her feelings.[26]

Thus, throughout her young years, Jane carefully emulated what she felt to be her father's strong traits and worked to live up to his expectations. His strong sense of loyalty to the family, his deep religious conviction, and his concern that his children should gain an education all became important values for the daughter.

Her father's death in 1892, when Jane was only ten years old, brought an end to the family life for which Harris had struggled. By that time, they had moved to the Carey Farm near Clemson College, where the father worked as a hod-carrier and the mother took in laundry for school personnel. The new location also had the advantage of being only five miles from the Silver Spring Baptist Church School. Family fortunes had finally changed from earlier bouts with abject poverty to a steady income, and, for the first time, the family had a cabin large enough that the children no longer had to sleep in the same room as their parents. Just at this point, Harris became seriously ill and died shortly thereafter. At his death, Jane remembered feeling that she had lost her truest friend.[27]

Rather than bringing Jane and her mother closer, Harris's death caused the family to break up and created an ever-greater rift between the two. Harriet Harris was not able to support the children without her husband's small income, so Jane and her sister Rebecca were sent to live with an aunt, while her brother and other sister went to live with other relatives. Only one month later, Jane was sent to Anderson, South Carolina, to earn her own room and board as a maid to the family of James Wilson. At the age of ten she was expected to cook, clean, wash, and iron for a family of six, while taking care of two young children. She said that she was so badly treated that neighbors (white as well as black) protested.[28] However, the one bonus during that period was that the oldest girl in the Wilson family taught Jane to write her name and to read nursery rhymes. Jane was grateful, since she had only gotten through the "First Reader" at the Silver Spring Baptist Church School.[29]

Jane was rescued from the hard labor and bad conditions by her mistress's sister, who had earlier taken an interest in the child. When she returned from studies in Europe, "Miss Ruby" was apparently horrified to find Jane in rags and wretched, her hair filthy with vermin. Miss Ruby found clothes for the child and had an old black woman clean her hair and rid her of vermin. Her tasks also became lighter after Miss Ruby appeared on the scene.[30]

Jane's tenure with the Wilson family ended abruptly when her mother, who had remarried, broke an ankle and sent for Jane to come back to Clemson and run the family household. After a year at home, Jane was sent off to Charleston to live with another aunt and uncle who were servants in a house on Franklin Avenue and who lived on the premises. Jane's responsibility was to care for her young cousin Ersie. She described her feelings of humiliation at having to push the child's carriage through the streets of Charleston. She said, "We presented a ridiculous contrast: I, a mulatto, barefooted, in rags; my charge, a full-blooded Negro, dressed in pink silk with streamers of ribbons."[31] This comment suggests Jane's feeling of superiority as a mulatto over the dark-complexioned baby, a superiority which she did not describe feeling when she later became the caretaker of a white professor's baby at Clemson.[32]

At the age of twelve or thirteen, Jane went to work as a waitress and chambermaid in a hotel near Clemson College. She described her terror as she dodged the advances of male patrons, who regularly pursued pretty mulatto girls. She was rescued from this job by an aunt who traveled from Pendleton to Clemson to convince Jane's mother that the child should not be in the position to be disgraced like so many other girls working in similar establishments. Jane returned with her aunt to Woodburn Farm where she had been born.[33] She earned her board by working the fields and picking cotton along with other family members. During her stay in the protection of her family, she became a member of the King's Chapel AME Church and enjoyed the church-centered social life of the community.

In 1896, when Jane was fourteen years old, once again fate seemed to set a new course for her life. Two black Presbyterian missionaries, Reverend and Mrs. E. W. Williams, who had a school in Abbeville, South Carolina, visited her uncle's home and met Jane. Even though she could barely read, they were very impressed by her earnestness and her desire to please.[34] No doubt Jane played an important role in their perception of her potential, as she was most eager to get an education. The Williams invited the young girl to come to the school and suggested a plan by which she could earn her tuition and room and board. With her aunt's intervention to gain her mother's consent, Jane was enrolled at Ferguson Academy in the fall.[35] The school was comparable to a high school preparation course where basic education skills were emphasized.

Jane spent four years at Ferguson. To earn her way, she worked in the student dining room and took care of the laundry for the Williams family. She also looked after the Williams's three daughters. Her contact with the educated and refined black family was very rewarding. She recounted the struggle of Reverend and Mrs. Williams to keep the school going as a real lesson to her in perseverance and dedication. Mrs. Williams's role at the school especially provided the young girl with a very positive role model.

Educated in New Jersey and at Howard University, Mrs. Williams was well prepared to play a significant part in the school's administration. When her husband went North to raise funds, Mrs. Williams was responsible for keeping food on the tables for the students and for maintaining the school program. She taught the young Jane many lessons in the application of Christian values and virtues to daily life. With her help, the young girl was taught to manage the school's dining room supplies and to use her imagination to find ways to bring funds into the treasury. These lessons proved to be extremely valuable for the life work which Jane later chose.

One incident from this period which Jane recounted in her autobiography is most reminiscent of the life story of Booker T. Washington, her idol.[36] It bears recounting because it emphasizes the role of the black community and its aspirations for its own.

After being away at school for one year, Jane came home for summer vacation. She earned enough money during the summer to buy the barest essentials and had no money left to pay the train fare back to school. A friend promised to buy the precious ticket for her. On the day she was to leave for school, about twenty of her neighbors came to the station to see her off. However, the friend who promised the ticket did not show up. Jane became anxious as the time for the train drew near, and she began to cry as the train pulled into the station, because she still had no ticket. When the neighbors and well-wishers learned what the problem was, they quickly pooled their meager funds and came up with enough money to buy the ticket and give Jane an additional half-dollar for the trip.[37] The community invested in Jane as one of their own who was on the threshold of breaking out of the pattern of poverty and ignorance. She represented the aspirations of many of her people and they were proud of her. Their willingness to give up very hard-earned money to send her on her way to school was a demonstration of their faith in both the education process and the young woman. At a time when the Southern states were retrenching from earlier commitments to public education for blacks, this demonstration of the black community's belief in the importance of education is especially poignant.[38]

Graduation from Ferguson Academy in 1900 was a glorious occasion for Jane Harris. She was crowned Queen of May of the little school, and she was chosen to recite Tennyson's "Queen of the May" on the first night of the graduation festivities.[39] On the second night, the school's principal talked about how Jane had been brought from Pendleton a little "pickaninny" and had matured into a fine dependable woman.[40] On the last evening, Jane was again the focus of some attention, as she led the boarding school girls in an industrial dialogue which exhibited their work. Since industrial education was the major thrust for educating blacks, this demonstration was undoubtedly the highlight of the graduation exercises.

On graduation from school at eighteen, Jane had approximately the equivalent of an eighth grade education.[41] Her training equipped her for one of two options available to blacks in the South. If she had the money, she could continue her schooling. The most common optimal degree would be that of a normal school certificate, which was required for teaching.[42] Or, she could become a domestic servant earning a little better salary than otherwise, since she had mastered the basic education skills.[43] Clearly, she preferred to continue in school, but there were no funds.

When she returned to Woodburn Farm after graduation, Jane felt somewhat out of place. She was no longer content to live in the crowded cabin of her generous aunt and uncle after exposure to the Williams family and a few of the amenities which existed as a way of life at the school. She was also bothered that she and her brother and sisters had not been reunited as a family, even though her mother was remarried and living in Georgia. The Harris children were dependent upon their extended family for shelter and nourishment. Jane longed for the home life she remembered from early childhood before her father died. In a pitiful attempt to arouse this sentiment in her mother, she wrote a letter begging her to come home because sister Rebecca was sick. Her mother came immediately and, upon learning that Jane had lied about her sister's illness, threatened to whip her. She did not stay to restore the family as Jane had hoped.[44]

At the end of the summer, Jane was sent to Tampa, Florida, to live with another uncle who ran a boardinghouse for Cubans and blacks. Once again she was faced with the problem of unwanted attention from male boarders. She was frightened, disappointed, and homesick, and after a few months she went back to South Carolina.[45] However, while she was in Florida, she attended Holloman Academy for a short time.[46]

Within the year, her dreams of further education shattered, Jane capitulated to her mother's urging and married a man forty years her senior.[47] Edward Hunter was kind and fatherly, but there was no love or mutual affection between the two. Jane quickly realized that she could not spend the rest of her life in such a marriage, and, after fifteen months, she decided to leave.[48] Hunter's comments about her marriage and separation in her autobiography are interesting for two reasons. First, their brevity. She only mentioned the marriage in one short paragraph, almost as an afterthought or a fact which required little note. Since this brief marriage was the only one in her lifetime and accounted for her adult surname, it is significant to point out that it was barely mentioned. She simply explained the marriage as an unsatisfactory arrangement which had taken place only as a result of her broken-off love affair with a man who did not have her mother's approval. The marriage also seemed to be an attempt by Jane to please her mother.

Second, Hunter's comments regarding the separation are certainly not typical for the early twentieth century. At a time when most women aspired to marriage and a stable family, she described her separation from Edward Hunter as, "a great weight [which] rolled away from my mind as I left him, determined to find and keep the freedom which I so ardently desired."[49] Hunter's attitude toward the separation indicated her fearlessness. She seemed to rejoice in the opportunity to make a life as a single female at a time when marriage was viewed as the ultimate protection for women. Her ability to recognize that she could not exist within the bounds of a loveless marriage was unique for her time, and her attitude toward its dissolution exceptional.

Jane Hunter also claimed that when she left her husband and went to Charleston to find work, she was subconsciously seeking to escape the curse of "mother's race."[50] Poverty, contempt, and subjection comprised her conception of the meaning of being black, and Jane was determined to break away from the cycle. She summed up her feelings about her own racial identity this way:

> Here again appeared the pattern woven in childhood by the dark and mysterious forces of the blood. Side by side with sympathy for Mother and my Mother's people, there grew up a desire to escape racial heritage as a Negro. The escape motive was unconscious—I would have denied it indignantly had anyone formulated it for me—but in the years to come it was to carry me far away from my native environment into new and strange ways of life. There, struggle and determination were to bring me the joys of success and the satisfaction of making my small will prevail in some measure against the buffets of chance.
>
> Then the miracle! Having escaped, as I thought, the curse of being a Negro—poverty, contempt, subjection, the badge of sufferance which my people had worn for so many years—I was overwhelmed by the realization that I was, above and beyond all, my Mother's child—a Negro; that I was proud of the blood of my black ancestors; that my life henceforth was to be a solemn dedication to the people of my Mother's race.[51]

This passage seems to indicate a resolution of earlier conflicts regarding her own racial identity. This is not to suggest that, in terms of the larger society, she had a choice; for she had inherited too much of her mother's racial characteristics to pass. However, in her own internal struggle with feelings about her racial heredity, white and black, she came to terms with the implications of being black and the limitations which blackness could imply. She seemed to affirm an acceptance that she was indeed a "Negro," but, rather than accepting the fact as an excuse for inferior status, would dedicate her life to improvement of her and her mother's race. She would use her race as a positive motivation to achieve. She viewed freedom from her marriage as a freedom to dedicate her life to helping others.

In Charleston, after she had left her husband, Jane was fortunate in her employment. She became a nursemaid to the children of the "very wealthy" Benjamin Rutledge family.[52] She was well-treated, and lived in the "Big House" while caring for the children. Her wages were good enough to allow her to send her sister Rebecca to Ferguson Academy. The Williams family also provided Rosa, the youngest sister, with Jane's old job. This meant that both sisters were safely in the hands of the Williams family, and Jane was left to pursue her own ambitions.[53]

While working in the Rutledge home, Jane met a very influential black woman, Mrs. Ella Hunt, who took an interest in her. She suggested to Jane that she should apply for nurse's training at the Cannon Street Hospital and Training School for Nurses. Mrs. Hunt used her influence to get Jane admitted ahead of eighty other applicants, and she was accepted within a month after filing the application.[54] She was delighted to have the opportunity to join the profession which had been practiced by her grandmother Milliner two generations before. She remembered her grandmother as a tremendously useful woman whose religious nature and life of service were worthy of emulation.

Only six months after beginning her training, Hunter was called back to the Rutledge family as nurse for one of the children. Following this first assignment, she came to the attention of a white surgeon, Dr. T. Grange Simon, for whom she worked after graduation.[55] As a private-duty nurse, Jane worked in Charleston and the surrounding vicinity, often for the very wealthy families of the area, and at times she was also called to the black slums of the city. She enjoyed great success during her two years in Charleston.

Having met the challenge of nursing school and with some practical experience, Hunter became restless once again, and again felt the need for more advanced training. Acting upon the advice of Dr. Simon, she entered Dixie Hospital and Training School for Nurses at Hampton Institute, in Hampton, Virginia. At Hampton, Hunter was exposed to an educational philosophy which glorified vocational training as a means for black people to gain entry into America's social and economic mainstream.[56] The school, which had molded the thoughts of Booker T. Washington, was also extremely important in shaping Hunter's personal philosophy. Hampton Institute promoted a four-pronged educational concept which seemed in a way to confirm the validity of Hunter's own experiences and formed a relevant and cohesive doctrine which might ensure success for blacks who were eager to improve their own situation. The goals of the school were

. . . to make Negroes of service to themselves and whites, to dignify human labor by reinforcing it with intelligence, to develop a sense of responsibility within each pupil by giving [him or her] specific tasks to perform, and to saturate the entire program with useful forms of manual training.[57]

These relatively simple ideals appealed to the young woman because they reinforced her notion of race progress and race relations. Hunter's beliefs were rooted in the context of three important variables: the people with whom she had interacted during her young life, the region of her birth, and the nature of her own work experiences.

Jane Hunter's formative years provided a near-perfect setting in which she could apply the Hampton doctrine to demonstrate the possibility of accomplishment for one who worked her way from plantation to the threshold of a successful career. Hunter had found a philosophical concept which she could use to inspire others who were to follow her lead. A summary of the above-mentioned variables offers an interesting commentary about her remarkable self-concept and her accommodationist attitude in relations with whites.

A factor which stands out in analyzing Jane Hunter's formative years is the dominance of women as role models and major influences. With the exception of her father, who played a key role until his death when she was ten years old, Hunter related to women as positive forces at critical junctures in her life.

When she was a child, there was her great-grandmother who played an important role. Her life and her personality symbolized black survival under the harsh yoke of slavery. Her grandmother furnished a model of usefulness, religious strength, and service to her community. Her mother, with whom she had the most difficult relationship, nevertheless dominated her life decisions. Attempts to atone for earlier estrangements from her mother were credited by Hunter as the source from which she derived the inspiration to dedicate her life to serving young women. Her aunts also played major roles. For example, when Jane was employed in the Clemson Hotel, it was her Aunt Carolina who came to rescue her from the possibility of sexual violation and took her home to Woodburn Farm. Mrs. Williams, wife of the president of Ferguson Academy, exposed Jane to gracious living in a black home and taught her about management while she worked in the school dining facility. Mrs. Ella Hunt, the clubwoman in Charleston, made it possible for Jane to go to nursing school.

White female employers were also positive models. Miss Ruby and Mrs. Rutledge stand out as examples. Although she mentioned uncles and a few men in the families where she worked, it is clear that Jane Hunter's inspiration came from the women who helped her through her formative years. Thus, her choice to spend the remainder of her life in a female-dominated environment, helping young women, can be traced to (1) the role models and support system which prevailed during her early life, and (2) the fear of sexual exploitation which dominated her limited experiences with men outside her own family.

Hunter's birthplace, Pendleton, South Carolina, is located in the Piedmont section of the state. According to Professor Richard Long, director of Atlanta University's Afro-American Studies Program, the Piedmont section was one which was less dominated by large plantations than some other sections of the South. There, the position of the black farmer was similar to that of the yeoman. The atmosphere between blacks and whites in the region was less fearsome than in some other parts of the South. Blacks lived in somewhat less of the threat of violence than their brothers elsewhere, and there was a general atmosphere of understanding between the races.

Hunter confirmed this relationship in her autobiography:

> In the years following the Civil War, the lot of the Negro was hard enough, it is true; still the majority of them I knew in my childhood lived somewhat happily on plantations their forebears had worked as slaves, the friendly interdependence of the earlier relationship of slave and master continuing to link tenant and landlord with ties that were personal and human.[58]

Thus, her early years were spent in an environment which did not create the kind of hostilities between the races which developed in some other sections where blacks were essentially reenslaved in systems of peonage. Her family's longevity in the area also provided a sense of safety and security. It allowed her to move freely among family and loved ones in a relatively protected environment.[59]

Hunter's relationships with whites varied from the extremes of excellent to poor—even within one family. Perhaps the most impressionable relationship was with "Miss Ruby," the sister-in-law of her mother's employer at Clemson when Jane was very young. Miss Ruby convinced Jane's mother that Jane should come to live as a part of their household. Jane's father was furious when he found out about the plan and secured legal papers to have her returned. Later, after Jane had gone to work for another part of the family after her father's death, Miss Ruby's role in her rescue made a lifelong impression on the child. Her "graciousness and kindness" provided a model of "noblesse oblige" which Hunter adopted as an acceptable relationship between upper-class whites and blacks who were striving to gain a place in the social order. This experience was somewhat repeated as Jane worked in other homes and found that hard work and a conscientious attitude usually were rewarded with better pay and good treatment. In addition, as she gained better domestic skills and, later, nursing skills, she was adequately rewarded.

By the time Jane Hunter left Hampton Institute, she had become a confident and skilled woman with a firm belief in the prevailing Social Darwinist theories of her time and in Washington's self-help credo. Her life experiences confirmed their validity and illustrated the rewards of following them.

THREE

A Nickel and a Prayer: The Working Girl's Home Association

Examination of the formative process for the Phillis Wheatley Association provides an excellent example of the conflict between two race ideologies which gained national attention during the early years of the twentieth century. Jane Hunter's experiences and responses to those experiences can provide a clue to dilemmas faced in many places, North and South, as blacks groped for solutions to such problems as shifting populations (rural to city and South to North), lack of adequate education facilities, lack of proper health care opportunities, and a great lack of social services. There was little response from traditional sources to the many problems inherent in these rapid changes in living patterns. Although the migration of black Americans from one geographic section of the country to another was not as dramatic a change as that experienced by Europeans who were flooding American cities, solutions to the problems of black Americans could not always follow the same models as those created for other groups, for a variety of reasons.

For example, European immigrants and white migrants from other places could, within one generation, become totally indistinguishable from the majority of the city's citizens; blacks could not look forward to similar assimilation. The children of the foreign-born could quickly move from a subordinate status to any class within their economic capability. However, black Americans did not have that kind of invisibility. Probably the most important difference was that no other group had the history of the justifications for enslavement, which included scientific, religious, and social explanations to ostensibly prove the racial inferiority of black people. In addition, post-slavery legal segregation in the South had served to compound the fears of blacks in the North that the country would soon be totally divided by race. The dilemmas which faced Hunter were replayed in countless other situations in the North during the same era. Thus, the ideological confrontation within the black community provides an example of the struggle for solutions to the problems of blacks and of the complexities involved in being a black leader.

In order to correctly evaluate events in Cleveland between 1905 and 1913, there is a need to recapitulate examples of the two national race strategies which were most often offered at the time, their spokesmen, and in one case a model of organization under which blacks were encouraged to operate. In each case, the strategy represented an attempt to address the need for blacks to come to realistic terms with a racial climate which spawned increasingly oppressive laws and acts of discrimination. Although both ideologies came to be identified with their chief spokesman, neither strategy was new; each was simply organized more soundly and articulated more forcefully under the sponsorship of its chief proponent in the twentieth century.

Undoubtedly, the most publicized strategy among whites as well as blacks was that identified with Booker T. Washington, an outspoken black Southern educator and principal of Tuskegee Institute in Alabama. His talented leadership as chief spokesman for a doctrine of racial solidarity and self-help was extremely influential, not only as an organizing ideology among blacks, but also as a persuasive device to draw positive white support for black efforts. Washington's use of the language of free enterprise and capitalism and his conciliatory manner with monied white persons made him a very popular model for the possibilities for black success.

Steeped in the American tradition of rugged individualism, out of his own background of ascendance from slave birth to a prestigious career in education, and convinced of the merits of the new progressivist organizational zeal for banding together individuals of similar inspiration, Washington played a singularly pivotal role in the formation of a number of all-black national organizations. Under his tutelage, and with the financial backing of white philanthropists and their foundations, Washington inspired such groups as the National Bar Association, the National Association of Funeral Directors, and the National Bankers Association, all all-black organizations.

One of the newly formed national bodies, the National Negro Business League (represented in Cleveland by the Cleveland Board of Trade, 1905, and its successor the Cleveland Association of Colored Men), provides an example of Washington's definition of the means to achieve racial progress for blacks. Perhaps no other single body was as influential in stimulating the belief that economic advancement could be the most important factor in demonstrating the race's eligibility for full citizenship rights.

Washington sponsored a great campaign to encourage the formation of local leagues as a means to support local black businesses and to emphasize the responsibility of the race to support their own businesses. By 1906, the annual meeting of the National Negro Business League attracted 1,200 participants to Atlanta, Georgia.[1] Resolutions at the convention affirmed the faith that blacks could depend upon the example set by other races by tying progress to demonstrations of advancement through economic growth. Emphasis centered on success and opportunities rather than failure and grievances. Delegates assured one another that economic laws of laissez-faire were blind to color. Resolutions and testimony provided outstanding contradictions as they urged black support of black business as the key to their own business success. Most conspicuous was the absence of resolutions aimed at political and civil rights.[2] Most important, perhaps, was the opportunity the organization provided to demonstrate solidarity among those blacks interested in advancement through their own businesses. By adapting this organizational model, Washington opened up for blacks a respectable avenue for contact and mutual support which engendered pride and a new spirit of confidence.

Definitions of racial solidarity changed radically with Washington's interpretation, from nineteenth-century militancy, which demanded political and civil rights, to a plan of self-help through mutual support. White philanthropic dollars were in plentiful supply to aid Washington's campaign to convince the race that they could master their own destiny by building a self-sufficient economic system. Encouragement to build their own banks, trust companies, insurance companies, and realty companies, as well as the more traditional service businesses such as barber and beauty shops, fostered an illusion of progress for blacks similar to that of parallel white institutions. By taking the focus off of white inequities, Washington supplied a spirit of hope that problems indeed had solutions which blacks themselves could control.

At the height of Washington's popular influence, another strategy, much older than the self-help notion, began to be expressed more forcefully. This strategy culminated in a 1905 meeting of black intellectuals at Niagara Falls, Canada, at which time William E. B. Du Bois led a movement to challenge the validity of Washington's strategy. Du Bois and his group clearly articulated the differences between the nation's black intellectual community and what some regarded as the erroneous assumptions of the Washington philosophy. They reasserted the more traditional view that only through political activity and the use of political leverage could blacks control their own destiny.

While not directly assaulting the notion of self-help, the Du Bois group vigorously challenged the idea that integration should be earned (or had not already been earned) rather than demanded. They reaffirmed racial solidarity, as it had more traditionally been defined, to represent a single voice demanding inclusion in the social, political, and economic mainstream. They also demanded inclusion in the services of institutions designed for the public consumption. They believed that the destiny of blacks was directly tied to the overall destiny of America, and vice versa. As proof of the country's obligation to its black citizens, they cited the need to enforce the Thirteenth, Fourteenth, and Fifteenth amendments to the Constitution. The Niagara group later joined a small group of white progressives to form the National Association for the Advancement of Colored People.(NAACP)[3]

The basic difference between the two doctrines was the perception of where responsibility lay for achievement of equality. This provided a basis for argument within the black community between those who maintained that blacks themselves were responsible for their own uplift and those who felt that the American government should respond to the historic rights of a group which had been denied. The fact is that both sides espoused self-help. The difference was in their definition of the concept. Ironically, Washington's definition of solidarity became the basis for argument in favor of separation, while Du Bois's argument pled the case for integration. This sharply contrasts with contemporary definitions which link separationism to militancy and integration to moderation.

In Cleveland, Washington's ideology became identified with a new, rising leadership group of blacks. The press for race progress through solidarity reached popular proportions somewhat late in comparison with Northern cities with larger black populations. The ideology of integration represented the older and more popular view, and continued to attract support from black leadership for most of the nineteenth century. Jane Edna Hunter's idea for a home for black working women, patterned after the YWCA, coming at the start of the twentieth century, brought the two ideologies into direct conflict in the city of Cleveland.

Black leaders in many cities grappled with similar issues when faced with the need to find a means for addressing the problems of their communities.

Jane Hunter's experiences can provide a clue to her dedication to what she perceived as the only practical course to follow. Her actions provide a model which was not unique at the time.

Jane Hunter arrived in Cleveland in 1905. After completing the nurse's training course at Hampton, Virginia, she planned to go back to South Carolina or possibly to Tampa, Florida, to resume her career. However, a chance visit with friends of her family in Richmond, Virginia, was to change the course of her life. Upon her arrival in Richmond, she found her friends packed and ready to move to Cleveland, where they had heard that blacks could find work. They invited her to come along with them, and she decided on the spur of the moment to join in their move to the North. Thus, the young nurse arrived in the city, looking forward to a new and free life.[4]

With her nurse's training and clinical experience, Hunter expected to have no problems settling comfortably in Cleveland, where she could use her skills to make a living. Her first realization that in moving North she had by no means escaped problems identified with her race came in the form of housing discrimination. When she and her friends arrived, they immediately went to Central Avenue to look for lodging. This area had served as a point of entry for many migrants to Cleveland, black and white. She and her married friends found rooms in a boardinghouse which Hunter later determined was being run by a family involved in prostitution. Hunter, whose plantation origins and education in a religious institution had made her quite puritanical, was appalled and shocked at the revelation that prostitution existed among black women in the city. She had given emergency medical treatment in Charleston, South Carolina, to white prostitutes, but was completely ignorant about the existence of black prostitution. She was also uncomfortable when she realized that the rooming house owners drank liquor and tried to encourage her to drink beer. She soon found a room in a "quieter and safer neighborhood . . . with another family far superior in character."[5]

Hunter's attempts to find adequate lodgings made her keenly aware of the economic plight of the single working women who entered the city. In her autobiography, *A Nickel and a Prayer*, she described her first months in Cleveland.[6] Her search for housing she recalled as "despairing . . . up one dingy street and down another, ending with the acceptance of the least undesirable room."[7] Her story was not unlike that of young white women in the previous century who moved into cities to find work in factories. Their problem was relieved with the opening of YWCAs in Northern industrial cities. However, there was no place for the young single black woman arriving in Cleveland to turn. The YWCA residence was not open to black women.[8] Hunter never forgot her feelings of defenselessness as a stranger at the mercy of boardinghouse owners. She later recalled that women roomers were considered less desirable than men. They were frequently relegated to the smallest rooms, and there was seldom a place where they could entertain gentlemen callers.[9] Often there were extra charges for use of the bathtubs, laundry, and gas.[10] Hunter concluded that the moral degradation of the black woman could often be attributed to the lack of a safe place to live and the lack of sufficient money to survive.[11]

Another concern for Hunter was the loneliness of the city. She recalled being lost for recreation with young people her own age, and after many months in Cleveland she accepted an invitation to a dance hall. Much to her chagrin, she discovered that the young women were "heavily painted . . . with indecently short skirts," and that the men were "slightly intoxicated and somewhat noisy."[12] A young man warned her that she was not in a place for nice girls, and invited her to meet his mother and sister. She later learned that the dance hall served as a recruiting station for prostitution for a notorious underworld figure called "Starlight," with whom she would later clash in a political confrontation.

Perhaps most distressing during Hunter's early days in Cleveland was her inability to secure work in her chosen profession. The North provided a curious twist to the racial barriers which Hunter had felt in the South. One physician whom she approached for work told her to go back to the South because "white doctors did not employ nigger nurses."[13] Hunter observed that in the South, black nurses were favored by white people (probably as an extension of the role of nursemaid during slavery); consequently, she was unprepared for the rejection she experienced in Cleveland.

She finally secured employment as a nurse after working at cleaning jobs in downtown office buildings. She got her first professional assignment after accidentally wandering into the office of Dr. L. E. Sieglestein, coroner for Cuyahoga County. She was also helped by a black physician, Dr. Christian LaTrobe Mottley, and Dr. H. F. Biggar, physician to John D. Rockefeller. Through these connections, Hunter was able to slowly build a clientele of wealthy white families. Recommendations from influential patients and prominent doctors afforded Hunter the opportunity to become self-supporting. Although she had gained experience as a surgical nurse at Dixie Hospital in Hampton, Virginia, her only reference to hospital experience in Cleveland was as an invited spectator during an operation at

Nurse Jane Edna Hunter (about 1910)

Huron Road Hospital. Hunter noted the resentment of white nurses at the hospital when she appeared.[14]

Hunter's early experiences as a single black woman from the South were typical for the period around the late nineteenth and early twentieth centuries. Notwithstanding her years of professional training prior to her arrival in Cleveland, her problems with housing, recreation, and limited opportunities for employment were the problems encountered by the vast majority of her peers. Especially during the years between 1900 and 1920, when Cleveland's black population grew from 5,988 to 34,451, or from 1.6 percent to 4.3 percent of the city's total, the problem of racial discrimination grew in the areas of housing, social services, and employment opportunities.[15]

For single black women, the effect was considerably more acute. In terms of employment, Hunter's nurses training eventually put her at a distinct advantage. The average black woman in the city had few alternatives to domestic service. Employment statistics in Cleveland between 1910 and 1930 reveal that although the female work force shifted from 21.9 percent in personal service in 1910 to a low of 14.8 percent in 1920, black women workers were represented in the category at significantly higher levels. While white women moved into clerical and white-collar positions between 1910 and 1920, from 22.6 percent to 40.2 percent, black women advanced from only 1.4 percent to 3.7 percent in those positions. However, in the category of personal service, black women were employed at levels of 72.8 percent in 1910 and 63 percent in 1920.[16]

Although there was a sizeable increase in the number of black women in the teaching profession and a small number of women proprietors, clerks, and skilled workers, they represented a minute proportion of the female working force.[17] Indeed, Hunter had to build up her nursing clientele while relying on interim cleaning and laundry jobs to sustain her.[18] As late as 1915, Cleveland could only list two black professionally trained nurses.[19]

Housing for blacks also followed a pattern of increasing concentration during the early years of the century. Although not totally restricted to the few identifiable all-black enclaves which existed prior to World War I, the trend of black migrant settlement tended to be more concentrated in those neighborhoods where blacks had been welcomed before the rapid increase in their numbers.[20] Studies in population density indicate that at the time of the 1910 census, for example, four census tracts in the Central-Scovil areas housed about one-half of Cleveland's black population, with densities ranging from forty-two to eighty-two inhabitants per acre, while that of Cleveland as a whole was only thirteen per acre.[21] Hunter's description of the lodging situation, where she paid $.1.25 per week for a "small, low-roofed, poorly furnished room" was the standard accommodation for the black migrant. Additional identifiable black enclaves offered no options to her or her category of migrants. One enclave was found in a vice district around Hamilton Avenue, which Hunter described as known to include gambling houses, dives, and brothels, and was the least desirable neighborhood to live in. The others were small settlements of middle-class families around Hough Avenue and Kinsman and East 105th streets. These families were not likely to rent rooms to strangers. Prior to Hunter's first Phillis Wheatley House, there was no social agency in existence which would provide or refer services for black newcomers.

In September, 1911, Hunter met with a group of black women friends to discuss the problem of housing for poor working women who, like themselves, were subjected to living conditions which seemed intolerable. The eight friends shared experiences such as having to turn lights out by 10:00 p.m., the lack of places to entertain friends, and no access to kitchen facilities in places which offered rooms to black women lodgers.[22] The women, although still involved in their own struggles to survive, felt that a solution must be found among themselves since "hundreds and hundreds of girls here in Cleveland are living in the most squalid surroundings."[23] They concluded that neither the city government nor whites could be expected to solve the problem, since "how could they know anything about the conditions which confront the Negro woman worker?"[24] They also did not feel that whites would understand that the conditions were not satisfactory, even if they knew what they were.[25]

The solution seemed to lie within their own group. The small group elected Jane Hunter president and pledged to each raise a nickel per week and to gather as many new members as they could find to add to their small pool of funds. Although the women were poor and mostly uneducated, they were enthusiastic. They decided that they would try to find a way to build a home "for all the other poor motherless daughters of our race."[26] The Working Girls' Home Association was the name chosen for the new project.[27]

Jane Hunter, who had called the small group together for the first meeting, had already begun to dream of a way to help young working women. Her early experiences in the city had been very disturbing to her,

43

and she had been recently reminded that the situation had not changed since her arrival. A few months before Hunter called the meeting, she tried to help a young woman who arrived in the city, poorly trained and destitute. Hunter's frustration, as she tried to find work and lodging for the woman (and her two babies) turned to resolve that she must find a way to remedy the situation which occurred so often among young black women. When Hunter asked for help from her friends, the dream began to take shape.

There were possibly also several other factors which motivated Hunter to try to start a home for women like herself. For one, the idea was not new, and there were examples in other cities of activities which had successfully solved similar problems. Although at no time did Hunter acknowledge any other inspiration than the above story, her idea was by no means original in Northern cities. As early as 1896, the idea for a home for young working black women was initiated in Chicago. Sponsored by a local black women's club and headed by their president, Elizabeth Lindsey Davis, the Phyllis Wheatley Home for Girls provided living accommodations, social facilities, and an employment bureau for single girls who migrated to Chicago and found themselves excluded from the YWCA and similar places run by white organizations.[28]

In New York City, a facility called the White Rose Working Girls Home was founded by a black woman activist, Victoria Earle Matthews, in 1897. The White Rose Home, besides providing lodgings and meals for female newcomers, had an active core of agents at the piers who met the boats from Norfolk to help young women find their places of employment and offer protection from "the dangers of our great city."[29] This establishment became a settlement house, providing classes in domestic training and "race history."

Concern about the vulnerability of black women who were being promised good salaries and good working conditions in New York City, only to arrive and find themselves victims of prostitution rings and shoddy employment agencies, also led to the founding of an organization which attempted to do on a national scale what the White Rose Home agents did on a local level. White progressive activist Frances A. Kellor helped to establish a society for the protection of black women, the National League for the Protection of Colored Women, with offices in New York and Philadelphia.[30] This organization is reputed to have virtually flooded Southern port cities with agents and literature to warn the young women of conditions which they might find in the cities. The League, which in 1911 became one of three reform agencies which consolidated to form the National League on Urban

Conditions Among Negroes (the National Urban League), was especially active along the Virginia and Georgia coast, where recruitment was most active.

Given Hunter's migration pattern, from inland South Carolina to coastal Charleston and later to Hampton and Richmond, Virginia, it is very likely that she was aware of the existence of either the White Rose Home, or the League, or both. Especially at Hampton, ideological birthplace of Booker T. Washington's philosophy, it is safe to assume that word of the mission was circulated. Victoria Matthews, founder of the White Rose Home, was an especially important supporter and admirer of Washington.[31] It is unlikely that such a valiant effort toward self-help would have been unnoticed at the college. Also, it is safe to assume that the League agents were active in Richmond's busy train terminal.

In addition to the likelihood of exposure to the work being done on behalf of black women through the White Rose Home and the League, there is no doubt as to Hunter's exposure to the work of the YWCA in Cleveland. Her arrival in Cleveland coincided with a building campaign and the subsequent building of a large new facility for the YWCA in downtown Cleveland. Newspaper publicity was extensive regarding the work of the women, most of whom represented Cleveland's wealthiest families, as they raised money to move from a headquarters at 314 Euclid Avenue to their new building at 18th and Prospect. Publicity about their work included details of their programs and activities, classes, organizational beginnings and current structure, and information about their new national affiliation.[32] There can be no doubt that Hunter was aware of their work with women in the city.

Hunter's own version of her inspiration to try to establish a place where young black women could find lodging and be trained to earn a living involved the unresolved relationship she had with her mother. Hunter's childhood identification with her father and her alienation from her mother had remained a source of emotional distress. Attempts to reach out to her mother in order to reconcile their differences were not successful, and her mother's sudden death in June 1910 left Hunter emotionally devastated. She said that she had to find a way to "give to the world what I had failed to give to her."[33] She claimed that when she was asked to help the young woman and her babies in 1911, she was not only reminded of her own plight a few years earlier, but she also thought of how her immature and impulsive mother would have been in a similar situation.[34] She decided that she would dedicate her life to "the supreme task for which God had designed me."[35]

During the early months of the Association, public money-raising efforts were centered entirely within the black community, as the young women sponsored concerts, meetings, and church activities to swell their organization's coffers. Notices of events were carried in the city's black newspapers, with frequent appeals for support. However, while Hunter claimed to believe that "the Lord will provide help," she also proceeded to test the idea with her wealthy white clients, seeking their reactions and testing their willingness to contribute money toward a home for black women. Hunter obviously was a careful student, not only of Washington's self-help plan, but she was also sensitive to her white employer's interest in maintaining racial separation.

As soon as the plan for a home for black women became known, the efforts of the small group became highly controversial within the black community. Supporters of the idea for the Working Girls' Home literally stumbled into the thick of a national ideological debate between those who supported Washington's idea of race separation and those who were demanding integration. Harry Smith, editor of the *Cleveland Gazette* and a staunch integrationist, launched an all-out attack on Hunter and her supporters. He labeled the plan segregationist and backward.[36]

Smith's outrage represented the traditional position of black leadership in the city. An almost blind faith that the city would continue to move toward racial integration and equality was based on that group's own nineteenth-century experiences in politics and education. Small gains, such as acceptance of a few leaders into the City Club and the election of a black councilman, were exaggerated to indicate progress, while the existence of a fast-growing pool of black workers who were being excluded from new unions and increased housing and job discrimination were viewed as only temporary setbacks.[37] The city's old-guard black leaders tended to focus on the advancement of a few individuals to indicate the possibility for race achievement. Any suggestion that the city was in fact becoming increasingly less hospitable to blacks was quickly attacked as regressive and self-defeating.

The outcry against Hunter and her plan was predictable and consistent with positions taken regarding similar proposals. In fact, there was already a controversy of at least five years regarding a black YMCA. A few of the city's young black men, including the editors of the *Cleveland Journal*, were determined to have a YMCA in the black community. Editorials and articles in the *Journal* heralded the coming of a YMCA.[38] However, weekly editorials in the *Gazette*, on the other hand, clearly warned of the opposition to such an institution. An editorial from this perspective, only months before Hunter's group first met, serves as an example of the sentiment of the traditionalists:

The Jim Crow YMCA

Those Negroes who insist on "flocking to themselves" because they fear general contact with other classes of people, and who in late years have located in Northern cities, have given greater impetus to "Jimcrowing" our people in this section, than our enemies in other classes. . . . This encourages our prejudiced enemies to increase the discrimination in all public places of entertainment, amusement, conveyances, etc. until the logical and natural result will be what Dr. B. T. Washington urges—a separation of the races such as now exists in the South. . . . Shall we sit supinely by and let a few selfish cowardly "Jim Crow" Negroes whose life in the South or in Southern environments makes it impossible for them to appreciate what the older Afro-Americans of Cleveland and this vicinity have enjoyed for many years, wipe out all the remaining advances our parents and their true white friends fought so long and so hard to secure?[39]

In this and numerous other editorials, Smith articulated not only the traditional black leadership view of the city, but also their biases against the intrusion of Southern blacks into leadership ranks. They believed that the newcomers were bringing segregationist ideas into the city with their espousal of "self-help" and race institutions to solve the problems of blacks. Smith and his peers failed to examine the impact of changes which were becoming evident in the racial attitudes of a growing white immigrant population as well as the changing sympathies of the white establishment. Smith also revealed the prevailing traditional attitude that Southern black newcomers had not been exposed to the cultural and social amenities available in the North. Thus it was felt that the newcomers lacked an appreciation for "what older Afro-Americans of Cleveland have enjoyed."[40]

Thus, the Southern black newcomer, perceived to bring a less refined and somewhat limited educational background, was felt to be unqualified to suggest solutions to Northern race problems. Hunter, a Southerner, proposing a race facility, was viewed by Smith and the traditional leaders as a typical outsider, forcing "Southern" solutions on to her newly adopted Northern community.

Perhaps the most vivid example of the confrontation between opposition to the Working Girls' Home Association idea and Hunter's supporters is described in her autobiography. Hunter said that at one of the meetings to which the general public was invited to discuss plans for the home, a small group of black club women appeared. Undoubtedly, the women were part of the "old guard," described by Hunter as "women who, blessed with prosperity, had risen from the servant class and now regarded themselves as the arbiters and guardians of colored society."[41] According to Hunter, the women arrived at the meeting and took complete charge of proceedings, attempting ". . . to inject discord into all that had been said or done in an effort to start a home."[42]

The spokeswoman for the group was quoted as saying, "We have never had segregation. Our girls must go to the YWCA along with the white girls. Why should you come up from the South and tell us what to do?" Another of the club women remarked, "We're club women, and we represent all the club women of Cleveland . . . and will not permit you, a Southerner, to start segregation in this city."[43] Clearly the sentiments expressed by the women echoed the Northern blacks' fear of racial isolation, as well as their resentment of what they perceived to be Southern black ideas.

Hunter's reaction to the women in the group and her description of them reflected her personal bias against the black elite. Although blacks of the "old guard" did not represent the great wealth of upper-class whites, they clearly symbolized an intra-racial stratification which was well recognized among blacks. Education, light complexion, genteel manners, upwardly mobile aspirations and community concern historically served to distinguish this group of blacks from the masses. Moreover, Northern roots were considered most desirable. Hunter's depiction of the women as ex-servants was mostly inaccurate, but indicative of a subtle hostility which she and many others felt because of their exclusivity and pretentiousness. As an "outsider" she resented their presumption that only one small group was qualified to lead all other blacks, and her description of the incident, written in 1940, reveals that she never forgot the implied rejection. When Hunter was confronted with the argument that she was bringing Southern ideas to a Northern situation, she wrote, "I kindly asked whether the group knew of the progress the Negroes had made in the South because they had worked together."[44] When the club women stated ". . . the YWCA is for all," Hunter's answer reveals the difference between the pragmatism of her solution and the idealism of the earlier leaders. She replied, "Yes, but can you use it? Will they be welcomed by white girls." Obviously, Hunter believed the answers to her questions to be "No." She also implied that the "self-help" alternative provided the more desirable opportunity for the race.

Despite opposition from many of the old-guard leadership, Hunter was apparently slowly gaining support from a few of their number, and she undoubtedly was finding support among a new class of leaders. Two notable exceptions, for example, of traditional black elite support came from Walter C. Wright, secretary to the President of the Nickel Plate Railroad, and John P. Green, attorney and former state representative. When Hunter appealed to Wright not only to use his influence to try to sway the sentiments of other leaders, but also to use his contacts to help her raise money for the home, Wright felt that the reality of the need for the protection of young women outweighed the probability of gaining entrance into the YWCA in the near future.[47]

Green, another member of the elite group, was chosen by the white donors to be the black representative on the first board of the Phillis Wheatley. Green had long been accused by blacks of race conservatism and a willingness to acquiesce in demands of white benefactors. His support of the home was consistent with his record of agreement with the white power structure. Although others of the elite slowly accepted Hunter's plan and helped with fund-raising activities to build future facilities, she never forgave them for their early attempts to block her efforts to begin the institution.[48]

Among the new elite, Hunter became a rising star. Business and professional men and women whose economic support came from their service to the black community saw the concept of an institution for black women as an extension of their idea of self-help. Quite opposite from their more traditional predecessors, the newer group of leaders were mostly newcomers to Cleveland from the South who had attended segregated schools and universities. Rather than demanding inclusion into white institutions and organizations, this group tended to emphasize race uplift through initiation of their own institutions. Their rhetoric of economic nationalism followed the Booker Washington theory that money should be made and spent within the black community, with significant benefits to the race as a result. While seeming to ignore their obvious exclusion from public facilities and services, this newer group seemed to accept separation as an opportunity to extend race cohesiveness (and incidentally created a built-in clientele for their businesses and services).

New leaders such as Thomas Fleming, the country's first big-city black councilman, and his equally active wife, Lethia; Mrs. Elmer F. Boyd, wife of a successful funeral director; Mrs. Cornelia Nickens, wife of a very active doctor; and J. Walter Wills, owner of the city's largest black-owned funeral home, were among Hunter's staunch supporters. Hunter also found support from a rival newspaper to the *Cleveland Gazette*, the *Cleveland Advocate*. The *Advocate* regularly featured the work of the Phillis Wheatley Association, considering it to be a vital and significant addition to the city for blacks.[49]

Traditionally, within the black community, the most influential group is the ministers. This was the case in the beginning years of the Phillis Wheatley Association. Hunter knew that her plan could not succeed without their support. With the exception of Reverend H. C. Bailey, pastor of Antioch Baptist Church (the city's most prestigious black Baptist church), the Interdenominational Ministerial Alliance, an organization of the black ministers in Cleveland, refused to endorse Hunter's plan.[50] The group stood firm in their belief in pressing for integrated facilities, even though Hunter conducted and presented to them a survey which indicated that no existing social agency would accept black women.

Frequent testimony about her own experiences as a newcomer to the city and their growing concern for the morality of young black women finally convinced the ministers to arrange a meeting between their members and the board of trustees of the YWCA. Only after the meeting did Hunter receive the group's full endorsement. The ministers were told in no uncertain terms that the YWCA would not encourage participation of black girls at their building for fear the white girls would withdraw. In addition, they were told that the YWCA board members felt that black girls should be cared for by their own race.[51] Subsequently, the ministers apologized to Hunter for opposing her efforts and became active advocates for the home. This represented a major victory for the institution's supporters.

With sentiment within the black community growing in favor of the home, Hunter and her group became more active in their fund-raising activities. While the idealistic dues of a nickel per member per week, along with small concerts and meetings in black churches, proved to be great psychological boosters, Hunter clearly understood the need for help from wealthy whites. Through contacts with wealthy patients, Hunter began her appeal for support for the home. Sarah C. Hills, a patient and wife of a prominent attorney, was credited as the first white supporter of the plan. Hills introduced Hunter to the Women's Missionary Board of the Second

Presbyterian Church, and later to the Presbyterian Society of Cuyahoga County. Soon she was asked to speak to various white groups, appealing for money and furnishings for the proposed new home.

An early communication from Hunter to her prospective white donors reveals that she made good use of her understanding of their interests. Her years as a servant helped to identify ways to use their personal concerns to make her case. While appealing to black leaders on the basis of their need to be concerned for the morality and protection of poor black women, and thus the necessity of providing a good Christian atmosphere, Hunter used an additional twist when she appealed for white support. A letter which she drafted and sent to prospective white donors (after having Mrs. Hills check it over), is quite revealing:

WORKING GIRLS' HOME ASSOCIATION
Miss J. Edna Hunter, Pres.
2167 East 76th Street
Miss L. R. Bailey, Secretary
J. S. Hall, Treasurer
Cleveland

Dear Madam:
After six years of study and thorough investigation, I have gotten at the root of the domestic problem involving the working girls and their inefficiency of service in well-governed and systemized homes. I found that lack of interest, ambition, training, and association is due largely to this trouble, which, perhaps, you and thousands of women have had to endure.

It is apparent that the time has come when something must be done to eradicate this evil.

The persons whose names appear on this letterhead believe that the only solution of this condition would be a Home Association where these women might have pure and pleasant surroundings when out of employment; a place where they can be taught the art of housekeeping, the techniques of hygiene, the beauty in personal neatness, the importance of loyalty, etc. The object of the board is to establish just such a place and to have the above mentioned subjects taught.

We are endeavoring to raise means by which we intend to lift the standards of working girls. It is earnestly hoped that you will cooperate with us in some way to help make this work a success.[52]

From this communication, it is obvious that Hunter had plans broader than providing a safe lodging. The letter, which promised domestic training for maids for white families, clearly established at least part of her agenda for the success of the institution. Also, the tone of the letter, which lays the blame for the lack of good servants on their own lack of ambition and preparation, is completely consistent with the style of her idol, Booker T. Washington. The emphasis on training for domestic help, with only incidental mention of the pure and pleasant surroundings for women out of work, is a clear indication of Hunter's perception of what would motivate white women to donate money to a home for black women.

Hunter correctly sensed that her black opponents would have disapproved more vigorously if they had known that the training goals of the prospective institution were limited to training domestic servants. Perhaps, in retrospect, she felt the need to justify what could seem a subtle betrayal of black aspirations, noting in her autobiography that it ". . . became my duty to harmonize . . . the purposes and desires of my people, and the policies of the white friends whose material support we sought."[53] Her method for bringing about the so-called amalgamation of interests required different tactics in the black community than could be used in dealings with the white community. Hunter carefully planned her strategy to gain white money and at the same time black support.

For the black community, the Working Girls' Home Association sponsored a series of public meetings in various black churches, sometimes featuring speeches by white supporters. One such meeting, which Hunter noted as an especially helpful session, featured the minister of Old Stone Church, Dr. A. P. Meldrum. Through his eloquence and influence, some blacks were persuaded that whites were sincerely interested in the welfare of needy black women coming into the city. He assured them that they had no need to fear the motives of white friends who supported the idea of a home for black women.[54]

In addition to the letter to individual white contacts, Hunter's strategy to gain help from the white community included an appeal to the YWCA. Rather than asking for memberships for black women, as had been tried before, Hunter asked only for advice and counsel from board members. She made clear her position that the city needed a separate institution, and appealed to the board only for help with planning and financing a facility which would house and train black women. Hunter based her appeal to the YWCA board members on her knowledge of their sentiments, gained during the time that she surveyed the community to document the lack of social services for black women. From her meetings with Elizabeth Schofield, president of the YWCA board, Hunter confirmed the board's position that they did not intend to encourage membership for black women, nor did they intend to allow blacks access to their various facilities. However, Schofield was impressed by Hunter's suggestion of a completely separate institution and gave a tentative promise to help with the project.

Shortly after her appeal to Schofield, Hunter was introduced to Henry A. Sherwin, president of the Sherwin-Williams Paint Company. She credited him with great generosity in advising her in the art of building an organization, a promise of financial support, and access to other donors. However, his aid was contingent upon the condition that she "must secure a group of white women to advise and work with the Negro women."[55] At that point, Hunter returned to Mrs. Schofield and informed her of Sherwin's offer.

Schofield, who had recently led a highly successful fund-raising campaign for a new downtown YWCA building (with Sherwin and his wife very active members of her committee), decided to join with Hunter to find a way to provide housing for black women. Disregarding the already-established board structure, which was composed of black women and men, Schofield suggested that she would be pleased to become a member of a group of ladies who would "head up and foster" Hunter's planned institution. Knowing of the interest Sarah Hills already had in the plan, Schofield recommended Hills, Mrs. Laura Goodhue, Mrs. Stevenson Burke, and Mr. J. R. Wylie as a core of whites to guide the efforts for the home.[56] All of the persons had been or were currently active members of the YWCA board or committees in the YWCA.[57] Schofield suggested that Hunter should appoint as many "representative colored ladies as she wished."[58]

The agreement which Schofield suggested brought Hunter's dilemma to the attention of the black community. She would have to waive the leadership of blacks who had long worked with her to make the planned facility a reality in order to accommodate her new white supporters. Her attempts to "amalgamate" the interests of the black and white communities were not as simple as she had anticipated. Hunter referred to the situation as a "tide of misunderstanding by misinterpretation of my relationship with white friends."[59] Another interpretation might well be that black supporters were beginning to recognize that financial support from the white community was inevitably going to threaten the blacks' ability to control their own "self-help" institution.

In spite of Schofield's initial proposal, the worst suspicions of supporters of the home were confirmed when the whites who were asked to serve refused to cooperate unless they were given the authority to select the blacks who would serve on the board. Hunter then was faced with finding a way to keep the support of critical black leaders who were only recently beginning to join her, as well as maintaining the staunch black supporters who had helped from the beginning. At the same time, she was trying to satisfy the demands of white financial and organizational supporters. This was not an easy job.

The dilemma was not new. Colleges, settlement houses, orphanages, hospitals, sanitariums, and a variety of service institutions for blacks had been faced with the same problem. Only a few of these could claim principal support from funds raised by black people. Although numerous organizations of blacks were formed to find ways to solve the seemingly insurmountable social problems of a race so recently out of slavery, with no federal plan for support to rectify the race's social ills there simply was not the money nor opportunity to accumulate wealth in the black community to begin to answer the needs of the people. In Cleveland, the only other service institution for blacks, the Home for Aged Colored People, was barely able to survive. With a total population of just under 9,000 blacks in the city, few blacks had sufficient income to donate substantially to charitable causes.

In his plan for the race, Washington never failed to provide for the accommodation of white conditions for philanthropy, thus retaining their financial patronage. By insisting that interracial harmony and goodwill were prerequisite to the advancement of blacks, Washington believed that those farthest down the socio-economic scale should be the ones to make concessions.[60] Hunter, Washington's true disciple, came to the same conclusion. In commenting upon the crisis, she stated:

> I was faced with a choice between offending members of my race who had given far more than they could afford, and yielding to influences which could give our organization a sound financial basis. I was called upon to make a decision which gave to us the support we needed. It seemed necessary to sacrifice personal feelings for the sake of the cause.[61]

Presentation of the new constitution to a crowd of over a hundred community citizens at the home of Mrs. E. F. Boyd, a black supporter, was frightening and challenging to Hunter. The constitution, written by Adin T. Hills (husband of Sarah Hills), virtually assured white control. Although the new constitution was in most ways patterned after that of the local YWCA, one glaring difference was found in the Code of Regulations, Section III, Membership.[62] In this section, membership was divided into two categories, regular and associate. Regular members were required to pay a membership fee of $5 at the time they joined, and $5 per year. Voting privileges were granted on the basis of one vote for every $5 contributed for the year. In addition, these members would be permitted to vote in person or by proxy. Trustees were to be chosen from members in this category only. A second classification of "associate" members who paid $1 per year would only have the privilege of participation in the activities of the association, and promoting its programs. [63] Opposition to the membership provision was vigorous from many blacks at the meeting. The idyllic nickel-and-prayer support had drastically multiplied. On advice from Reverend H. C. Bailey, the vote on the constitution was deferred for two weeks.

Hunter stated that during the crisis she first turned to a potential white trustee in an attempt to find a compromise which would be acceptable to both sides. She was told firmly that there would be no compromise on the part of the whites. Hunter then used the time to gather support from within the black community to approve the plan as it had been presented. At the meeting which followed, Hunter's opponents did not appear. The constitution and its by-laws, complete with the disputed membership code, was approved. At that time, the official name of the home became The Phillis Wheatley Association, both to give recognition to the slave poet, and to avoid confusion with a rival organization which filed for a charter to start a settlement house under a name almost identical to the Working Girls Home Association.[64]

The new board of trustees elected Mrs. Levi T. Schofield president; Mrs. Adin T. Hills, vice-president; Mr. J. R. Wylie, treasurer; and Jane E. Hunter, executive secretary. Other members of the board were Mrs. Laura S. Goodhue, John P. Green, and Robert E. Lewis. Jane Hunter was the only black woman on the board, joined by one black man, Green. The constitution was signed by Jane E. Hunter, R. K. Moon, Charles Bundy, Mrs. Thomas W. Fleming, John S. Hall, T. M. Farlice, Mrs. Minerva Taylor, Miss A. B. Cohen, Miss R. E. Johnson, Mrs. Ida M. Burton, Mrs. Cora Boyd, Howard E. Murrell, Thomas W. Fleming, John P. Green, Blanche Johnson, and Lula B. Cox.[65] All signers of the constitution were black.

Thus Cleveland gained a black institution, financed mainly by whites and controlled by the donors. It seems no coincidence that the white officers almost duplicated the leadership of the city's YWCA. Also, complete exclusion of black girls from YWCA programs and classes directly coincided with the creation of the Phillis Wheatley Association, during the time that

Mrs. Schofield served as president of both organizations. George Myers, an old-guard black leader, commented that the home was "fostered by a few misguided whites endeavoring to relieve their consciences of the discrimination of the YWCA."[66]

It seems reasonable to conclude that black opposers did not lose the fight to stop Hunter and her supporters because of ambivalence about integration as a goal. Rather, they were willing to compromise because accelerating anti-black sentiments, both locally and nationally, made it increasingly more difficult to achieve a better short-term solution. The rapid growth in the number of blacks entering the city, with few social services available to them, meant that the old solutions simply would not be effective. However, it is important to note that while at the same time support was growing for the Phillis Wheatley in 1912, a chapter of the integrationist-oriented NAACP was established. R. K. Moon, a major supporter of the Working Girls Home Association, and Hunter's Phillis Wheatley, was elected the first president of the new chapter.[67]

Moon's affiliation with both of the organizations serves as a reminder that lines were not hard drawn in the black community as to the best method for blacks to achieve integration in the long run. Although some leaders were convinced of one means or another, others seemed willing to work with equal vigor on short-term solutions to the problems, as well as on longer-range plans such as the new NAACP proposed. In any case, integration of blacks into the economic and social mainstream was the ultimate goal.

The names of black leaders were often found on the rolls of seemingly opposite ideological efforts to find direction for the newly burgeoning population. There simply was no single answer to the complex problems of a race beset with a history of slavery in a country that defined worth in terms of individual achievement while at the same time supporting practices and policies which continued to bar blacks from opportunities for success. Hunter's compromise with white financial supporters was a survival tactic. If she had failed to make the decision to accept the conditions which the donors set, there was little chance that her dream would have been realized.

A specific example of a similar effort during the same time further illustrates the complexities of solution-seeking within the black community, as well as some of the contradictions among a people struggling to conform to a value system which did not suit their particular situation. During the time of the debate in Cleveland's black community as to the acceptability of the plan for the Phillis Wheatley Association in the form which Hunter presented, a social settlement house on Central Avenue at 25th Street was announced. The City Federation of Women's Clubs (an affiliate of the National Association of Colored Women) was the sponsor. Sarah Mitchell Bailey, a well-respected teacher in the public school system and wife of the pastor of Antioch church, signed the announcement.[68]

Even though by its sponsorship and location the settlement house was clearly intended to aid blacks in the city, the new institution was welcomed by the traditional leadership. Harry C. Smith spoke at the dedication of the house and editorialized favorably on its behalf in his newspaper. Even as he passionately objected to the Working Girls' Home Association, or any mention of a black YMCA, he favored the work of the Federation. His response to the effort (which probably reflected that of the old guard), raises a question as to the seeming contradiction in his statements and sentiments. One could speculate that Smith and his peers expressed a trust in the leadership of the Federation. The women of the Federation represented the more traditional upper strata of the black community. Wives of leading doctors, ministers, lawyers, and businessmen were included along with schoolteachers. The women were very acceptable "leading ladies" representing a federation of literary clubs, sewing circles, and church clubs. Smith did not see their efforts as "race exclusive," but rather lauded them for making a valuable contribution to the life of the city.

The difference was that the women claimed to be interested in the neighborhood, which was multiracial in population, and did not specify the race as their target clientele. Also, as members of the black elite, their efforts merely extended into the black community the model of charitable work being done by the white women of the city. Theirs was not an intrusion of separatist Southern ideas, but was rather an expression of concern from within the black community for their less fortunate members.

Hunter, a Southerner, a semi-professional, without the benefit of a Northern education, was an outsider. Her original group of supporters included maids and laboring women to whom the community was not accustomed to look for leadership for race solutions. In addition, Hunter's idea offered a directly parallel service to that offered by the YWCA, an established institution which had provided at least limited access for black women to white services. In contrast, a settlement house on Central, sponsored by black club women, would not duplicate, but merely imitate, similar efforts of elite white women who sponsored settlement houses for the foreign-born who were entering the city. One could make a fine distinction between the obvious separation of facilities for blacks and an extension of services to blacks, sponsored by a group of established black women. The settlement house closed in February of 1913, for lack of funds and lack of support.[69]

FOUR

The YWCA and the Phillis Wheatley Association: Separate Institutions for Cleveland

Between 1910 and 1920, Cleveland's black population increased 308 percent, from 8,448 to 34,451, a gain of 26,003.[1] The increase represented a gain in percentage of the city's total population from the historic 1.5 percent to 4.3 percent. It has been estimated that as much as three-fourths of the increase in the black population occurred between 1916 and 1919. Thus, the city was faced with the difficult task of absorbing and assimilating a large number of black citizens at a time when racial segregation was gaining as a social and legal norm at both the local and national levels. Precedence was set by a Southern president, Woodrow Wilson, who undertook the task of officially segregating the nation's capital in its public facilities and government offices. The model of separation was duplicated in many parts of the country.

Locally, the racial climate grew increasingly hostile. Cleveland's black *Gazette* editorialized weekly against theaters showing such racist moving pictures as *The Nigger* and *Birth of a Nation*, and such practices as barring blacks from the popular Euclid Beach and Luna parks.[2] Exclusion of black workers from the labor unions prior to World War I also served to create an economic disparity between black and immigrant laborers.

Although the causes of the great population shift were varied, historians have cited and grouped together "push" factors, which contributed to the out-migration from the South, and "pull" factors, which attracted blacks to Northern urban centers. Among the "push" factors were such economic realities as the mechanization of agriculture and the general economic depression in the South, which was aggravated by floods and the depredation brought on by the boll-weevil. Social injustices such as the dual-education system, the disfranchisement of black men, and the fear of lynching and terrorism were also important factors. Among the so-called pull factors were the opening of jobs in industry, better schools, and the general perception that blacks could live better in the North.[3] Intricately involved in all of the causes for movement was the attempt by black Americans to find relief from the racism which prevailed in Southern life. The desire to make decent wages was frequently cited as the primary motivation, along with the opportunity for a decent education.[4]

Cleveland, with its concentration of heavy industry, was very attractive to black workers. The outbreak of hostilities in Europe in 1914 ended the flood of Eastern and Southern European immigrants which had provided a supply of workers. As a result, black workers, who had traditionally been labeled as "inherently unfit for industrial work" were suddenly sought after as an untapped "reserve" labor force. For the first time, blacks had an opportunity to gain employment on a larger scale, in jobs which had the potential for skills development. Although skilled trade unions routinely excluded them for the most part, this did not prevent blacks from entering industry at the lower occupational levels.[5]

Announcement of the opening of the Phillis Wheatley Home coincided, almost as if planned, with the phenomenon of mass movement of blacks into the city. When Mrs. Levi T. Schofield, newly elected president of the board of the Phillis Wheatley, announced in March, 1913, that nearly $800 of the $1,000 needed to establish a home had been pledged, she was optimistic that the entire amount would be raised within a few weeks.[6] Election of the new white-dominated board seemed to ignite a virtual whirlwind of activity for Hunter and the Association. Her new friends moved quickly to introduce the plan for black women to numbers of church groups, especially women's clubs. Speeches recounting her own struggles against the hardships and temptations of city life served as testimony to the need for help for women of her group. Contributions began to pour in, and within a very short time, $1,500 was added to the little treasury.

Henry A. Sherwin, whose conditions for donation forced Hunter to accept a white-dominated board, was obviously impressed with her success in carrying out his suggestions. He personally donated $600 to be used for rent for the home for the first year. When he made his contribution, he remarked to Hunter that "Colored people often ask for fifty cents when they need five dollars."[7] Hunter never forgot his advice. She said that Sherwin taught her to decide upon what was needed for a given project, and then present the facts.[8]

The new board of trustees selected a house adjacent to St. John's African Methodist Episcopal Church, at 2265 East 40th Street. This was a twenty-three room building which housed fifteen girls along with a house matron and Hunter. There was a kitchen, space for the women to entertain guests, and laundry facilities. A dining room was added later.[9] Included in the fee charged for rent at the home was use of the laundry, parlor room, and the kitchen. Later, when the dining room was added, there were group dinners prepared by the residents. The women were encouraged to attended free lectures offered by the Association to the community, and they were requested to participate in weekly vesper services which were conducted in the home. Hunter and her board were interested in furnishing not only a safe shelter for the women, but they also wanted to provide opportunities for recreation and religious training.

The first year of operation of the Phillis Wheatley Association proved a phenomenal success. An opening-day reception with Mayor Newton D. Baker in attendance served to bolster the spirits of board members and supporters, despite the death of President Schofield only a few days before the opening. With a meager budget of $1,500, donations of used furniture, and the hard work of a few persons, the demand for services proved far greater than anticipated. The small board of trustees elected Sarah C. Hills (Mrs. Adin T.) as their leader. They labored hard to disperse the income of approximately $200 per month, collected at a rate of $1.25 per week for rent.[10] Some of Hunter's staunch black supporters, like Mrs. Elmer F. Boyd and Amy Cohen, helped with refurbishing furniture, painting, and scrubbing to make the house habitable. Almost before the doors of the home opened, there were more requests for lodging than there was room available.

Perhaps the most interesting response to the opening of the home was the outpouring of white sentiment and monies to support the venture. While the black community seemed to have mixed feelings about Hunter and her activities, whites, especially white church members, endorsed the plan wholeheartedly. Especially helpful and supportive were those men and women who were involved with the Cleveland YWCA.[11]

Schofield, first president of the Phillis Wheatley, was also president of the Cleveland YWCA. She had served on the Building Committee for a new downtown YWCA headquarters, working closely with Mr. and Mrs. Henry A. Sherwin (Mrs. Sherwin chaired the committee), Laura Goodhue, Mr. Adin T. Hills (Chair of the Committee of Management for the Central Building), and Robert E. Lewis, general secretary of the Cleveland YMCA. All of those persons became trustees of the Phillis Wheatley. Even before the Phillis Wheatley had obtained a home, the YWCA general secretary, Mary E. Rathburn, was a speaker at one of the open meetings on behalf of the Phillis Wheatley Home.[12] From the earliest announcement throughout the history of the Association under Hunter's direction, the YWCA played an important role, with YWCA staff and volunteers providing leadership for both institutions. The relationship between the two provides an interesting example of the complexities of relationships between the white and black communities before 1950.

Before the Phillis Wheatley opened, the question of membership and service for black women had not been officially addressed by the YWCA. Founded in Cleveland in 1868 as a "Home for Working Women" and a "Retreat for Erring and Unfortunate Girls," the organization was led and nurtured by prominent families such as the Mathers, Eells, Sherwins, Chisholms, and Stones. Before 1900, the organization had grown to sponsor additional facilities for women, including a home for aged women, day nurseries, a home for incurable invalids, an employment bureau, a camp for women and girls, and a home for transient women. Although there was no written policy regarding blacks, there are no records indicating service for black women at any of these sites. The Association was clearly intended to aid protestant white women. In addition to their boarding facilities, there were such classes as bookkeeping, cooking, table service, stenography, millinery, and tailoring, and there were numerous small club groups. A few black girls were apparently allowed to participate in some of these activities.

Evidence of their lodging practices comes from Hunter's own experience when she arrived in Cleveland in 1905. The YWCA was not available to her for lodging or for aid in finding employment in her nursing profession, though their stated purpose was to aid young female newcomers to the city. In addition to her own personal experiences, Hunter documented in a survey of social services for blacks, prior to presenting the Phillis Wheatley plan to

FOR WORTHY GIRLS   NON-DENOMINATIONAL

First home of the Phillis Wheatley Association, 1913-1918

the community, that the board of trustees of the YWCA had no intention of allowing more than a very few black women to attend classes. Board members stated the fear that "if the black girls came to the 'Y' building in large numbers, and were the majority in any activity, the white girls would withdraw."[12] Further, they informed the black Ministerial Alliance, which met with the YW Board to discuss the issue, that they felt that "Negro girls should be cared for by the Negro race."[13] However, the same women could not ignore the fact that the city had *no* facilities for black women. Their closed doors literally could seal the fate of many in need of such services which only they, the YWCA, were equipped to provide.

It seems safe to speculate that Hunter's approach to YWCA trustees, timed three years after the completion of the large downtown facility, gave the Christian ladies some relief from what could be anticipated as a problem, as black migration to the city accelerated. The fact that the idea for a proposed separate facility came from a black woman surely helped to legitimize its validity. Hunter, with her sincere and humble plea for help, was to provide a near-perfect answer to any Christian guilt the women may have felt for their exclusionary policies.

Hunter's request for "counsel" from the women also coincided with affiliation by the local YWCA with the newly organized National Board and National Association. The new national structure attempted to pull together all local and student organizations using the name YWCA, including a few in cities with already-established black centers and/or work with black women. Consistent with their mission to aid working women, some cities, at the time of national organization, already had extensive programs for black women. The new National Board found that they had acquired a black student constituency when they merged with the National Student Association. In response, the board hired the first black female social worker to work as a national staff member, to survey black colleges where there were active student associations. By 1913, a national field secretary for "colored work" had been hired and black branches were being built in New York City, Baltimore, and St. Louis.[14] Cleveland's avoidance of a policy regarding work with black women at the early stages of a black population explosion could only be temporary at best. Hunter clearly offered an alternative which could delay official action on the part of the board on the one hand, while relieving the serious lack of services for blacks on the other.

YWCA policies in Cleveland seemed to be typical of the ambivalent yet hardening racial atmosphere in the city. Earlier inclusion of a few blacks in classes which the institution sponsored was consistent with inclusion of blacks in the Cleveland public school system. As well, a few social service agencies in the city boasted in 1905 of having given aid to black citizens.[15] Although agency records do not indicate the extent of black participation or receipt of services, it is likely that the limited inclusion of blacks in the YWCA and YMCA was typical. Russell H. Davis, in *Black Americans in Cleveland*, described the policy of the YMCA:

> A few young men were accepted, but some of these were refused renewal. However, most applicants were turned down without reason being given, although Negro leaders appealed directly to the General Secretary.[16]

YWCA policies often mirrored the YMCA's in such matters.[17]

Hunter's decision not to approach YWCA leaders to ask for membership for black women, but only to appeal for their "advice and counsel," gave the women an opportunity to provide service to blacks, while at the same time allowing time for them to consider what, if any, official policy could be worked out. The question of the relationship between the two Associations was raised continually for ten years until 1922, when an agreement was reached for each to remain autonomous. Although local leadership of the two institutions was the same from the outset, Hunter credited the YWCA National Board with initiation of official negotiations between them. While attending a conference at Summer Land Beach near Columbus, Ohio, in 1914, Hunter came to the attention of a National Board worker, Miss Florence Simms. Upon learning from Hunter of the new home for black women, Simms reported to the National Board the possibility of incorporating the work of the Phillis Wheatley into that of the Cleveland YWCA.[18]

The June 9, 1914, minutes of the Phillis Wheatley Board of Trustees recorded a vote to grant Hunter two weeks to study in New York City, presumably at the YWCA National Board's Training School. No further reference was made to the YWCA until April 13, 1915, when the board again voted to give Hunter six weeks leave of absence with salary to study in New York. Hunter specifically referred to the latter study course as a special training opportunity to help her to fully understand the policies of the local and national YWCA.[19] After the summer training course, the National Board was very actively involved in trying to persuade the Cleveland Association to make the Phillis Wheatley Association its colored branch.[20]

Their interest in the Cleveland situation intensified after a national conference in Louisville, Kentucky (November 23, 1915), which was specifically called to deal with work with colored women. A plan for the inclusion of separate branches was recommended, with a structure designed to assure ties to Central Boards of Trustees. The promotion of black leadership was an important consideration.[21] Cleveland was in the unique position of having not only a strong Central YWCA, but also a ready-made black institution which paralleled the work of the YWCA, with essentially the same leadership in both. With but a few structural adjustments, Cleveland had a nearly model situation, at least in the opinion of the National Board. Eva Bowles, national secretary for colored work, came to Cleveland several times to aid in the negotiations between the YWCA and the Phillis Wheatley. On one occasion she challenged the Cleveland YWCA to assess how they were going to meet the needs of black women in order to fulfill the YWCA mission in the highest sense.[22] Assuming responsibility for the Phillis Wheatley was seen as a very natural step toward achieving this goal.

During the negotiations between 1915 and 1917, it is not clear how Jane Hunter felt about the proposed merger of the institutions. In later recollections, she often mentioned the lack of housing accommodations for black women at the National Board headquarters, and this made quite a negative impression as to the YWCA's real commitment to "amalgamation" of the races.[23] However, there is no indication that she was opposed to merger in the early months of negotiations. Mary Parsons, president of the Phillis Wheatley board (1915-17) and an active YWCA board member, is on record as being very much in favor of the merger, as were Phillis Wheatley board members Dr. Paul Sutphen, minister of the fashionable white Second Presbyterian Church, and Charles Chesnutt, noted black author and civic leader.[24] Minutes of the Phillis Wheatley board suggest that its leaders and the National YWCA staff were more enthusiastic about the possibility of merger than was the local YWCA board.[25] The minutes contain frequent references to requests by the Phillis Wheatley board members for meetings between the two organizations.[26]

The YWCA Board of Trustees minutes of January 19, 1917, note an appeal by Dr. Sutphen for merger of the two institutions. Subsequently, a motion was passed that an invitation be extended to the Phillis Wheatley Association to become a member of the YWCA. Following the vote, however, YWCA board members again raised the question of membership privileges for blacks if the Phillis Wheatley was absorbed. Questions were also raised regarding the financial responsibility which would be assumed if the YWCA took the Phillis Wheatley organization under its structure. Dr. Sutphen reportedly reprimanded the women, stating that the question between the two organizations was "not one of money but of amalgamation." Even so, a motion was passed to table action to merge the two organizations until a subsequent meeting.[27]

In her account of the early negotiations between the Phillis Wheatley and the YWCA, Jane Hunter recalled that she was out of town in 1916 when the meetings were held. Until this point there is little evidence that she did not agree with the efforts of her board to seek the protection and financial security inherent in being a part of the YWCA. However, when she returned to town, Hunter's position had become very firm: the Phillis Wheatley should remain independent of the YWCA. Hunter later recalled:

> With no rancor, but with a deep sense of the rightness of my belief that we could stand on our own feet, and that only as an independent organization would we win a full measure of justice for colored girls, I made my position clear.[28]

Moreover, as she "made her position clear," Hunter also announced that she had secured pledges of $13,000 toward purchase of a larger facility for the home. The pledges, coming at such a sensitive time during negotiations between the two institutions, point to a strong sentiment against the merger on the part of at least a few major benefactors. It is evident that Hunter's support for independence for the Phillis Wheatley was greatly influenced by the promise of funds.

When Hunter turned over the pledges to her board, she threatened to organize another Phillis Wheatley if the board decided to join the YWCA. Within a week, the Phillis Wheatley board withdrew their motion to become a part of the YWCA, and the YWCA announced on March 20, 1917, a willingness "to concur in any motion to defer action on the subject of amalgamation of the two organizations. . . ."[29] The question came up again in 1922, with similar committee meetings between the two institutions, and again resulted in a decision for the Phillis Wheatley to remain independent.[30]

Resistance to the merger in both cases may be attributed to Hunter as well as the YWCA board. During the negotiations in 1916, Hunter was persuaded by the offer of funds for her organization if the Association remained independent. However, by 1922, her reasons for maintaining autonomy appear to be a bit more complex. When asked in a joint meeting in 1922 to discuss the possible merger of the two institutions and ways that the merger could benefit the Phillis Wheatley, Marie Wing, then general secretary of the Cleveland YWCA, responded that it would provide an opportunity to secure trained workers for the colored branch. Lack of trained workers was a frequent criticism of the Phillis Wheatley. The YWCA required that its workers have a college degree as a prerequisite for being trained for work in their associations. Hunter responded to Wing that she could probably get help from colleges of higher education for colored girls.[31] However, Hunter seemed threatened by the requirement of the YWCA that staff have college degrees. Although she graduated from Ferguson-Williams "College" in 1896, the degree was considered equivalent to high school only.[32] Her nurses' training also did not qualify as a college course. This deficiency in her education was frequently cited by co-workers as a continuing source of insecurity for Hunter.[33] Although concessions might have been made for her experience if the YWCA had taken over the Phillis Wheatley, there remained the possibility that she could lose the administrative position which she had created as founder of the institution.

In addition to the education requirements of the YWCA, the structure for colored branches would have essentially made Hunter an employee of the Central Branch Board of Directors and its general secretary. Although there would be an all-black board of managers for the Phillis Wheatley, they would have reported to a Committee for Colored Work, chaired by a Central Board member (white).[34] This structure would have undoubtedly usurped Hunter's authority and position. It would have also curtailed her association with wealthy white supporters, and would have made her more responsible to black supporters and critics.

The fact that she seemed reluctant to share certain responsibilities and opportunities with other black women surfaced when on at least one occasion, at an all-black fund-raising meeting, the women expressed concern that Hunter was not training anyone to take over the Association in the event of her absence. "It was found that no one else can handle the white people and get the money we need in order to run the home," stated the minutes of the meeting.[35] YWCA affiliation would have clearly eliminated the problem of depending on one individual for access to funding sources. Monies would automatically be funneled through the Central Board to the black Phillis Wheatley, with most of the control as well as responsibility for raising funds at the Central Board level. This new structure would have removed Hunter from most direct contact with wealthy whites and, consequently, the status which she clearly felt she gained from association with them. Having so carefully cultivated her wealthy supporters, Hunter was not interested in this loss of contact.

Another benefit for Hunter for having the Association remain autonomous was the on-the-job training in management and administration which she received from intimate contact with board members who represented not only wealth, but also business acumen. The board's treasurer, J. R. Wylie, for example, headed the Women's Division for Cleveland Trust Bank. Wylie's careful investments for the board were very instructive to Hunter for her own personal small investments. Also, Mrs. Hills and Mrs. Parsons and others were married to very successful businessmen. Hunter observed their business and administration practices very closely, adapting at least some of them for her own use in administrating the business of the Phillis Wheatley. In addition, Hunter attended YWCA National Board training events at various times, and attended many conferences relating to social agency administration. The board was generous with time for Hunter to attend conferences and skills-building training events, sometimes paying fees and travel expenses. There seemed to be no problem of access to YWCA national resources, even though there was no official affiliation.[36]

Locally, the YWCA staff and volunteer resources were easily accessible to the Phillis Wheatley. Beginning with Elizabeth Schofield, who held the presidencies of both institutions, the Phillis Wheatley board was dominated by members of the YWCA board. In addition, a Phillis Wheatley Cooperative Board was formed, made up almost exclusively of YWCA board members. The Cooperative Board was to supplement the work of the board of trustees in aiding the work of the Phillis Wheatley. Beginning with Mary Rathburn in 1913, the general secretary of the Cleveland YWCA was always included as a member of the Cooperative Board. Prominent YWCA names such as Mrs. Stevenson Burke, Mrs. H. A. Griffin, Mrs. H. A. Sherwin, Mrs. Paul Sutphen, Mrs. Robert E. Lewis, Mrs. Fred A. Glidden, Mrs. Hylas S. Janes, Mrs. A. B. Teachout, Mrs. Bertha L. Bailey, and Mrs. Gertrude Hayes were joined by only a handful of prominent black women such as Mrs. Thomas Fleming and Mrs. E. F. Boyd.[37] The women gave generously of their financial and moral support, balancing their effort for white women in the YWCA with help to black women through the Phillis Wheatley. YWCA staff members often gave reports of conferences and activities to the board of the Phillis Wheatley, and, in at least one instance, a YWCA program, the

Girl Reserves (clubs for teenage girls), was installed at the Phillis Wheatley.[38]

When the question of merger was first raised, the Phillis Wheatley was seriously considering expansion into larger quarters. The small band of six board members feared that the move might be too much of a financial burden for their meager resources. Merger with the YWCA would have provided valuable financial and administrative support. By the end of 1916, 50 percent of the girls and women who applied for shelter were being turned away because of lack of room.[39] Hunter and the institution were, in the meantime, becoming well known by blacks throughout the country. As blacks poured into cities, models for aid for the newcomers were widely publicized by the national black press, and Hunter's home for women was recognized as one of a growing number of new institutions, North and South, to which blacks could turn for help. In fact, before 1923, the Phillis Wheatley served as a model for work in Youngstown and Toledo, Ohio, and Greenville, South Carolina.[40] Although the YWCA was rapidly increasing its work with black women through its branch structure (in cities where the black population was over 15,000), the independent Phillis Wheatley provided an alternative institutional model. Whites could control and finance work with blacks without integrating the clientele or services, while, blacks, at the same time, could boast of having interracial boards for their "self-help" institutions.

While YWCA board members worried about what their responsibility would be if blacks became members through the Phillis Wheatley, Hunter became convinced that the work could be carried out quite as effectively without a merger—and without jeopardizing her own position. Her negative reaction to YWCA affiliation by 1917, when the matter was officially being negotiated, was probably related to her increasing self-assurance as an administrator, her growing influence among blacks as the institution became well-known, and most importantly, her assurance from wealthy whites that they would continue to finance the separate facility, especially if it remained independent from the YWCA.

At the March, 1917, joint meeting of the board of trustees and the Cooperative Board of the Phillis Wheatley, a decision was made to purchase the Winona Apartments at the corner of Central Avenue and East 40th Street. The building contained seventy-two rooms and could easily triple the work of the Association. Hunter recalled that the decision was not easy because of a still-strong belief by some that the Association should be under the supervision of the YWCA. This sentiment complicated matters because so many members of the Cooperative Board were also members of the YWCA board. After much discussion, Mrs. Robert E. Lewis, wife of the YMCA general secretary, finally made a motion to purchase the building. The decision was made. By April, $14,061.33 had been pledged, and Hunter was assured that the remainder was forthcoming.[41]

Although the list of donors for the building could not be secured, one must assume that many of the donors were members of the Cooperative Board, since most of the women represented Cleveland's wealthiest families. Hunter's threat to withdraw and begin anew certainly was made on more than faith. She had come to the March meeting with $13,000 in pledges, which means that she had been talking with donors and had some knowledge of their sentiments. Mrs. Stevenson Burke, one of the city's wealthiest and most influential women, offered the motion to raise funds for the building on the same day that Woodrow Wilson declared war.[42] Hunter said that she went to "friends" and was able to obtain enough money not only to purchase the building, but also to refurbish and remodel it into an eighty-eight-room facility. By spring of 1919, a campaign among blacks raised enough additional money to purchase an adjacent two-story building to provide activity and meeting rooms to accommodate the black community.

The expansion of the Phillis Wheatley closely paralleled Hunter's personal development and involvement in the community. She was asked by the board in 1915 to give up her nursing profession and to devote full time to the institution, joining the one other paid worker in their employ.[43] However, the rapidly increasing demands by the black community soon dictated expansion of the staff from the two workers in 1915 to twenty by 1922. Hunter closely supervised all workers. In addition to her administrative responsibilities, Hunter served as the institution's chief fund-raiser. She also was a liaison between the black and white communities during the period of the city's most dramatic black population rise. Her position as head of the city's major black social agency made her highly visible in both the black and white communities. Consistent appointment of affluent whites to her board of trustees and Cooperative Board assured Hunter of regular interaction with the city's most powerful families, while the mission of the agency and its position in the black community kept her in close contact with all strata of black life. Her leadership was formally recognized when the Welfare Federation accepted the Association for membership in 1918, thus confirming its status as a full-fledged social service agency, and guaranteeing financial support from the Community Chest.[44]

By the time negotiations to merge the Phillis Wheatley Association and the YWCA were initiated in 1922 at the suggestion of Marie Wing, YWCA general secretary, Hunter left no doubt that she was against the merger. Once again the Phillis Wheatley was exploring the possibility of a large fund-raising drive, this time to build a permanent home. Hunter expressed her delight when the joint committee for both institutions recommended that the two should not affiliate, but should continue to cooperate. When the question was settled, Hunter expressed her belief that "the Phillis Wheatley could best serve the interests of the Negro people by remaining independent."[45] There is no doubt that her position had been influenced by her belief that the YWCA was not willing to take the Phillis Wheatley when the need was greatest (1914-16), and the fact that neither she nor the institution needed them any longer. In addition, she was confident that she had the support of the white monied community. Hunter's stand was confirmed when Mrs. B. S. Milliken, chair of the joint committee (and active on both boards), reported to the committee that "businessmen had advised that affiliation would be a calamity for the Phillis Wheatley. They would rather give separately than through the YWCA."[46] Clearly, Hunter's interest in autonomy and authority coincided with the will of her major donors. They had found a way to keep the YWCA all white, while she maintained control over the city's most successful black social service agency.

In light of the phenomenal growth of the city's black population, the city's lack of services for black newcomers became a concern not only for established black citizens, but also for the city's organized white leadership. When the Welfare Federation recognized the need for more adequate social services for blacks, Hunter was among the first called to join an integrated group to form the Negro Welfare Association.[47] She remained a member of the board of trustees for many years. The association's first office was housed in the Phillis Wheatley Building.

The philosophy of the new Negro Welfare Association closely resembled that of Hunter and the Phillis Wheatley. Like its parent organization, the National League on Urban Conditions Among Negroes (later known as the Urban League), the primary purpose of the association was economic improvement for blacks flocking to the country's urban areas. Through its industrial department, hundreds of jobs were found for the unskilled laborers, as well as some skilled jobs for the better educated.[48] Though it was billed

Second home of the Phillis Wheatley Association, 1918-1926

as another "self-help" organization, its leadership and funding came from white industrialists. In addition to providing a pool of laborers, the organization performed such diverse functions as keeping statistics on housing and employment patterns among blacks and sponsorship of community recreational facilities and lodging for soldiers returning from the war. At least part of its functions so closely paralleled for men the services provided for women by the Phillis Wheatley that a facility was turned over to them by the city to house returning black veterans. The building eventually became a black branch of the YMCA.[49] Hunter's support of the Negro Welfare Association was typical of her support of the concept of separate institutions for blacks. Their emphasis on "race-uplift" and teaching the newcomers acceptable middle-class values and behavior was consistent with the mission of the Phillis Wheatley.[50]

In addition to her logical role with new community agencies, Hunter saw herself as a self-appointed defender of morality among blacks, particularly in the area surrounding the Phillis Wheatley. She was especially vehement in her opposition to vice which involved young women. Prostitution, a major problem for unsuspecting migrant women who were lured North by unscrupulous employment agencies, made her especially angry. Because of her experiences as a newcomer to the city, she campaigned vigorously to get the city to provide recreational outlets.[51] She felt strongly that supervised recreation would help to reduce temptation to the younger members of the race.

Hunter's main opponent during the early years of the Phillis Wheatley in her battle for "Christian morality" was a man she described as an "unsavory creature who thrived upon the tolls which he extracted from prostitution and vice dens."[52] The man she described was Albert D. Boyd, known as "Starlight," a successful tavern owner with strong political connections. His influence with local Republican boss Maurice Maschke was strong enough to assure the "privilege of naming a councilman to be elected to that body from our [eleventh ward] district."[53] In 1910, his choice was Thomas W. Fleming, first black to receive the support of the party in a city-wide council election. Fleming's election to the council made him the first black councilman in a major American city. Boyd's payoff for his support of the Republican slate was Fleming's appointment as chairman of the committee which oversaw the police and fire departments. This put him in an ideal position to protect some of Boyd's business interests and to assure entrenchment of vice conditions in the developing black ghetto.[54] It also happened that "Starlight" owned the dance hall which had enticed Jane Hunter to pause for a little recreation in her first days in Cleveland. After finding the hall to be a "recruiting station for the notorious 'Starlight,' procurer for wild-wealthy men," Hunter never forgot her embarrassment nor the circumstances of loneliness which led her into the predicament.[55]

Hunter's determination to thwart Boyd's illicit activities led her into the midst of Republican politics. With a Democratic victory, led by Newton D. Baker in 1911, Fleming lost his bid for reelection until 1915, when the Republicans returned to city office.[56] Almost immediately after Fleming's first election in 1910, a "reform" group was organized through St. John's AME and Antioch Baptist churches, along with other interested citizens. By 1919, they were able to field a candidate to oppose Fleming.[57] Hunter campaigned enthusiastically against Fleming, even though he had been one of the earliest supporters of the association and his wife was currently heading the drive for furnishings for the building. She claimed that under Fleming's tenure, first as an at-large councilman and later as the councilman representing the eleventh ward, scarcely a week went by when she was not summoned to police court to help some girl who had been arrested for prostitution in one of Boyd's brothels.[58]

Although the crusaders were defeated in that election, they remained organized and backed Howard E. Murrell, a businessman in the area in the election of 1921.[59] According to Hunter, her involvement in the latter campaign was marked by a direct confrontation with Boyd. She claimed to have shaken her finger at Boyd's face announcing, "Someday I'll get you, you rascal."[60] Defeat of Hunter's political allies that time was climaxed with a parade down Central Avenue led by Boyd and his forces. Marching in front of the Phillis Wheatley, they threw their searchlights on the building, and someone in the crowd rushed forward to strike Hunter. Although a spectator warned that no one should touch her and she was not harmed, Hunter was furious. She later charged that the election was "stolen" from the voters.[61]

This dramatic confrontation with "evil and immorality" added to Hunter's reputation as champion of good government against vice and corruption. It also gave her important exposure to Republican politicians with whom she later collaborated as a member of the party's executive committee.[62] Although she maintained her independent posture, sometimes backing candidates who did not have the party's endorsement (especially black candidates), she was active enough to be considered a party loyalist, campaigning vigorously for Republican candidates in city, state, and national elections. Hunter's politics also served to keep her and the Association in the good favor of many wealthy white Republican supporters.

FIVE

A New Building:
Fulfillment
of a Dream

By 1922, it was apparent to Jane Hunter that the Phillis Wheatley would again have to consider larger quarters. Never a modest dreamer, Hunter, in that year, began to press the board of trustees to consider how they could best approach the community to raise funds to build a permanent home for the association. She repeatedly pointed out that it was "quite time for Negroes to discontinue the custom of taking over secondhand buildings and trying to adjust them to their needs."[1] Secure with assurance from her board that the Phillis Wheatley would remain independent from the Cleveland YWCA, Hunter suggested a feasibility study for a capital funds campaign in the near future. The board agreed that Hunter's suggestion was valid.[2]

Hunter's request was well justified. In the nine years since the first small home opened, the Phillis Wheatley Association had experienced extraordinary growth. The lodging space was always 100 percent occupied. Hunter reported at the annual meeting in 1922 that the association turned away about fifty young women each week who would be worthy applicants for rooms.[3] The dining room at the Phillis Wheatley was currently the most popular facility for blacks in the city. A summer camp on the shores of Lake Erie in Lorain had been successfully in operation for two years.[4] The association had acquired a building and grounds on East 105th Street (the Doan Branch) to serve blacks who lived in the more easterly section.[5] Also, outreach activities had grown to serve black residents in Mt. Pleasant, the downtown Hamilton Avenue district, and the near west side.[6]

A 1923 report, written to support the need for the capital campaign, noted that the Phillis Wheatley provided the only respectable boarding home in the city for colored women and girls. During that year, the home accommodated 1,188 persons; the cafeteria served 39,378 meals to more than 5,000 people; and 3,791 persons attended literary, musical, and social activities. The same report noted that 20,000 white employers had inquired at the association for colored help, resulting in the placement of 8,654 workers. Instruction in Domestic Science was received by 1,923; sewing lessons attracted 723; and piano instruction was provided for 687. At the Doan Branch, 6,756 persons attended the Phillis Wheatley for activities similar to those at the main building.[7]

Another internal report indicated that it was almost impossible to use public school buildings often enough to carry on programs for school-age youngsters:

> . . . there is discrimination against the colored people and unless we have certificates from people of the highest social status it is difficult for colored people to get the public school buildings.[8]

The increase in black population since the establishment of the Phillis Wheatley in 1913 was also cited as having affected the phenomenal growth of the institution. The report stated that "the refusal of the white institutions, because the people are colored [is] the strongest evidence we know for asking for double space."[9]

Increasing symptoms of overt racism in the city of Cleveland can be easily documented from items in black newspapers. For example, in April, 1917, Harry Smith charged in the *Cleveland Gazette* that "Afro-American pupils are segregated (jim-crowed) at Sibley School and have been it seems, for some time. There are two other such classes in our local public schools, all organized in recent months."[10] Although the charge drew a quick reply and apology from Superintendent Fredrick of the Cleveland Board of Education, in which he assured George Myers (prominent black Republican barber) that "the segregated classes . . . will be abolished just as soon as practical," the problem existed nevertheless.[11]

Indications of deteriorating employment opportunities in the city could also be found in the black newspapers. In 1917, the *Cleveland Gazette* noted that Wm. Tayler & Sons, a local department store, had recently released six black male employees and was gradually dismissing their eight black female employees. The article stated that no fault had been found with their work, but they were told that a change (presumably in racial policy) was to be made.[12]

Women waiting to be assigned to jobs. (1920s)

Basketball team, 1923

Most hotels, restaurants, and theaters also began openly to segregate black patrons. Perhaps the most well-known cases involved two black dignitaries visiting the city. In 1919, because of Cleveland's reputation for racial liberalism, the NAACP chose the city for its national convention. While visiting the city, James Weldon Johnson, then a field secretary for the organization, was refused service in a Cleveland restaurant because he was black.[13] The other incident involved Robert R. Moton, successor to Booker T. Washington as principal of Tuskegee Institute. Moton visited Cleveland in 1923 at the invitation of the Chamber of Commerce. Although he was housed at the Statler Hotel, officials agreed to accommodate him only if he took his meals in his room.[14] Gone were the days when there was strict enforcement of the nineteenth-century Civil Rights Bill. Accommodations for blacks were to be found only through a few businesses downtown and black-owned establishments. By 1924, a discussion at the Phillis Wheatley indicated that all hotels, club houses, and the YWCA were closed to black women and girls in the city.[15]

Hunter formally presented a request to the board of trustees in December, 1922, that they consider a capital funds campaign to raise $550,000 for building and equipping a new home. In April, 1923, they bought an option to purchase property on Cedar Avenue, between East 43rd and East 46th streets. The decision to build in that location was based on speculation by the board that blacks were permanently ensconced in the Central-Woodland Area.[16] A Building Committee was immediately formed, with David E. Green, a young white attorney, as chairman. Fannie Frackelton, president of the board and wife of a bank president (and daughter of a former president of the Pennsylvania Railroad), set the tone for the campaign in its early stages when she spoke to a group of potential donors. Quoting the poem "The East Is East and the West Is West" in its entirety, she made clear the point that support for the Phillis Wheatley Building Fund would assure separation of the races. Frackelton's formula for race relations was that separation plus cooperation would equal success.[17] Frackelton and the predominantly white board then proceeded to plan the campaign strategy and the building "in behalf of the colored women and girls."[18]

The first step toward building a case for the campaign was suggested by Building Committee Chairman Green. In July, 1923, he presented an extensive questionnaire to the board of trustees "relative to the needs of colored people and their accomplishments throughout the United States."[19] This was intended to help the board fortify themselves in their argument for the need for special work among blacks. Board members were expected to be knowledgeable about blacks in order to justify requests for donations to aid the black community. They were told to read about Booker T. Washington, George Washington Carver, and Phillis Wheatley as examples of black accomplishments and success.[20] Hunter registered no complaint about trivial issues such as the questionnaire or other discussions about black people by white board members, although discussions at meetings were sometimes graphic in their use of black stereotypes.

For example, at a Preliminary Gifts Committee meeting in 1924, a Mr. Sidall urged solicitors to try to convince potential donors of the value of the Negro for common labor. To illustrate his point he recalled a conversation with Mr. Bradley, a wealthy Clevelander. He said that Mr. Bradley had the impression that the Negro was lazy, extravagant, and shiftless, and that he would not save his money. His own chauffeur, who was extravagant and indifferent about his work, was Bradley's prototype.[21]

It can be assumed that Hunter chose to ignore the racism implicit in much of the campaign strategy. Rather, she concentrated on the goal of a successful campaign and conceded that the means by which success was gained were less important. Her own role in the early planning and preliminary gift period before the public campaign was announced exemplified her belief that financial aid to the Phillis Wheatley could be a step toward racial uplift. The money provided by whites would act as an important curative for the ills of poverty and laziness so often associated as racial characteristics of blacks. Hunter, a frequent speaker at churches and women's organizations, constantly used case histories to make the point that the Phillis Wheatley alone served as a refuge for destitute young black women in the city, making useful citizens of potential social misfits. Her own story of struggle made her a popular symbol of the upward climb for the race. Like her idol, Booker T. Washington, Hunter's life was proof to blacks and to whites that hard work could remedy the plagues of poverty and racism.

Between 1923 and 1926, plans for the capital fund campaign proceeded. The professional fund-raising firm of Ward, Wells, Dreshman, and Gates directed the effort. In a letter to Board President Frackelton, the firm suggested that advance gifts in the amount of at least $250,000 be secured. The firm suggested that trustees should be analyzed as to their own ability to donate and to solicit donations from others. The following description of board members was compiled for the campaign:

Mrs. D. W. Frackelton: President, Daughter of late President of Penn. R.R., brother big in Penn Co. Wife of Pres. of Equity Savings and Loan and V.P. of Chandler Printing Press. Has mind of her own; young.

Mrs. W. H. Merriam: Middle age. Very influential and wealthy. Pres. of YWCA, active in Welfare Fed., can be persuaded to go along with majority. She also stands in with women with money.

Mrs. Hylas S. Janes: Well to do but not rich. Well acquainted in Unitarian circles. Very interested in PWA.

Mrs. Paul S. Sutphen: Wife of minister of Church of the Covenant. Influential with a lot of wealthy people. She and Dr. Sutphen interested in colored people.

Mrs. Bertha L. Bailey: Moderate means. She has no money.

Mrs. J. R. Reaugh: Out of towner. No money. Influence in political organizations.

Mr. J. R. Wyllie: Head of Women's Dept. of Cleveland Trust. No money, but has some influence.

Mrs. R. H. Bishop: Daughter of Samuel Mather. Great deal of influence and money.

Mrs. Dudley Blossom: Daughter of Mr. Bingham. Extremely wealthy. Young. New Board member.

Mrs. Edwin S. Burke: Was Miss Josephine Chisholm. Influential and wealthy. Young. New Board member.

Mrs. Stevenson Burke: Very wealthy. Long interest in Phillis Wheatley. Sixty years old. Hobby is art. She is widely acquainted and can give largely.

Mrs. A. T. Hills: Widely acquainted. D.A.R. No money.

Mrs. B. L. Milliken: Daughter of S. L. Severence. Wealthy family. Active Trustee. Forty-five years old.

Mrs. Frank Lloyd: New Board member. No money.

Mrs. Fred L. Taft: Daughter of Frank A. Arter. Wealthy. Widely known in Methodist Church.

Frank A. Arter: Millionaire. Very peculiar. It takes a genius to handle him.

M. A. Bradley: Millionaire. Interested in PWA.

John Drummond: Princeton Univ. Not well known. Do not believe he has money.

Mr. D. W. Frackelton: Big church man of Calvery Pres. Church. Fifty years old.

David E. Green: Outstanding young lawyer. Forty-five years old. Just beginning to make money. Limited acquaintances.

Mr. F. W. Ramsey: Has money. Not a big giver. Good friend to PWA.

Remainder of no consequence.[22]

The board was led by early donations of $25,000 from Mrs. Stevenson Burke, $10,000 each from Mr. and Mrs. A. D. Baldwin and Mrs. Dudley S. Blossom, and $5,000 gifts from Mrs. Merriam and each of the wealthy Van Sweringen brothers, developers of Shaker Heights and the Terminal Tower complex. Preliminary Gifts Chairperson Mrs. Robert H. Bishop secured a gift of $12,000 from her father, Samuel Mather.[23]

Cleveland donors were somewhat reluctant in the first few months of the preliminary gifts effort. Committee members grappled with ways to interest potential donors, as well as trying to find an effective organizational structure from which to run the campaign. It is important to note that throughout the early planning process, Hunter was the only black person in attendance at committee meetings. The serious lack of input from the black community, alleged beneficiaries of the effort, demonstrated the paternalistic attitudes of the predominately white board. Planners for the institution, to serve exclusively a black clientele, never considered that there could be an active planning role for the consumers of the services of the agency. The Preliminary Gifts Committee, working with the professional fund-raising firm, concerned themselves solely with appealing to the self-interest of potential donors and their willingness to help "the colored." The self-interest of whites was, of course, to maintain an all-white YWCA, while at the same time addressing the need for housing and training for black women. An adequate facility for the Phillis Wheatley would assure the maintenance of racially separate services.[24]

One of the first efforts of the Preliminary Gifts Committee was a trip by Mrs. Robert Bishop and Mrs. Edwin Burke to the New York offices of the Laura Spellman Rockefeller Foundation to solicit a preliminary pledge for the campaign. In preparation for the meeting, materials were sent which described the institution, its function in the Cleveland community, and its organizational and financial status and structure. In exhibits accompanying the materials sent to the Foundation, the Phillis Wheatley was described as "a society for colored girls and women similar to the YWCA and operated in Cleveland with something like an interlocking directorate with the YWCA. . . ."[25] The exhibit explained that the Phillis Wheatley grew out of a great need for a Christian home for the Negro girls who came to Cleveland strangers, and were not housed at the YWCA because of their color.[26] The institution's separate organizational structure was explained:

> There has been since the beginning the most pleasant working relation with the YWCA, and its President and General Secretary have always been officers or members of our Board of the Phillis Wheatley Association, and four other members of our Board are also members of the Board of that Association. For racial and financial reasons it has been thought best that the two Associations should not be organically united but should be operated in entire harmony and upon similar lines.[27]

Unfortunately, the request did not fall within the guidelines of the work of the foundation, but officials there were so impressed with the request that they brought it to the attention of John D. Rockefeller, Jr. The women reminded Rockefeller of the friendship between his mother and Elizabeth Schofield, first president of the Phillis Wheatley board. Schofield had appealed to John Rockefeller, Sr., to do something for Negro girls by giving to the Phillis Wheatley. John Jr., personally pledged $100,000 to the effort in memory of his mother's interest in the colored race.[28] As was his custom, Rockefeller made the pledge with the following conditions:

> First: that $450,000 should be secured by the Association on or before February 1, 1928.
> Second: that his pledge should become due and payable only pro rata with the amount received in cash from other contributors to the building fund.
> Third: that if the balance of the sum pledged should not be paid on or before the above date, his pledge would lapse and all his obligations thereunder would terminate.[29]

The Rockefeller gift gave the campaign the boost it needed. When the public campaign was announced on January 1, 1925, preliminary pledges amounted to $235,000.[30] Donors were separated according to race, with a goal of $50,000 from the black community and $500,000 from whites.[31] Initially, the campaign chair was wealthy socialite Dr. Robert H. Bishop. However, when he was hospitalized early in the campaign, Mrs. A. D. Baldwin, another prominent supporter, took over the leadership. White team captains were Mrs. Fred L. Taft, Mrs. Walter Merriam, Mrs. D. W. Frackelton, Mrs. Charles Thwing, Mrs. Edward S. Bassett, and Mrs. Charles E. Brush. The black campaign team captain was Mrs. W. S. Biggs, wife of a prominent dentist.

The decision to run a segregated campaign posed a few problems. While strongly recommending the strategy, the campaign manager outlined to Chairman Bishop the peculiar characteristics of such an effort.[32] The racially separate campaign necessitated higher expenses and a great deal of duplication of effort and campaign materials. For example, brochures for prospective white donors were different from those for black prospects. As a result, a dual mailing system and two sets of workers was required. Mailing expenses included addressing, postage, and circulars and was calculated to be five times greater than normal because of the necessity of educating whites about the work of the Phillis Wheatley and the needs of black people.

Another added expense was the result of hotel segregation. Since campaign meetings could not be held in hotels, the Chamber of Commerce Auditorium had to be rented. Also, report meetings for colored workers had to be held at night, with the added expense of dinners, because workers were not available for noon luncheon meetings.[33] Campaign strategy called for an organization of 350 white workers who would call on 10,000 prospects and 250 black workers to call upon 5,000 or 6,000 prospects. The added expenses were considerable.[34] Further, campaign officials often met at the all-male segregated Mid-Day and Union clubs to plan strategy. Ironically, when Hunter was invited to speak at the campaign meetings, she had to enter the Union Club from the "women's entrance" at the side door, and at most hotels she was forced to use the freight elevators because of her race. Also, the segregated YWCA was another meeting place which was favored by white fund-raisers.[35]

The short life of the official campaign (January 1 to February 1, 1925) was nearly ruined by an incident which typified the tenuous nature of race relations in the city. Just after the public announcement of the Phillis

Wheatley campaign, it came to the public's attention that a black undertaker had purchased a home in the Shaker Heights, Van Sweringen Allotment.[36] The purchase was considered an outrageous breach of racial protocol. White workers and donors, many of whom lived in the suburb, threatened to withhold pledges and funds from the Phillis Wheatley campaign if the black purchaser did not give up the deed to the property. Black leaders (who while supporting the Phillis Wheatley still held some deep reservations about building a segregated facility) were deeply insulted by threats made to the property holder. Claybourne George, an attorney and president of the local NAACP, issued a statement in the form of a resolution to the Phillis Wheatley board:

> The Cleveland Branch of the National Association of Colored People understands that there are a number of white people in Cleveland who are refusing to pledge, and some of them have withdrawn their pledges to the Phillis Wheatley Association, an institution which they have always fostered as a definite social need, because a colored man owns a home in the Van Sweringen allotment in Shaker Heights.
>
> We also understand that certain pressure is being brought to bear upon the gentleman in question to compel him to dispose of his home, before certain elements of whites will contribute to the campaign.
>
> The Cleveland Branch of the NAACP wishes it distinctly understood that if those are the conditions upon which the pledges of the white citizens are to be made, then all self-respecting colored citizens want it understood that they would rather not have the contributions.[37]

The black property purchaser was J. Walter Wills, active participant in Phillis Wheatley affairs as a member of the advisory board of the association. It is not clear whether the purchase was intended as an effort to secure a home for his family or to call attention to the racial hypocrisy of the city's white leaders, or to make money. Hunter's version of the story indicates that Wills's motives were less than honorable. She accused him of parking a funeral hearse in the front yard and placing a large sign on the house to attract attention.[38]

On the other hand, the NAACP resolution describes the purchase as a "home" for Wills. Nevertheless, whatever the motives for the purchase, the outcome was that a group of white Phillis Wheatley supporters gave $1,500 to Jane Hunter to purchase an option on the property. Hunter quickly acted to dispose of the matter by offering more than the original purchase price.

At the close of the campaign, a resolution was entered into the minutes of the board which credited Wills with a pledge of $1,000. He was also paid $500 in cash. The full amount ($1,500) was entered on the books as a "necessary campaign expense."[40]

A *Plain Dealer* article noted that a group of citizens had appointed a committee to restrict purchase of Shaker Heights property from "undesirable" persons, stating "There is an ever present menace to every resident of Shaker Heights and throughout Cleveland."[41] Membership on the committee included David E. Green, chairman of the Phillis Wheatley Building Committee, along with Newton D. Saker, former mayor of Cleveland, Mrs. H. K. Ferguson, Reverend Charles H. Meyers, Louis A. Wells, W. K. Stanley, and H. G. Cannon.[42]

A few months later a similar situation arose when Dr. Charles Garvin, a black physician, purchased a lot in the Wade Allotment near Western Reserve University. Although Garvin's home was bombed and his family threatened, they moved into the house upon its completion and remained as residents. Once again, a committee was formed to prevent purchase by blacks.[43] When news of the Garvin purchase reached the newspapers, Phillis Wheatley contributions were again under possible threat, even though there was no connection drawn between their capital drive and the housing incident.[44]

In spite of these distractions, when the campaign ended in February, 1925, the total amount of subscriptions was $645,378.45. The amount pledged was far more than enough to ensure Rockefeller's $100,000 gift. Of the total amount, black citizens had pledged $169,000 to the new building.[45] Pledges by blacks undoubtedly assured white supporters that blacks desired a role in financing the institution which served the needs of their community. Perhaps on the strength of the black pledges, Hunter finally requested that a black person be placed on the Building Committee. She informed the committee that "since they were making history for the race, it would look well to have a representative of the colored people to assist in the planning of the building."[46] Attorney David E. Green, Robert E. Lewis, Mr. and Mrs. D. W. Frackelton, and Jane Hunter were joined on the committee by R. K. Moon, the choice of Mrs. Frackelton.[47]

Moon's appointment to the committee in May, and a motion by Green to deposit "$3,000 to $5,000 of the $224,530 collected so far from the donors into the Empire Savings and Loan Company," a black-owned business, served as another symbol of the uneasy relationship between blacks and whites on the committee. The token deposit was meant to satisfy a growing spirit of economic self-reliance among blacks. Moreover, Hunter was a stockholder and officer of the savings and loan company.

At the same time, the Phillis Wheatley board took care to protect the "racial investment" which contributors had made. When they voted a resolution to include in the building contract the phrase, "erection and completion of a building to be used by said association for the housing, education and physical culture of *colored girls*" (italics mine), the purpose of the facility was to be clearly defined for posterity.

On June 19, 1927, the cornerstone of the new building was placed with great ceremony. Mrs. Stevenson Burke, the largest local contributor, attended along with Dr. and Mrs. Sutphen, longtime supporters of the association. Burke's generosity was acknowledged along with the Sutphen's hard work in behalf of the Phillis Wheatley.[50] Articles included in the cornerstone box were as follows: a list of 3,689 names of persons who had paid toward their pledges, headed by John D. Rockefeller, Jr.; the names of all past and present trustees; names of all members of the Co-Operative and Advisory committees; a copy of a letter from Mrs. Schofield; endorsement of the Colored Ministerial Alliance; a copy of everything used in the campaign of 1925; pamphlets signed by Dr. R. H. Bishop, Jr., chairman of the campaign; papers signed by Mrs. Baldwin; a story of the Phillis Wheatley from its beginnings; a copy of Mrs. Baldwin's picture; and a program of the ceremonies for laying the cornerstone.[51]

When the building was ready for occupancy, there was much concern that black pledges had not been collected in sufficient amounts. For example, in February 1927, only $11,000 of the $169,000 had been received by the association. Hunter was humiliated, but continued to express her belief in the race. Mr. P. W. Lemon took on the task of collecting the delinquent monies.[52] Because of the cash flow problem, only a small amount of money could be spared for furnishings. With the help of individual donations specifically to furnish rooms, one hundred women moved into the building on December 15, 1927. Dedication services were held in April, featuring a speech by R. R. Moton, successor to Booker T. Washington.[53]

Work to make up the deficient collections from the black community was taken on by a small committee of black women led by Mrs. Wingate Todd. Their goal was to pay off the remainder of the mortgage of $86,500 as quickly as possible. The committee finally reached their goal in 1936, the year of the silver anniversary of the association.[54] This was accomplished through numerous fund-raising activities in the black community such as style shows, dances, rummage sales, club activities, food bazaars, and the like. A final interracial effort during the silver anniversary involving the Cleveland Bar Association, the press, the parent-teachers association, post office workers organizations, and city and county employees, helped the association to achieve its goal.[49]

The triumph of the 1925 campaign and the move into the new building in 1927 were real victories for Jane Hunter. Even though she had endured racial tensions, insensitivity on the part of white Phillis Wheatley supporters, and a failure on the part of the black community to fully live up to its financial promises, Hunter had lived to see fulfillment of her dream of a new facility for the association. She pointed out to friends that all hardships had been quite well worth the accomplishment of building the largest facility of its kind in the country. Despite disagreement about some of the policies of the association, Hunter was convinced that her contribution to the self-help ethic was paving the way for immediate survival for the race and future race relations. She believed that blacks would be in a better position to become part of the American mainstream if they were more firmly entrenched in the values which the Phillis Wheatley demonstrated.[56]

Although the *Cleveland Gazette* continued to challenge the need for black institutions, Hunter's admirers seemed to outnumber her detractors, and her demonstration of success at the Phillis Wheatley seemed to spur new discussion among blacks as to the possibility of other institutions which could serve the needs of black citizens. However, the question which continued to plague blacks in the city was whether such institutions served to increase the practice of race segregation or, by extending much-needed services to blacks, they equipped race members to better fight for integration. This question dominated all discussions which concerned social services for blacks. The issue often split blacks from their well-meaning white supporters because of a basic philosophical difference in their understanding of how a black-dominated institution could function in a Northern community where there was no legal segregation.

The basis of continuing opposition to Jane Hunter's activities and the Phillis Wheatley was that it was expressly "for Negroes," offering accommodations and services which duplicated those of the YWCA "for whites." Thus, blacks were compelled to use the services of the institution because there was no alternative. The Phillis Wheatley Association was perceived by many blacks to be an institution which was dominated and

The new Phillis Wheatley Association (1926)

Entrance of the new Phillis Wheatley Association (1927)

supported by whites in order to maintain segregation of the races. While the institution was supported by the black community, there remained much resistance to the essence of its function. Likewise its leader, Jane Hunter, was seen as a "tool" of the white community.

Hunter's emulation of Booker T. Washington extended to help her to rationalize accommodation to whites' insistence on control of the institution as a means which justified the end result—the survival of the institution. She seemed willing to overlook excessive racist demands, preferring instead to accentuate the contributions (especially financial) made to the Phillis Wheatley by whites who were willing to help her. She was always at the beck and call of the white establishment, attending meetings where she was most likely not welcome to dine (such as at the Union Club), siding with those who refused housing to blacks in select areas (such as in the Wills incident), and telling stories which reflected negatively on poor blacks. With Washington as her example, Hunter kept a perspective which enabled her to do whatever was necessary for the fiscal health of the institution.

However, the existence of the Phillis Wheatley Association posed a near-classic dilemma for Cleveland's black community. This was especially demonstrated when a group of black doctors proposed a hospital where they could admit and treat their patients. The facility was also to serve as a place where black doctors and nurses could be trained. The difference between the hospital and the Phillis Wheatley was that the hospital was to be open to all who would choose to use it. Based on the model of denominational and ethnic controlled institutions such as the Jewish Mt. Sinai Hospital and Catholic St. Vincent's Charity Hospital, but without the racial segregation which many of those institutions perpetuated, the hospital was proposed as a means to fulfill a community need, with blacks as principals. The question posed by this proposal essentially challenged traditional definitions of integration, which always presupposed white control and domination.

The controversy deeply involved all persons, black and white, who were concerned with race relations in the city. In addition to the important health service which would be rendered, black supporters saw the issue as germane to the definition of their position in the life of the city. Of the nineteen black physicians in the city in 1920, only one was on the staff of a hospital dispensary and none was able to admit patients to area hospitals.[57] By 1927, a 40 percent increase in the black population had attracted a total of forty-three doctors, with only three on hospital dispensary staffs and none with hospital privileges.[58] Also, black patients were routinely put in segregated sections of hospitals.[59]

The issue of prestige for the black physician was also raised, somewhat symbolizing the desire of the black community to command respect for its professionals.[60] Without institutional affiliation, this group would continue to be viewed by white peers as second class. The black professionals, who by virtue of education and income comprised the highest status group among blacks, were the logical pioneers to demand respect from whites for themselves and their mostly black patients.

Complicating the issue of separate versus integrated facilities was the existence of the Phillis Wheatley and its function in the community. Opponents of the hospital feared adding another black institution to the already segregated facility for women. White liberals fought against the proposal, calling it a "Jim Crow" plan.[61] Fearing that the effect would be to close the doors of existing institutions tighter, as had occurred with the YWCA and YMCA, opponents used the fact that Jane Hunter favored the hospital as an example of the kind of mentality which would assure that segregation would follow. Especially as the time neared for work to begin on the new Phillis Wheatley building, some felt that Hunter saw an opportunity to sell her old building.[62]

Proponents, however, argued that discrimination existed in every large hospital in the city against black physicians as well as black patients. The new hospital would be manned and controlled by blacks, but would admit patients of all races.[63] Although this particular plan fell through, the issue of hospital care and professional privileges remained unresolved for many years. Hunter's model for the "self-help" institution, where whites clearly were in control of policy and funding undoubtedly served to remind potential supporters that the hospital could easily become just another segregated facility which would keep blacks out of the mainstream.

In spite of the controversy which she and her institution constantly engendered, Hunter unfailingly supported separate institutions. For example, when a group of black Presbyterians gathered to begin steps to form a separate congregation, Hunter eagerly joined them. Because she had been educated by Presbyterian missionaries at Ferguson-Williams College, Hunter sought out the familiar denomination when she first arrived in Cleveland. However, there was no black Presbyterian church. After attending the predominately white Bolton Avenue Presbyterian Church for a short time, she decided to join the African Methodist Episcopal Church. Even though members at the other church had been helpful and kind, Hunter was uncomfortable among so many whites.[64] Later, she played an important role in founding the black St. Marks Presbyterian Church.

Much like the example of Washington (who continues to baffle his biographers with his seemingly contradictory behavior in his public and private life), there was another side of Hunter which bears examination. While she projected a clearly stereotypical image of the black who bowed to white notions of racial superiority in her public behavior, always humbling herself in their presence, and constantly accommodating to their demands, Hunter, too, contradicted the negative behavior. True to the old slave axiom of "wearing the mask," Hunter followed the example of thousands of black predecessors: accommodating to white perceptions of black inferiority and acting out the role, while skillfully using every opportunity to gain knowledge and information which could be helpful personally, or which could strengthen her position in the association. Her interpretation of "race uplift" seemed to continually involve using the Phillis Wheatley as a base to make the institution *and* Jane Hunter powerful entities in the city. Hunter's best tools were an extremely keen instinctive sense about dealing with people to her own advantage (both black and white) and an overwhelming drive for power and local and national prominence.

If one examines only the facade, Hunter could be profiled as a strong, enduring, and highly motivated female. Through her struggles to obtain a basic education in the South and her efforts to build an institution to aid young black women, her strength and character emerge forcefully, depicting her as an individual who had faith in herself and who could gain the confidence of persons who could aid in accomplishment of her goals. Another view might be that of a "handkerchief head," the kind of black person known to bow to the will of the majority, sometimes sacrificing her self-respect. A third version could depict Hunter as a very insecure individual—one who was plagued by feelings of inadequacy, and who constantly worked to position herself to seem more important than she felt she really was. Some remember her as a "saint," and some called her a "sly fox." Both descriptions seem to fit. As a single woman dominating a single-sex institution, her sexual preference was openly questioned by blacks. As a black who was at the beck and call of whites, her racial loyalty was suspect. She created her own seemingly impenetrable facade, and few were allowed beyond her self-imposed boundaries. Every contact seemed to have a purpose, and there was little hint of sentiment. Examination of her activities outside of the association may reveal how she kept her own ego intact, while seeming to ignore the racism which dominated her relations with whites and the sexism within her own community.

It is much too simple to view Hunter's ability to ignore the many demeaning remarks and actions of whites by attributing her behavior to her simple Southern plantation origins, where blacks were conditioned to show no emotion to whites. Hunter indeed "wore the mask" well, revealing little of herself to white benefactors. In no case did they seem to be concerned with Hunter's personal responses to their behavior. She was the perfect obedient servant type, one who would do their bidding, without rebellion. However, like many of her counterparts, Hunter worked hard to elevate herself to a position which could not be threatened by loss of their support.

For example, in the same year that Hunter began to urge her board toward finding financial means for a new building for the Phillis Wheatley (1922), she also began to work toward a law degree at Cleveland's Baldwin Wallace College. The two simultaneous moves on her part suggest that Hunter was interested in securing her position as a visible and qualified leader among her own race. Since coming North, Hunter had been faced with a class structure within the black community which relied, in large measure, on educational achievement as the basis for acceptance into the upper ranks. As a single woman, Hunter had no family connections which would automatically admit her into the very closed social circle. Education and position were her only entrees to the ranks of the upper group.

Hunter's few years of school in the South did not compare with the education of her black women peers in Cleveland. Public schools in the city were well known to be outstanding for their college preparatory courses, and many of the women in the black community had graduated not only from the high schools, but from colleges as well. Phillis Wheatley activists like Hazel Mountain, the city's first black school principal, and Hunter's own assistant Edith Wright had such credentials. Hunter's decision to continue her education was consistent with her ambition to be considered a bona fide leader among blacks.

In addition, the tenuous relationship between the YWCA and the Phillis Wheatley served as a constant reminder to Hunter of her deficient education. A requirement by the YWCA that their workers must have a college education before entering training in their school could have threatened Hunter's directorship of the Phillis Wheatley in the event of a merger between the two institutions. Relationships formed at national YWCA conferences for black workers must have served to motivate Hunter to "qualify" herself for the position which she held by virtue of her role as founder of the agency.

Hunter's choice of law for her course of study brought together her interest in securing her financial future, her desire for higher education, and very likely her competitive spirit against men. Working closely with businessmen and lawyers who were on her board had introduced Hunter to a world of contracts and investment, with fiscal and legal jargon dominating many of the meetings of financial advisors. Evidence of Hunter's personal interest in such matters can be documented by her early association with a black investment company, the Union Realty Company.[66] Correspondence indicates that Hunter took an active part in the company's real estate speculation. She also began to purchase property in the Central area in 1924, and eventually she personally owned at least six properties.[67] Hunter evidently paid careful attention to investments which the experienced businessmen made in behalf of the Phillis Wheatley and utilized the knowledge to build her personal fortune.[68]

Hunter passed the Ohio Bar in 1925, just in time to plunge full-force into building campaign activities. Now she had unquestionably, at least in her own mind, demonstrated her qualifications to direct the agency. While her board members denied her the respect which usually accompanied such a position, Hunter must have felt some satisfaction in her academic accomplishments. As a matter of record, Hunter had surpassed many of her "superiors" in educational achievement and was at least on par with many of the men.

Further evidence of Hunter's "coping mechanism" is probably indicated in her application to affiliate the Phillis Wheatley Association with the prestigious National Association of Colored Women, through its Ohio Federation of Colored Women's Clubs.[69] The organization represented a federation of assorted women's clubs all over the country, and the national officers were a virtual "who's who" of black women leaders. Hunter's affiliation in 1925 gave her the opportunity to become a part of a strong network of women who were involved in community, state, and national issues and activities on behalf of black women. Hunter quickly capitalized on her position as head of the independent social agency for black women and girls by participating in state and national meetings. By 1928, Hunter headed the organization's national Big Sister Department (affiliated with the National Big Brother and Big Sister Association), and by 1934 she headed a national

Phillis Wheatley Department designed to use her institution as a model for similar homes in cities where the YWCA did not have a black branch.[70]

Eager to secure a position in the ranks of national leaders, Hunter cultivated the friendships of Mary McLeod Bethune, founder of a college in Florida and national president of the NCNW (1933-35); Nannie Burroughs, founder of the National Training School for Women and Girls in Washington, D.C.; and Charlotte Hawkins Brown, founder of Palmer Memorial Institute, a finishing school for upper-class blacks in North Carolina. Hunter was fond of placing herself in the ranks of the other founders, referring to the four (including herself) as "the Horsemen." She corresponded with the women frequently, and they often exchanged visits. Hunter's letters to Bethune were very formal at the outset, and she openly flattered and ingratiated herself to the well-known woman. Hunter clearly cultivated friendship with Bethune and with her approval, felt free to woo the other two women. By securing the support of women who were involved in similar struggles to build institutions, Hunter provided herself with a peer network and recognition beyond the black rank and file. In reality, she was protecting herself by expanding her position from one of local recognition to that of national leadership. A fringe benefit, to be sure, was protection of her self-esteem, which could have easily been damaged by white "supporters" who, out of their own belief in white racial superiority, frequently failed to concern themselves with responses which they surely engendered from the blacks they purported to help.

When the new Phillis Wheatley building was completed, white newspapers heralded the event as a major step toward black uplift.[71] Eleven stories (nine above ground and two below), built exclusively for the purpose of housing and training black women and girls, it surpassed any similar institution in the country. When the keys to the building were turned over to the Phillis Wheatley board, one hundred young women moved into their new home. Meeting rooms, club rooms, a reading room, lounge, sewing rooms, a model dining room, and a domestic science kitchen were available to serve a much-expanded clientele. The dining room, already popular in the old building, became the most popular meeting place for blacks in the city. The building was one of the few places in the city where black and white could comfortably meet together. Without a doubt, Jane Edna Hunter had scored a personal triumph, despite problems from the inception of the idea. Her goal to head the largest agency of its kind in the country was fulfilled.

The most fittingly symbolic activity at the formal dedication services for the building, in April, 1924, was not the speech by Moton or the presence of Bethune. It was the presentation of an American flag by the Daughters of the American Revolution (D.A.R.).[72] This organization was to gain national infamy in 1940, when they refused to allow Marian Anderson, an internationally acclaimed black contralto, to sing in their Washington, D.C. Constitutional Hall.[73] Their gift of a flag to the Phillis Wheatley could serve as a daily reminder of the prevailing belief in white superiority and racial separation, which, of course, were the bricks and mortar of the Phillis Wheatley.

SIX

"What Shall We Do?": Training Black Women for Domestic Work

With some notable exceptions, the trend toward increasing discrimination in public and semi-private institutions, agencies, and services which had emerged in Cleveland between 1890 and 1929, coincident with the dramatic growth of the city's black population, appeared to level off in the thirties and early forties.[1] By the beginning of the nation's Great Depression, the pattern of discrimination was evident in practically every facet of life in the city. Retail stores, hotels and restaurants, transportation facilities, entertainment spots and the like all had become inhospitable to the black population.[2]

Although there were no written laws favoring the practice of segregation in places of public accommodation, frequent protests from the city's NAACP and black newspapers document the situation faced by blacks in their daily encounters.[3] Narrow interpretations by the courts of the 1884 Ohio Civil Rights Law and its 1894 amendment, the potential for embarrassment of persons violating the segregationist practices of local establishments, and the cost in time and money for seeking legal redress for violation of the law all served to discourage blacks from breaking the rapidly solidifying customs of race segregation in the city.[4]

Although segregation was hardest to document in private establishments because of the threat of suit and the subtlety of some discriminatory practices, its penetration into the systemic lifeline of the community resulted in a city divided by race. For example, discrimination and mistreatment from law enforcement agencies, particularly the courts and police department, were widespread.[5] Discourtesy, indiscriminate arrests, clubbings and shootings, and a lack of fair enforcement of gambling, liquor, and prostitution laws in densely populated black areas, created mistrust and hostility among black citizens toward the law and its enforcement. While the courts seemed to administer justice with a more even hand, the assignment of black court officials to handle only all-black cases and the scanty acceptance of black jurors attested to the existence of discrimination on the part of the system.[6]

Likewise, the city's social welfare and health care agencies, educational institutions, and recreation centers pursued a pattern of segregation and discrimination.[7] Officially sanctioned segregation in hospitals and city-run health clinics was well known in the black community. Separate wards in the hospitals which accepted blacks at all and separate days set aside for black patients in the city clinics were common practice.[8] Schools became increasingly identifiable according to racial lines, with black personnel assigned to all-black schools and black students held in neighborhood schools while their white neighbors were granted transfers to schools in other parts of the city.[9] Black leaders complained of gerrymandering of school boundaries into racially segregated districts.[10]

Cleveland's recreation and amusement centers held perhaps the most rigid color line. Dating back to the turn of the century, complaints of discrimination persisted for skating rinks, bowling alleys, and amusement centers such as Luna Park and Euclid Beach Park, which either had separate days for blacks or turned them away altogether.[11] The practice of race separation was widespread enough that even black entrepreneur, S. Clayton Green instituted separate nights for white and black patrons at a skating rink that he owned.[12] City-owned playgrounds, swimming facilities, and parks employed a variety of segregationist ploys, including separate sections at beaches, harassment at the parks and playgrounds, and outright exclusivity at pool facilities, with two pools in the Central Area informally designated for black use.[13]

Social welfare agencies were also blatantly discriminatory, particularly those which provided living accommodations.[14] The Home for Aged Colored People, a home founded and operated by blacks, was the only facility open to the black aged. The YMCA refused to admit black boarders or to serve black members except at the segregated Cedar Avenue facility and the YWCA regularly referred black women who needed aid to the Phillis Wheatley Association. Settlement houses excluded blacks except for those located in the heart of the black ghetto. And, even some of those did not necessarily provide extensive services for blacks. Hiram House, for example, located in the middle of the Central Area, registered blacks at a rate of only 21 percent of their clientele. Hiram House also ran a segregated camp.[15] The Playhouse

Settlement was the rare exception as an agency committed to the ideal and practice of racial integration.[16]

Employment opportunities dwindled with the onset of the country's worst economic depression. During the prosperous twenties, the rate of black employment was high, even though the occupational color line restricted them at or below the semi-skilled level.[17] Among black males, approximately 79 percent were employed below this level and approximately 93 percent of females who were employed worked below the semi-skilled level.[18] Of the males, almost two-thirds held jobs as laborers in Cleveland's iron and steel mills, and the remaining third worked in domestic and personal service or as janitors, porters, or elevator operators.[19] Among the women, approximately three-quarters of those working were employed as servants, while the remaining quarter worked at jobs such as seamstress and laundry operator.[20]

With the onset of the depression, the black labor force suffered devastating rates of unemployment. While blacks made up only 10 percent of available workers, they constituted 27 percent of the unemployed.[21] In areas of the city with a high concentration of black workers, unemployment figures reached 50 percent to 90 percent.[22] Even among those workers who remained employed, domestics who at one time had earned up to $15 a week were now paid as little as $3 or $4.[23] As the decade wore on, unemployment remained the biggest problem of the black community.

National recovery programs initiated before Roosevelt's New Deal did not provide any appreciable relief to the situation, since Cleveland's participation was minimal. The pattern of private funding for social welfare limited the scope of penetration, through funded agencies, to meet the severe needs of the city's unemployed.[24] City- and county-financed efforts provided only token solutions.[25] Only after 1933, when the federal government entered the field of public relief through emergency works projects, was the unemployment picture for blacks in Cleveland alleviated to any significant extent.[26]

While the earlier part of the century was characterized by rapid growth of the city's black population, from 5,988 in 1900 to 71,899 in 1930, the 1930s saw only a 16.6 percent increase of blacks.[27] Census figures indicate that by 1940 the black population was 84,504, of which only perhaps half could be attributed to migration.[28] The problems and excitement of great growth gave way to the reality of survival and adjustment, as blacks became an entrenched segment of the city's population. Major issues for the decade among blacks included the unemployment crisis, limited access to housing, segregation of public and semi-public facilities and institutions, uneven health care, and crime and vice in the Central Area.[29]

The Phillis Wheatley Association, as the largest social service agency for blacks in the city, found itself both beneficiary and victim of the attitudes of white citizens toward blacks. Its existence as a safe refuge for black women and a center for training and activities took it out of the category of agencies with geographic boundaries and placed it in the somewhat unique position of being on a par with its counterpart, the YWCA, as a city-wide institution. However, as an institution serving only blacks, located in a predominately black ward, it was vulnerable to the racism and neglect which characterized the city's attitude toward its black citizens. Typical of such racism were the disproportionate cuts in funding during the 1930s by the Welfare Federation, planning and fund allocator for social agencies.[30] As the economy became more depressed, the Phillis Wheatley required more sacrifices from an already underpaid staff and more vigorous fund-raising activities from a community which could barely sustain itself.

Through the 1930s and 1940s, Jane Hunter's activities, correspondence, and speeches, as well as the minutes of the Phillis Wheatley Board of Trustees and committees, reveal Hunter's involvement in a personal struggle between values and behavior which had served her well in the past and new realities and circumstances which pressured leaders to reexamine problems and means for solutions from the perspective of experience in the urban environment. As the leader of an institution with a significant influence not only in the lives of hundreds of women and girls, but also in race relations in the city, Hunter either did not comprehend or chose not to incorporate new definitions and strategies into her consciousness. Holding on to values inspired by another era, she remained loyal to the purpose of "racial uplift," and maintained a demeanor which suggested accommodation to the demands of white board members and supporters. However, occasionally she could be found at the forefront of militant protest, even though she rationalized such actions from a traditional perspective.

Several specific incidents help to illustrate Hunter's responses to events and issues during the years leading up to World War II. Her frustrations and anxieties, as well as her actions, help to demonstrate the dilemma of traditional leadership in the face of economic crisis and race polarization.

Hunter's interaction with members of her board, black and white, provides a good example of the often tenuous position of a traditional conservative black leader in the pre-war era. Association minutes and an unpublished narrative help to indicate some of Hunter's difficulties and some attempts on her part to cope with subtle and not-so-subtle changes in relations, especially among blacks.

The decade opened for the Phillis Wheatley Association with two major events. One was a dramatic drop in funds from the Welfare Federation to support the building and its activities, and the second, the ascendance of a black woman to the presidency of the institution. Although the former caused a serious disruption in the functioning of the agency, it was the latter which best illustrated Hunter's struggle with changing attitudes of blacks and her own relationships with whites.

Jane Hunter left the city in May, 1930, for Europe. Upon her arrival, she received the news that the president of the association, Mrs. J. A. Reaugh, had died suddenly. Sadie (Mrs. William J.) Anderson, a black woman, was first vice-president at the time. With the death of Reaugh, there was much discussion among board members, black and white, regarding "whether or not it would be advisable to have a colored woman serve out Mrs. Reaugh's term."[31] Some of the board apparently felt that the president needed to be a person who had good financial contacts and wide influence. Hunter, whose later recollections strongly indicate that she agreed with that position, could not participate in the decision due to her absence from the city. In a private informal meeting, Anderson agreed to consider declining the presidency in favor of a white woman (Mrs. A. D. Baldwin), but when the meeting was called Anderson informed the board that the constitution provided for her succession to the presidency and she expected to be elected. Her only concession was that if Hunter, upon her return, felt that she could not work with the new president, she would resign.[32] Although many of the women were shocked by Anderson's response, two of the more influential white women spoke up in defense of Anderson's position and averted a potentially unpleasant situation. Thus, the first black president of the Phillis Wheatley was elected by demanding her rights. This represented a change in the attitude of at least one black board member.

Hunter's response to Anderson's election and the manner in which it was achieved was predictable. Her account of the incident indicates that she was incensed by Anderson's assertive conduct. Hunter accused Anderson of "exercising her constitutional rights and her desire for social advancement in preference to the welfare of Negro girls."[33] She also raised an old resentment which dated back to the earlier controversy within the black community regarding the wisdom of supporting a separate institution for blacks.

According to Hunter, "The Phillis Wheatley . . . no longer had to beg for Presidents and especially from that group which had rejected it in its early struggles for existence."[34] Anderson, the wife of a well-respected minister, was apparently one of the class of black women who earlier opposed a separate race facility, but who later gave in to support the institution. However, when she returned, Hunter consented to work with Anderson as she completed the term of the previously elected president.

When the time came for Anderson to seek election in her own right as president, Hunter, in typical fashion, consulted two people before she supported a new term for Anderson. She talked with her pastor, who advised her to stand behind the capable black woman by all means; and she sought the advice of Constance Mather Bishop, the wealthy white woman who had helped to raise the money to build the new facility. Bishop, too, confirmed that it was all right for Anderson to be reelected. She assured Hunter that the white board members would continue to work with the black president, and she used her influence to keep the board true to her promise.[35] By consulting these two, Hunter avoided controversy and criticism from either the black or white community. She set aside the old personal hurt and gave full support to Anderson, complimenting her administrative term and calling her a "splendid presiding officer."[36]

Throughout Hunter's administration, the board's composition remained predominately white and conservative. Wealthy and influential white women and well-educated (if not so affluent) black women were carefully selected by a process of members nominating their friends for the board. It was one of the few (if not the only) opportunities in the city for a peer association between women of the races. From the beginning of the association, white women worked diligently to raise funds and set direction for the institution. As blacks were brought on to the board in small numbers, they joined in the board's activities and seemed to participate at all levels of decision making. Hunter's meticulous selection of black women who would not offend the white patrons of the institution by "outrageous" demands or actions (as well as those who likely agreed with her view of race matters) ensured that there would be no major upsets. Anderson's bid for the presidency signaled one of the first evidences of assertion on the part of a black.

There is no doubt that interaction between the women of the two races served to raise some awareness of individual as well as group concerns and differences. Although the board rarely recorded discussions other then those pertaining specifically to the functions of the agency, there seemed a gradual

Cooking class, Sarah T. Hills Training School (1937)

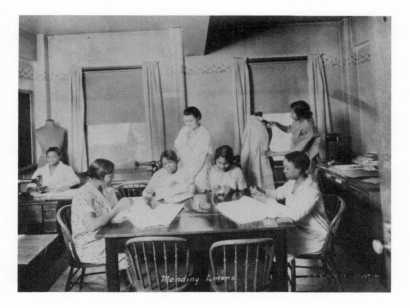

Sewing class, 1930s

heightening of awareness about issues, especially after the beginning of the economic depression. Perhaps because of the tight money situation, board members were forced to evaluate activities and functions and set priorities based on the needs of their particular clientele. There were more frequent occasions after 1930 when the board was confronted with requests to take a position on issues directly affecting the black community. Hunter, while continuing to pamper her white financial contributors, also seemed more inclined to confront the board with the realities under which a black agency in the Central Area had to operate. On a few occasions, she asked them to officially endorse actions in which she was personally involved.

One such issue was in regard to a Central Area Citizens Committee for which Hunter provided leadership. The Committee, composed of concerned individual and institutional citizens of the area, became controversial in 1936. They decided, as a course of last resort, that they would oppose a city operating levy of 5.5 mills in order to bring to the attention of the entire city problems which were growing because of the city administration's neglect of the district.[37] Problems of crime and vice and poor law enforcement, haphazard trash removal, abandoned properties, and inefficient transportation systems caused the district to decline. At a time when whites were moving out of the Central Area, blacks found themselves more confined to its limited housing resources. Discriminatory real estate and banking practices made it increasingly difficult for blacks to move to newer, less congested residential sections. City services seemed to deteriorate in direct proportion to the decrease in white occupancy and to the increase in black population density.

Hunter frequently complained of the city's practices in the Phillis Wheatley's publication, *The Open Door*, and at times pointed out the area's problems to the board.[38] She also kept them informed about deteriorating school conditions in the area. The Citizens Committee's decision to try to defeat the levy was a drastic departure from earlier tactics which had always included support for increased taxes in hopes of better services.[39] In December, 1936, Hunter presented a statement to the board which set forth the position of the Committee in its opposition to the levy. She asked the board to vote to support the statement which bore her name as secretary of the Citizens Committee. The board voted their support after a brief discussion.[40] However, at a special meeting called shortly after the regular board meeting, the board held a lengthy discussion of the matter and voted to rescind the original decision and not to support opposition to the levy. Instead, they decided to support the efforts of Mayor Harold H. Burton, an independent Republican who was at odds with the black political leadership, in his work to correct conditions in the community.[41] No more than two months later, the mayor's wife joined the Phillis Wheatley Board of Trustees.

Hunter's request to the Phillis Wheatley board to support the action of the Citizens Committee seemed to serve the purpose of raising their awareness of the serious problems faced by the Central Area. Although she did not succeed in steering her board into taking a stand, the discussions resulted in the appointment of a Phillis Wheatley Committee on Community Activities.[42] With Constance Mather Bishop as chair, the committee reassured the political powers that there would be no radical action taken by the board which would jeopardize an already shaky relationship between the mayor and the black leadership. The new committee quickly involved itself in an assessment of recreation space available for children in the area and, subsequently, working through top city officials, acquired a lease for city property on which a playground could be developed. It was appropriately christened The Booker T. Washington Playground.[43]

There is no indication that the board ever took advocacy action in matters related to the Central Area. It is ironic that while the board shied away from becoming embroiled in issues which affected the Central Area, it did not hesitate to endorse a "great peace rally" at Public Square in January, 1937.[44] Hunter was instructed by the board to participate in the more popular cause, even if she had to send a designated substitute to planning meetings.[45] Her presence on the Committee of One Hundred, which sponsored the rally, was no doubt an important token gesture of support from the black community.

As the leader of a black self-help institution with a white-dominated board, Jane Hunter found herself caught between her traditional accommodationist role and her desire to be viewed as a race leader. The two roles were fast becoming incompatible. Although she never deviated from her loyalty to the Washington conservatism which had always influenced her thought and actions, shifting strategies among blacks to achieve racial integration and equality made it more difficult to serve two masters. Controversy, which had always surrounded the institution, became focused more specifically on the actions of Hunter, the leader, who was expected to use the power of her position as a means of making social and economic gains for the race. As a conservative, she was carefully scrutinized by the race newspapers, which often pointed out inconsistencies between her espousal of race unity and self-help and her concessions to whites. For example, the black community took careful note of the fact that the Phillis Wheatley building was designed and built by white architects and contractors who did not hire black workers.[46]

When a small fire damaged the building which formerly housed the Phillis Wheatley, Hunter's difficulties in carrying out her philosophy once again were the subject of discussion within the black community. The fire, which occurred in the winter of 1934, necessitated the hiring of a contractor to repair the damages. Over Hunter's objections, the chairman of the Properties Committee and a member of the Phillis Wheatley Fiscal Advisory Committee awarded the contract to a white man. Despite the fact that the job was estimated and bid lower by a black contractor, the decision was made by the two fiscal advisors, without a meeting. Hunter's old adversary, the *Cleveland Gazette*, was quick to call the situation to the attention of the black community, pointing out that the so-called self-help institution was "controlled by whites who look out for themselves while Negro laborers and contractors remain unemployed."[47] Hunter brought the article from the paper to the attention of the board of trustees, along with a written request from the Negro Board of Trade and the Housewives League for an explanation.[48] She requested that the board investigate the decision, because it had been made over her recommendation.

Response from the two who made the decision was simply that they desired to see the job well done and gave the contract to a company whose reputation they knew.[49] It did not matter to them that the institution stood for race self-help, or that opportunities were so limited for black contractors. Their lack of attention to such obvious details perpetuated a racist cycle which confirmed the complaint that black workers lacked experience. The committee members failed to apologize to Hunter or the board. The incident demonstrated both the community's perception of Hunter's version of race solidarity and also her dilemma when dealing with the insensitivity of the whites who dominated her institution.

Hunter's conservatism, which encompassed gradualism, conciliation, cultivation of middle-class values, racial solidarity, self-help, and cultural pluralism as the means for achieving race equality, was gradually being replaced by new definitions among black leaders. Race solidarity came to mean block voting and the demand for representation in decision making and jobs. Self-help came to be a more militant consciousness among blacks as the economic depression deepened, and was increasingly associated with drives to encourage blacks to patronize the race's businesses and professionals.

As a result of worsening conditions during these years, some formerly conservative black leaders adopted more militant strategies to solve economic and social problems. Indeed, Hunter's activity with the Central Area Citizens Committee was a good example of a somewhat militant strategy. However, even when she participated in movements designed to gain greater opportunities for blacks, she held to a conservative rationale which considered blacks largely responsible for their own deficiencies. Hunter felt that blacks should prove their ability to perform services and conduct business in a manner befitting their entry into the economic mainstream. While at times she challenged the racism of the systems in the country, she was inclined to accept those circumstances and, instead, to emphasize ways that blacks could overcome such realities. Hunter often stated that it was "important to squarely face conditions as they exist, while at the same time using energy and intelligence to improve them."[50]

While this approach to race problems had predominated through the first decades of the century, a new, more direct-action oriented leadership, inspired by the success of such organizations as the NAACP, was setting more tangible and timely goals. Such strategies as court actions, boycotting of businesses, and heightened political activity were achieving gains which could be experienced immediately. The slower—time will take care of all—attitude was no longer acceptable. Most importantly, in an age of industrial domination, changes in marketable skills, training needs, and personal values were affecting the practicality of adjustment to circumstances which could be obsolete before they could be achieved.

A specific illustration of conflict between Hunter's personal philosophy and the changing aspirations of blacks can be found in her continuing advocacy of domestic service training programs for black women, which she envisioned as a means for increasing their employability. This sensitive issue created for Hunter and for the Phillis Wheatley an image both positive and negative, which lasted throughout her tenure.

Hunter's advocacy of women entering into the job market via servant status can be traced back to her own personal experiences. Her tenure as a maid in South Carolina, while sometimes very difficult (as in the case of the Wilson family's expectations of a ten-year-old), had also presented her with (1) exposure to middle-class life and manners; (2) the opportunity to finance an education for herself and her sisters; (3) a means of becoming acquainted with the personal interests, biases, and tastes of her employers, on which she later capitalized when raising funds for the Phillis Wheatley; and (4) opportunities to broaden her own experiences and step up into higher paying and higher status jobs, such as her promotion from maid to personal attendant to the Rutledge children in Charleston. Time as a maid during her formative years predisposed her to view the master/servant relationship in a positive fashion. In addition, it was her belief that blacks could use such humble beginnings to build a foundation upon which they could support much higher aspirations.

While Hunter by no means believed that training for blacks should be limited to vocational and industrial education, she felt strongly that those of limited mentality or opportunity should be taught to consider jobs in the domestic category as important positions which should be held with dignity. Looking realistically at employment opportunities available to blacks in the years during the depression, Hunter feared that lack of proper training and exposure could lead to loss of these lower skilled positions to foreign-born workers who offered stern competition to blacks in the labor pool at each level.

Using the background of experience in employment placement which had been sustained at the Phillis Wheatley since it opened its doors in 1911, Hunter vigorously advocated a full training program for the institution in order to make the women more competitive and competent. Although the institution had always had both an employment department and a domestic science department, they had never really coordinated the two in a way which would encourage the women to relate the training which was offered to the possible reward of a better-paying, longer-lasting employment opportunity. When the job market tightened during the early depression years, Hunter was able to press her board to consider a special training program which could both improve opportunities for the women and also build a better reputation for the institution among potential employers.

In addition to the practical applications of the training plan, Hunter's own credo included a strong belief that training to one's capacity improved self-esteem as well as performance. Better-trained individuals had better opportunities to control their own lives and thus could become better citizens. In a statement appealing for expansion of training facilities at the Phillis Wheatley, Hunter's ability to generalize and summarize a complex problem, such as the plight facing many black women, and to find a simple solution is illustrated:

> When we realize that in the North there are no openings except personal service for the masses of our girls, and that so few of them are qualified to do this kind of work, we know that we face a very serious future. We hope

that our own people will be co-operative, if only to make the girls keep their own homes clean and sanitary. The exceedingly high death rate among Negroes is due largely to unwholesome and unsanitary conditions in their homes. The Phillis Wheatley Association through its Training School has a wonderful opportunity to help the race lift its standard of living and to reduce its death rate.[51]

Hunter thus viewed training in domestic science as a means not only to improve job opportunities, but also to prepare the women to be better and more responsible homemakers. The training would improve black home life, health standards, and employment opportunities, which would then result in uplifting the race.

Although Jane Hunter's first appeal to the white community for support for a home for black women had included an implied promise to provide better-trained servants, a job market which favored newly arriving, cheap black labor in the homes of the wealthy did not provide an atmosphere conducive to the sacrifice required to be trained before seeking employment. Also, although the institution placed large numbers of domestic workers, pressures from the black community against the separate institution would have damaged its gradual acceptance by black leaders, if domestic service training had been a major emphasis. At a time when blacks were actively seeking to expand their opportunities in industry and business, the Phillis Wheatley, the largest black agency in the city, could not afford the stigma of being a training institution for maids. Instead, the training in cooking, sewing, nutrition, and housekeeping was promoted as an aid to urban living skills. Neighborhood women and high school girls were taught good manners, hygiene, and modern scientific approaches to the art of homemaking as a means of helping them to adjust from their customary rural life-style to the more sophisticated techniques of urban family care. Although early residents of the home were required to attend sessions in the Domestic Science Department in order to train for potential employment, lessons in proper living were often stressed more as a way to mold new city life-styles.

Classes in domestic science also served as a social outlet for residents and for neighborhood women and girls. Since money was an endless problem for the association, participants found themselves involved in bake sales, teas, clothing and notions sales, and other fund-raising activities. New acquaintances formed mothers' clubs, music clubs, usher boards, girls clubs, and the like, with strong allegiance to the association. Meeting rooms at the Phillis Wheatley were in constant demand. Staff workers for the association

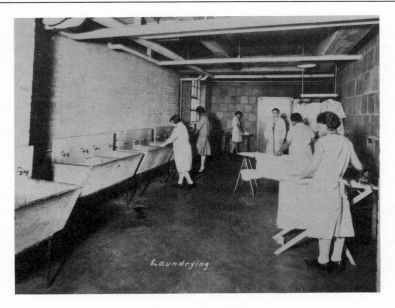

Laundry class, 1930s

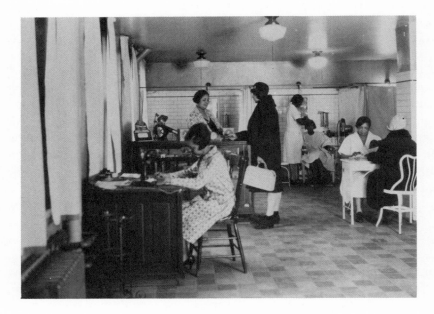

Edith Wilkenson Beauty School, 1930s

were expected to serve as resource persons for the many activities, keeping the participants "morally tied up" to the ideals of the association.

Though the Domestic Science Department was successful in reaching neighbors and residents, Hunter was disturbed that the majority of women who came for placement by the Employment Department did not seem interested in taking advantage of the domestic science offerings. Of the women who were placed by the Phillis Wheatley, by far the largest number were day workers. In Hunter's view, day work was the least desirable form of domestic service. This group seemed to offend her strong conviction that race uplift could best be achieved by making the best of even the most menial circumstances. The women were constantly encouraged to seek permanent maid positions with one family. Hunter deplored any display of lack of ambition. Failure to heed her advice to upgrade their circumstances was especially disturbing. Lecturing to the women daily as she made her morning rounds through the Employment Department, she tried to show them how much more they could control their own lives if they knew where they were going each day and could anticipate their employer's expectations.

The association was often criticized as merely a job placement service for domestics. Some blacks felt that instead more energy could be spent trying to open other employment opportunities for the women. Hunter felt, however, that the reality of the job market, which must be "squarely faced," was that black women needed to work, and there was very little access to jobs outside of domestic service. Examination of census statistics tends to support Hunter's analysis of the employment situation before World War II.

Employment statistics in Cleveland between 1910 and 1930 reveal that although the female work force shifted from 21.9 percent in personal service in 1910 to a low of 14.8 percent in 1920 and back up to 20.3 percent in 1930, black women workers continued to be represented in the category at significantly higher levels. Black women in the work force were in the personal service category at levels of 72.8 percent in 1910, 63 percent in 1920, and 69.8 percent in 1930. While white women moved into clerical and white-collar positions, between 1910 and 1920, from 22.6 percent to 40.2 percent, black women advanced from only 1.4 percent to 3.7 percent in those positions. When the proportion of the total female work force in clerical positions slipped to 35.9 percent, the meager gains of black women before and during World War I were practically wiped out. In fact, in 1930, the occupational status of black women was not much different than it had been in 1870, when 65.7 percent of the total female work force was confined to domestic service. As late as 1940, 76.2 percent of the black women who worked in Cleveland held jobs in domestic service.[52]

The evolution of the Domestic Science Training concept at the Phillis Wheatley can be traced by viewing its various definitions over the first twenty years. For example, when the department was opened in the agency's first building, three goals were listed:

> First, to help a girl earn her own way; second, it tied the girl morally up with our ideals; and third, it gave us an opportunity to study a girl.[53]

By 1923, the Annual Report of the Phillis Wheatley listed three different purposes for the domestic science classes:

1. To train women interested in the catering business.
2. To upgrade those women who are already employed.
3. To aid housewives and prospective housewives.[54]

The listing of catering as a business opportunity and its prominence as a purpose for the department seems an attempt to respond to the business aspirations of women clients. The other purposes were also attempts to lure prospective students to acquire skills which were applicable to the job market, while at the same time appealing to the desire of the women to be better homemakers.

A 1925 list of activities reflects an even more sophisticated appeal. "Economy and Efficiency Classes" grouped Household Economics and Domestic Science, and included them with such courses as stenography, millinery, dressmaking, music, and charm school.[55]

In 1931, Hunter was finally able to carry out her original plan to institute a training program which was specifically designed for domestic workers.[56] The depression had become the catalyst to carry out the plan originally conceived at the inception of the institution and proposed again in 1925. The focus of the program was women between the ages of sixteen and eighteen years whose job potential was restricted because of their poverty and lack of education and exposure. What originally was planned as a six-week course in the main building was extended to six months in a rehabilitated house adjacent to the institution. The women were trained to clean, cook, serve meals, and do laundry in a very strict and scientifically oriented course. The rate of success for the program was high. Out of 178 girls admitted in 1931, 102 completed the course and found immediate employment. Hunter took great pride in the fact that the women went on to become creditable citizens in the community.[57]

While her emphasis was based on concrete training programs at the Phillis Wheatley, Hunter extended her crusade to make black women more competent and competitive in domestic service into the public schools. As the influential head of a female institution, she was often called upon to speak on issues affecting women in the city. Vocational and industrial education were already a part of the Cleveland Board of Education's curriculum pattern, and Hunter's plea for more opportunities for black participation simply called for expansion of opportunities currently available for white students. However, rather than pressing for full integration of black girls into the school's existing programs, she chose to place her emphasis on the responsibility the school board had to upgrade facilities at Longwood School, a public school specifically set aside to enroll black girls from Southern states who were overage and poorly prepared. Despite the fact that Jane Addams, a girls' vocational school located at the boundary of the Central Area, trained white girls in such areas as practical nursing, cosmetology, dental hygiene, and domestic science, Hunter chose to stress needs at the black school. A statement by the assistant superintendent of the Cleveland schools that "teachers should have the same nationality or racial background as their students" served as her rationale.[58]

Hunter urged the public schools to train Negro girls for domestic service for the same reasons that she emphasized the training at the Phillis Wheatley: "As we study the opportunities for Negro working women in Cleveland, we are convinced more and more that the only field open to them is that of domestic or personal service."[59] She later chided black parents in an article about Longwood School:

> The writer regretted to see that fewer Negro girls are taking advantage of the opportunity to receive the training in homemaking offered at Longwood. . . . Negro mothers have withdrawn their girls from such classes because of vicious propaganda against vocational training, spread by special groups in the past years. Some of the race's outstanding women leaders got their start by using domestic service as a stepping stone.[60]

Hunter's priorities for the education of black girls clearly conflicted with the growing sentiments of the black community, which wanted to put an end to the segregated facilities at Longwood School and to open admission to black girls at Jane Addams School.[61] There was also much community pressure to open opportunities to blacks in industry and white-owned businesses.[62] While Hunter admonished the school board for not including more black school administrators and personnel, she based her criticism on her belief that they were better equipped to respond to the needs of black students.

Hunter's advocacy of increased training for domestic service seemed, on the one hand, a practical solution to the existing circumstances of limited employment opportunities for black women and the need for greater competency among those who were competing for the available job slots. However, on the other hand, her limited view revealed a shortsightedness which seemed typical of Washington ideologists. Her failure to use her position in the city and her persuasive faculties to try to penetrate the system to open a greater variety of opportunities for black women not only demonstrated a failure to correctly assess an economic phenomenon, but also revealed a limited view of changing social conditions.

A shrinking market for domestic services was related not only to the depressed economy and increased competition from foreign-born workers, but also to changing life-styles among the upper and middle classes. Modern appliances such as washing machines and vacuum cleaners were making household chores less demanding; newer homes tended to be smaller than the mansions of the earlier part of the century; and the automobile gave younger women a mobility which led to a less formal pattern of visiting and entertaining. Never again would the large complement of household workers of an earlier time be required to serve the needs of employers.[63] Hunter's incorrect analysis of the changing demands for domestic services placed blame on the women seeking employment, rather than recognizing a new trend. She continued to blame the potential employee for the lack of jobs available, as her synopsis of the problem in *The Open Door* reveals:

> We have discovered that so many Negroes are inefficient, restless, unwilling to sacrifice for the convenience of their employers and to stay on the premises. . . . The Negro race as a whole has somehow lost ambition, to pursue vocational education, while other groups are bidding strong for the few jobs open to the Negro group. With the many opportunities being offered by night schools, WPA schools, and the Phillis Wheatley Association, there is little excuse for Negro women not to be prepared for the work at hand.[64]

Hunter's concern about the decline in demand for blacks for domestic service went further than decrying a loss of job opportunities. While she

Dining room, the new Phillis Wheatley Association (1920s)

Training for domestic service, 1930s

acknowledged that blacks faced a severe financial loss if they lost their major occupations to foreign-born whites, she saw an even more ominous problem for the race.[65] In an address on NBC's popular "Wings Over Jordan" radio program, Hunter stated:

> . . . This financial loss has severely affected the economic life of the Negro race, both from the standpoint of the professional and the layman. In my attempt to analyze this situation, I find that the $500,000 is not our greatest loss, but the loss of contact with the white race has materially curtailed interracial understanding.
>
> In referring to those of my race who are privileged to serve in the homes of others, there is a need today for the qualities they contribute to American home building. They speak and understand the American language. They sympathize with the ups and downs of the American white man. They are loyal to him. . . . I am sure they will conclude that the Negro servant, who by similarity of nativity and environment, will remain the potent factor in keeping the American home happy and contented.[66]

Hunter's belief in the value of the master/servant relationship could not have been stated more explicitly.

If Hunter's understanding of philosophical, social, and economic phenomena was at times somewhat limited and askew, her ability to steer the agency and her personal fortunes against the tide of economic depression was equally remarkable. Except for an occasional year-end deficit, she consistently kept the agency active and solvent at a time when the demand for services was greatest and financial resources were most limited. Also, the agency filled a very important need in the black community. Hunter's management of the politics of survival for her institution and for herself cannot be overlooked. Her sense of race solidarity, although flawed in its interpretation, expressed a nonetheless sincere belief that the race could only thrive by sticking together, supporting their own businesses, and building their own economic and social systems. If Hunter's rural plantation background made her somewhat naive in regard to the serious limitations of her philosophy of self-help and separatism and contributed to an inordinate trust in "the master," it also nurtured a strong sense of Sunday school morality, fundamental religious beliefs, belief in thrift and frugality, and a basic mistrust of big government. Also, lessons learned from her cunning great-grandmother in survival and manipulation gave her a political instinct which served her well.

When the stock market crashed and the depression started, Jane Hunter found herself in the position of having little to lose except dreams of a paid-off mortgage for the association and her desire and determination to have a home of her own. Although she had dabbled in the stock market with some of her earnings, she had begun to invest in real estate early in her career and simply had to hold on to the properties until more prosperous times. Also, she had always lived extremely frugally, so there was no adjustment to be made in her own life style. The most important consideration for Hunter during that time was to find ways to keep the Phillis Wheatley open and independent and to continue to serve what she and her board perceived to be the needs of the black community.

When, for example, funds to the association were cut by 75 percent in a drastic move by the Welfare Federation, Hunter complained that little was left except enough to keep the building open with lights and heat, with no money for staff.[67] She did, however, manage to keep a skeletal staff in place, even with constant complaints about low salaries. It can be speculated that employees had few alternatives for jobs and elected to stay with one which at least provided cheap room and board.[68] Since the majority of the employees were single women, it is logical that the association provided relative safety and companionship with others in similar circumstances.

An Auditor's Report in 1933 strongly suggests another way in which Hunter kept the agency afloat. The report criticized the intermingling of the Phillis Wheatley's financial resources with Hunter's personal assets, and threatened to cut off funding altogether if the bookkeeping and administration departments were not completely separated. The report cited unrecorded collection of rent from Phillis Wheatley-owned properties, unauthorized work on properties owned by the association, and even noted that a garage and a filling station had been built on association properties without the consent of the board. Further, it was noted that a water meter on the Phillis Wheatley property at East 46th Street was attached to property owned by Hunter. The auditors concluded that, while Hunter's fiscal administration was well intentioned, it was less than professional or ethical.[69]

This author would suggest that Hunter's survival instinct would compel her to do whatever she felt necessary to save the agency which represented her life work. Also, at times it is hard to recognize a separation between Hunter and the institution. In her mind, and in the minds of black and white citizens, Jane Hunter was the Phillis Wheatley. There is little question that

Hunter managed her own finances and those of the association, by using whatever resources were available to either, to keep afloat. Hunter's personal fortunes were tied to the fortunes of the association.

Hunter's dream of a fully-paid mortgage for the association's building did not subside with the advent of the depression. Instead, she continued to press toward its accomplishment. It seems incredible that in 1932, with a mortgage indebtedness of $34,000, she was able to reduce it by over $12,000. This feat was accomplished by a special appeal to John D. Rockefeller, Jr., who forfeited the conditions of his original pledge, that the community must raise all the funds to match his gift, and sent a check for the balance of his pledge, $5,631.98, thus completing his gift of $100,000. Another $3,355.39 was raised by "staff and friends," and $3,652.39 was borrowed from the Cafeteria Reserve Fund.[70] Vigorous fund-raising continued until 1936, when the entire debt was paid in time for the 25th anniversary celebration.[71]

Hunter's resourcefulness did not stop with her management of finances for the Phillis Wheatley during the depression. Her decision to carry out plans to build a new residence for herself further demonstrated her determined optimism, fiscal creativity, and political astuteness, all of which were fully utilized in the project. The house was built in 1934 on property directly behind the new Phillis Wheatley building.

Original drawings for Hunter's home were a gift from a local white architect, Walter McCornack.[72] The gift came at precisely the time that citizens were proposing rehabilitation plans for the city's Central Area. Hunter, prominent in Central Area politics and aligned with the Republican Party, was extremely grateful to McCornack for the gift. In exchange, she invited the architect and his wife to an informal evening at the house with Maurice Masche, chairman of the county's Republican Party, to discuss housing plans for the Central district.[73] Obviously, Hunter's gratitude provided adequate pay for the architect, since it resulted in the opportunity for an informal, personal chat with the city's chief political power broker.

Drawings for specifications, a cost estimate, and labor for the house were negotiated with her alma mater, Hampton Institute. In a letter to W. E. Carter, head of the Department of Architecture, Hunter promised summer jobs, close supervision, and room and board in exchange for Hampton students' participation in the project.[74] Carter was amenable to Hunter's suggestions, but made her promise to keep the arrangement confidential, since they did not want local architects to think that the school was competing for jobs.[75] It seems logical to speculate that Hunter's public loyalty to the school, as well as an earlier $1,000 donation to a Hampton-Tuskegee fund drive, made the school eager to cooperate. Hunter named the house Elli-Kani, an African tribal name which translates as "house of faith."[76] The house served as a private retreat for numerous black luminaries who would have otherwise been limited to all-black hotels or the Phillis Wheatley building because of the current segregationist policies of the local white hotels.

The Phillis Wheatley's prominence as a center for the black community during the 1930s can be documented by the variety of programs and activities advertised in *The Open Door* and reported in Annual Reports. For example, a 1931 advertisement entitled "Tempt Her with Decency and Clean Fun" announced activities such as mothers' clubs; Negro history lectures; a Music Department which offered piano, voice, and violin lesson; an Industrial and Business Department for working women; and clubs of many kinds for girls, including dramatics, basketball, tennis, and dancing. Along with the home economics offering, the agency seemed to run the gamut of interests for women and girls.[77] A similar listing in 1940 indicated the addition of lectures on health education (presented by black and white health professionals), political history and economy, and announced a health fair to celebrate National Negro Health Week.[78]

The building also served transient guests who came to the city. By this time, with few exceptions, hotels and restaurants were not willing to accommodate blacks. Therefore, although a lower occupancy rate of the traditional young women clients of the association was noted because of a decrease in migration during the depression years, the residence still brought in its share of income. Especially the ninth floor was made available to transient guests of both sexes.

Also, the dining facility remained popular with black professionals. Lunch at the Phillis Wheatley gave this group the opportunity to meet and swap information, much as private clubs served their white counterparts. A popular "round table" of black professionals met there regularly to discuss race issues.[79] On Sunday, after church time, the dining room became the center for black social activity. Everyone wanted to see and be seen at the Phillis Wheatley. The home-style meals were well prepared and cheap, and the atmosphere was inviting to people of all walks of life. Moreover, this was one of the few places in the city where the races could meet together for a meal.[80]

In addition to the local prominence of the institution, Hunter used her affiliation with the National Association of Colored Women to enhance its national image. Following her selection as head of the National Division of Big Sisters for the organization, Hunter soon moved to create a Phillis Wheatley Department in 1934. With the motto, "A Phillis Wheatley in every city where there is not a branch of the YWCA," the organization succeeded in establishing or affiliating at least nine additional houses and numerous Phillis Wheatley Clubs in cities across the country.[81] The houses were in Chicago; Greenville, South Carolina; Minneapolis; Winston-Salem, North Carolina; Toledo, Canton, Oberlin, and Steubenville, Ohio; and New Haven, Connecticut. A national statement of purpose proclaimed objectives for the houses:

> . . . to maintain a home with wholesome surroundings; to afford colored girls and women an opportunity for fuller development; to promote growth in Christian character and service through physical, social, mental and spiritual training; to create a social understanding which operates unceasingly for the extension of the Kingdom of God."[82]

Hunter's affiliation with the National Association of Colored Women also helped her to avoid pressure to affiliate the Phillis Wheatley with the YWCA. Mounting criticism from the Welfare Federation's Group Work Council strongly suggested the need for a more professionally run agency with a clear cut purpose and plans to carry out the purpose. There was also criticism of the qualifications of staff and board members. The council strongly recommended that the association needed to be affiliated with a national organization.[83] When affiliation with the Social Settlement Union was considered, there was a fear, on the part of the board and staff, that they might be required to include work with boys.[84] However, when affiliation with the YWCA was again proposed, Hunter was adamant in her assertion that the National Association of Colored Women was already affording the Phillis Wheatley national contacts.[85] Independence and autonomy for the institution seemed closely tied to the success of the national Phillis Wheatley project.

Perhaps the most impressive testimony to the fact that Hunter held the respect of a number of blacks, despite disagreement among some with her conservative philosophy and servile behavior, were the honors bestowed upon her during her most prominent years of active leadership. At a local level, she was invited to be an honorary member of Alpha Kappa Alpha

Officers of the National Association of Colored Women, 1937
Jane Edna Hunter, back row, second from right

Sorority, an organization of black college-educated women who were committed to civic involvement.[86] This honor represented acknowledgment of Hunter's achievements by a group whose exclusive membership might have opposed her separatist activities in an earlier time. In 1938 and again in 1940, Hunter's friendship with Mary McLeod Bethune gained her invitations to meet with Eleanor Roosevelt and women heading up government activities which particularly concerned girls and women in Washington, D.C.[87] She was also invited to participate in a four-month federal government sponsored training in connection with projected federal housing projects.[88] These invitations were issued despite her prominence in local, state, and national Republican politics.[89]

In 1937, Wilberforce University conferred upon her the Master of Arts degree. Perhaps her most meaningful honor was from Tuskegee Institute, which conferred a Master of Science degree, in recognition of her achievements in the development of the social and vocational program conducted at the Phillis Wheatley Association, as the embodiment and essence of the industrial philosophy maintained by Booker T. Washington.[90] This honor indeed gave her national recognition and approval for holding fast to the traditional conservative philosophy and values. It also confirmed that a still significant segment of the black population felt that her program and ideas for race uplift were valid and relevant.

SEVEN

Applause and Abandonment: A Career Ends

The story of Jane Hunter, the Phillis Wheatley Association, and race relations in the city of Cleveland during the 1940s illustrates the radical changes which the nation experienced as a result of the depression, World War II, and the war's aftermath. The most appropriate descriptions of the era for blacks must include "flexibility, indignation and impatience," as the nation rode the crest of a wave of nationalism brought about by the serious implications of world events. Totalitarianism, Nazism, and Fascism posed immediate threats to the American dream of democracy for "all."

Within one decade, American blacks were subjected to exclusion from the war effort, inclusion when the nation needed their labors, and exclusion again when the country settled back into normality. Racial sentiments in the country ran the gamut from complete separation in institutions, jobs, housing, the armed services, public accommodations, and virtually all phases of life, to disappointment in a nation which fought for democracy and freedom but refused to grant equality to her darker citizens.

However, the rhetoric of wartime significantly changed America's political and sociological perception of racial justice and tolerance. A forced examination of the "American way of life" followed the war which was fought to preserve human dignity and against the principles of racial superiority as espoused by Hitler. Black Americans, the country's largest racial minority, became the focus of self-conscious liberalism and pompous patriotism, especially in Northern areas where their potential as a voting bloc was recognized and exploited.

The war also changed the perceptions of black Americans and their notion of a more just and equitable society. Hundreds of thousands of soldiers and their families who participated in the national war effort began to dream of full citizenship rights. Returning black soldiers were able to attend college on the G.I. Bill, creating a far broader base of educated black Americans than ever before. The NAACP, in a careful strategy which began in 1934 to challenge the exclusion of blacks from the law school at the University of Maryland, steadily chipped away at the legal concept of "separate but equal" through court battles. These efforts would culminate in a ruling that would require institutional integration in the second half of the century.[1] The decision rendered in *Brown* v. *Board of Education of Topeka* ended the myth of "separate but equal."

Perhaps most significant, however, was the change in geographical distribution of black citizens, described as possibly the most rapid and extensive shift by any large population group in modern history.[2] The proportion of blacks living in the South fell from over three-quarters in 1940 to a little over half by 1970.[3] Primarily, this change removed a large number of blacks from the jurisdiction of political districts where voting was actively discouraged to urban centers where they were more able to exercise the franchise.

Blacks gained a political advantage from this largely because they were crowded into segregated wards and precincts in large cities, thus forming a voting bloc. For the first time since Reconstruction, black voters were openly wooed by white politicians, and concessions of major and minor significance were won. Perhaps the most symbolic indicator of the new importance of black urban voters was the dramatic action of President Harry Truman in signing Executive Order 9981, ordering the desegregation of the armed forces, in anticipation of the 1948 election.[4] The new status of the black voter was notable when he began to recognize the potential power which could be wielded at the ballot box. Between 1948 and 1952, political organizations in the South battled a newly awakening black awareness, employing any means possible to bar blacks from voting, at the same time that voter registration drives doubled Southern black registration.[5]

In addition to recognition of their potential at the ballot box by blacks, a new style of race activism became an important strategy in the battle for civil rights. As the decade of the forties opened, blacks used the threat of a massive March on Washington as a means to call attention to their desire for full participation in the apparent coming change in the nation's economic fortunes. As mobilization for the war accelerated, blacks keenly felt that the mood of race exclusivity in the country would deny them access to both employment in war-related industry and participation in the armed services. Jobs became the focus of the black press, the NAACP, and local and national leadership. When appeals to the federal government yielded few results, A. Phillip Randolph, founder and president of the Brotherhood of Sleeping Car Porters, sent out a call for black Americans to march in the nation's capital to dramatize their determination to be included in the war effort. Backed by every major black organization, the threat of the march resulted in President Roosevelt's only tangible act against racism, the signing of Executive Order 8802, creating the first Committee on Fair Employment Practices.[6]

Locally, the issues and experiences of black citizens reflected many of the changes taking place across the nation. The decade opened with a slowly recovering economy as factories began tooling up for war production. High unemployment figures in the black community were little relieved, as white industrialists and union officials alike overlooked the black worker. According to the city's Negro Welfare Association, a decline in industrial activities during the depression had virtually eradicated blacks from the blue-collar work force. Those companies making airplane parts and tool and die makers, which began an early recovery from the recession, rejected efforts to place black workers.[7]

Cleveland's white retail business community also failed to consider blacks for jobs, even in the Central Area where blacks were most heavily concentrated. While the main streets in the area's commercial sector were well dotted with white-owned retail stores, few blacks were employed as clerks. A campaign to secure jobs was organized by the Future Outlook League, a militant protest organization which had been founded in 1934 by John O. Holly. Tactics ranging from private negotiations to picketing and boycotting opened up hundreds of clerical positions during the thirties and forties.[8]

Living conditions for blacks grew worse during the late thirties and forties with acceleration of black migration into the city. High absentee landlord ownership and high density in the central city were major factors. One of the most bitterly fought race battles during the period centered around a slum clearance project, sponsored by the federal government and administered by a city housing authority. While thousands of poor black ghetto dwellers were displaced by the project, only a few middle-income blacks were able to relocate into a segregated portion of the newly built dwellings.[9] Black Clevelanders were enraged when they realized what the plans would mean to many, and even more infuriated that the city and federal governments would sponsor such a blatantly racist undertaking.[10] Pressure from the city's black political leadership, which was mostly Republican at a time when black voters were shifting to the Democratic Party, resulted only in obtaining a single appointment of a black to the housing authority and no substantial change of the segregationist practices.[11] Displaced families were left few alternatives except to crowd into areas already heavily populated with the poor. The city's Central Area expanded its ghetto boundaries to include a few more streets and hundreds more residents.[12]

Thus, the Central Area, center of black living accommodations and businesses, became a haven for vice and crime, a target of black protest, and a living hell for the numerous black families who were crowded into its borders. Calls from social workers and politicians for reform of city administration policies which allowed the situation and for relief for the inhabitants became commonplace. Studies of the area between 1942 and 1944 indicated that major problems included underemployment, poor education facilities, a breakdown of family relations, and, most important, the problem of racism in all systems operating in the city.[13] Only a few black business and professional families trickled into nearby predominately white areas, because of severe difficulties with restrictive covenants, discriminatory mortgage policies, and harassment.[14]

Jane Hunter and the Phillis Wheatley continued to provide much of the recreational and training outlets for the burgeoning community. Before the declaration of World War II, the agency participated in National Youth Administration (NYA) programs to train youth for limited vocations requiring some skills. Classes in sewing, cooking, cleaning, practical nursing, and clerical skills were offered in the program through the agency.[15] They were also involved in the Works Progress Administration (WPA), using the skills of sometimes highly trained women who were out of work.[16] The agency also continued to provide a very well-attended camping program in the summers for neighborhood children, a pre-school for working mothers, an Industrial and Business Girls Department, a beauty school, and a music school. There were also lectures on health and hygiene, Negro history classes, and a number of social clubs and activities. The board constantly tried to find ways to better serve the rapidly growing community. Phillis Wheatley workers were sent out on door-to-door recruitment campaigns to talk with their neighbors and to find ways to attract them to the agency.[17]

The nation's entry into the Second World War did not immediately signal a return to the job market for blacks in Cleveland. Despite the national FEPC order, until 1943, black workers continued to be excluded from jobs in industry at approximately the same rate as in 1939, before the order.[18] The Negro Welfare League reported "no increased opportunities for Negroes in private industry" despite their vigorous efforts.[19] As late as early 1942, the *Call and Post* reported that "The New Year still finds the Negro battling for a foothold in the economic programs of the nation. . . . The War for the Negro is a serious question mark."[20]

When federally sponsored training was attacked in the *Cleveland Press* as being of dubious value, Jane Hunter wrote in response that the criticism was unfair, considering that 65 percent of the youth being trained by NYA schools were black.[21] She also noted that the Board of Education "has limited facilities for vocational training in predominately Negro schools, consequently Negroes are kept on relief."[22] Lack of training, however, was only a facade under which lay the deeper problems of race discrimination. There were obvious flaws in the training programs sponsored by the NYA and the WPA, especially their failure to include training for industrial work. This does not account, however, for the report by the NYA training center in Cleveland in 1942 that "Placement . . . of both Negro men and women in the field for which they were trained was infrequent."[23] Racial bigotry and intolerance still predominated among union and corporate officials, and, as a result, black workers were not hired.

The *Call and Post* brought in the new year of 1943 with an announcement which would change the employment situation for blacks for the remainder of the war. The headline, "Job Freeze Announced," signaled action from the federal government which would force industry to utilize all available manpower in the metropolitan area before recruiting out of state to fill jobs.[24] With production of war-related products as much as nine months behind schedule, the national War Manpower Commission stipulated in its plan that war-related industry must prove that there was no manpower available before any recruitment could take place.[25] The net effect of the program was to benefit black workers, who for the first time returned to full employment. By 1944, the Commission reported that the number of Negro men employed in private industry had increased from 4,500 in 1942 to 29,000, and the number of women had grown from 2,000 to 6,000.[26]

While the war era produced a change in occupational opportunities for blacks, Christopher Wye in his study of Cleveland's black population concluded that comparison of the census data from 1950 with the census of 1940 suggests that the permanent effect was modest.[27] Black males holding jobs above the semi-skilled level increased by only 6 percent and for females the increase was only 4 percent. However, among black women, an 18 percent decrease in domestic and personal service employees, together with an increase of nearly 14 percent in clerical occupations, represented a significant shift in employment opportunity.[28] Black women were finally able to break into jobs above the level of personal and domestic service.

The shift in opportunities for employment for blacks was accompanied by a 76 percent increase in the black population in the forties. Growth from 85,000 in 1940 to 148,000 in 1950 changed the portion of the population which was black from 10 percent to 16 percent of the city's total.[29] The increasingly visible minority, crowded into basically three wards within the city limits and fully employed during the war years, brought with them the need for business and professional services unprecedented in the city's history. Small businesses that had been able to hang on during the depression were once again able to thrive, and they were joined by newcomers who opened up to meet the needs of the community. The influx of blacks from the South, conditioned to patronizing race enterprises, made the businesses and professionals thrive.[30]

Among blacks in business and professions, a new organization appeared which actively promoted the concept that black customers should spend their dollars within their own community in order that the race could build a strong economic base. The Progressive Business Alliance sponsored a weekly radio program, "The Negro Business Hour," as one effort to promote race consciousness among the growing population. It also assumed the function of monitoring the community. Jane Hunter felt the power of their wrath when the Phillis Wheatley was boycotted by their business luncheon roundtable because of the institution's "unwholesome" attitude toward Negro business.[31] Hunter had refused to purchase bread for the institution from a black-owned baking company.[32]

Emphasis on racial tolerance, stimulated by Hitler's war to empower the world's "master race," served to stimulate examination of race policies no less in Cleveland then in the rest of the nation. Although discrimination did not suddenly disappear, slight changes in attitudes and in practices could be discerned. The city began to recognize that inexcusable inequities existed, which made the cause of the war seem incredible to those who truly believed in justice. Examples of support for more equitable race relations could be found in some actions on the part of city government, in the tone of newspaper articles and headlines, and in some changes in the race code in social agencies.

An illustration of the change in political dynamics came when Democratic Mayor Frank Lausche yielded to the pressures of an increasing black leadership and appointed a Cleveland Metropolitan Fair Employment Practice Committee in May, 1942. Although the committee could only investigate cases of racial discrimination and had no power to penalize companies for such practices, it served as a symbolic reminder to the business community that practices of racial discrimination would not be condoned by the city administration.[33] White newspaper support for the city's position on employment of black workers echoed the appeals of black leaders for greater equality. Editorials such as one in the *Cleveland Press* argued that ". . . if we are actually fighting against the Hitlerian notion of a 'master race' predestined to rule 'inferior peoples,' we cannot permit discrimination toward our fellow Americans."[34]

A change in the policies and practices of the Cleveland YWCA toward black women demonstrated a significant change in race attitudes among social agencies. Since it was initially the YWCA's refusal to serve black women which provided the impetus for founding the separate facility and the individual financial support of many YWCA members which sustained it, one might observe that in many ways the history of the Phillis Wheatley indicated a dependency on the race position of the other institution. In addition, events indicating a change in attitude toward service for black women by the white institution also helps to illustrate a basic flaw in the model of "integrated" or predominately white control of a black self-help institution.

As has been pointed out in previous chapters, the history of race practices by the Cleveland YWCA is completely intermingled with the history of the Phillis Wheatley Association. From the inception of the idea for the Phillis Wheatley, the duplication of leadership for both organizations and the continued interaction of both boards and staffs created an unusual situation of parallel though not duplicate institutions. In effect, except for its organizational independence, for many years the Phillis Wheatley, for all practical purposes, was a Negro branch of the YWCA. Despite Hunter's determination to retain control of the Phillis Wheatley and her affiliation with the National Association of Negro Women, the net result of her early relationship with the YWCA and its leadership may have contributed to the

131

demise of the institution for black women as originally conceived, since the association was continually perceived by the public to duplicate the services of the YWCA.

The slow change in racial policies at the YWCA began when a group of young campers wrote to Mrs. Judson Stewart, president of the association, to question policies regarding Negro girls' use of the facilities, especially the pool. They pointed out that following the philosophy of the national organization they had included girls of all races as members of their group in order to build a fellowship of *all* girls. They were embarrassed to learn that they could not all enjoy the same privileges.[35] As a result of the letter, Mrs. Stewart promised to put the issue on the agenda of the first fall meeting of the board of trustees.[36] At the September meeting, when the letter from the girls was read to the board, it was decided that the interracial policies of all departments should be considered.[37] A new Committee on Race Relations was assigned to investigate the policies and practices of the association, and to make recommendations to the board as to what could be done in the future.[38]

At a subsequent meeting, the committee discussed the fact that the association had included Negro girls in its Younger Girls Department through school clubs at integrated schools, and in the Industrial Council and Industrial Clubs where women worked on the same job. These mostly "off site" activities had not required a review of the policies related to use of facilities. On the other hand, the Health Education Department had assumed that Negro girls who were part of club groups could use the pool. Even so, only one Negro girl had used the pool. It was also brought out at the meeting that Red Cross Life Saving groups had discontinued using the YWCA facilities because of the Y's restrictive race policies. The committee briefly considered the history of the Phillis Wheatley, but there was no comment as to the YWCA's responsibility for or relation to the other institution. The committee concluded that the YWCA had never had a written policy regarding service to black women, but there was no doubt about their practices.[39]

The committee's report to the board in October again raised the issue of the Phillis Wheatley. The sentiment of the board seemed to be that "We are a different agency doing a different work than the Phillis Wheatley. They come for what we have to offer and go to the Phillis Wheatley for what they have to offer."[40] The board felt that there was no conflict or comparison between the two institutions.

In 1942, the YWCA race relations committee recommended that the following resolution be passed by the board.

In view of the critical world situation in which democracy hangs in the balance and

Whereas, the Young Women's Christian Associations of the United States of America assembled in Convention at Columbus, Ohio, in 1938 took action that "Associations should continue to work for the building of a society nearer to the Kingdom of God:

By attempting to create within the Association a fellowship in which barriers of race, nationality, class, education and social status are broken down in the pursuit of the common objective of a better life for all; and by attempting to create an understanding this objective in the community."

Whereas, this action was reaffirmed in the Convention at Atlantic City in 1940,

Whereas, interracial practice now exists in many parts of the Cleveland YWCA; be it

Resolved: That interracial policy and practice be extended as rapidly as possible in those parts of the organization where such policy and practice are not now operative.[41]

Passage of the resolution symbolized a considerable change in the official posture of the agency toward black women. While there was no rush to integrate the association or to solicit black membership, the door was opened which would allow the participation of all racial groups in the YWCA. Appointment of a black woman, Mrs. Joseph Gomez, to the board of trustees, in 1944, followed discussion about the role of a black board person. The board made clear that a black member was not to be expected to represent any group. She was to function in the same way as all others on the board. The appointment marked a first step toward including black participation in the association's decision-making process.[42] Gomez was joined the following year by Mrs. Robert P. Morgan, a staff worker at the Phillis Wheatley.[43]

Changes in the YWCA's race policy did not immediately affect the work of the Phillis Wheatley. Rather, the war effort which brought increases in the black population caused an acceleration in demands for services for black women and girls. The residence at the Phillis Wheatley filled to overflowing between 1943 and 1945. At one point, Hunter complained that beds were in office rooms and there was no longer space for club and class activities. Also, a shortage of recreation facilities in the area put a serious strain on the limited recreation spaces at the Phillis Wheatley.[44] During the same period, the association listed an active Elementary Department which offered such activities as cooking, dancing, knitting, sewing, story hours, and a children's evangelism program. There was also the Music School; gym and physical fitness; dramatics and modern dance; Girl Scouts; a Business and Industrial Girls Department; arts and crafts; a homemaking department; and numerous club and class activities.[45] The inclusion of boys in some of the classes and activities, and the sizable Elementary Department, had the effect of making the association seem more like a settlement house than a YWCA. The Phillis Wheatley was indeed a duplication of neither. Instead, it had evolved into a multi-service center which was utilized for different purposes by different segments of the black community.

Hunter was somewhat vindicated, during the war years, by the extensive use of the agency. Criticism by those who had objected to the separate facility gave way to acknowledgment that indeed the Phillis Wheatley filled a unique place in the growing black community. Problems of adjustment for new urban blacks were critical enough to command the attention of not only the Phillis Wheatley, but also the Negro Welfare Association and the Cedar YMCA (all black). There was frequent cooperation between the three major social service agencies which served the black community.[46] Although the Phillis Wheatley never deviated in its focus on service for women and girls, the problems of race discrimination sometimes seemed to compel services to both sexes.[47]

Hunter did not express concern about the YWCA's plans for integrating their services. She felt strongly that there was room for both agencies for women in the city.[48] She was concerned, however, that the Phillis Wheatley's facilities limited the kind of services that they were able to offer to the community. Describing overcrowded conditions at the building, she complained that neither she nor the building's architects ever took into consideration that they would be challenged to provide social services on a large scale. Rather, she said, "the building was planned to earn money."[49] The dream of a home and training center for young women had been far exceeded by the reality of multiple uses for the facility. The residence was only one part of a large operation.

With the use of the association's facility at an optimal level, Hunter turned her attention to ensuring the future of the institution. She felt that there were two very important problems for the association. One, the need to update and expand the physical facilities, and two, the burden of constantly looking for money for the agency's operation. She wrote to her friend

Nannie Burroughs (who also headed a large training school for black women):

> Somehow I wish that you, Mary Bethune and myself could give up raising money and could devote all of our strength and spiritual life to the building of God's kingdom. This money business destroys so much of one's real self, that we cannot do our best, feeling that we need money all the time.[50]

The Phillis Wheatley was without an endowment fund until a modest gift of a few shares of stock was received in 1943.[51] This gift formed the nucleus for a fund which Hunter hoped would relieve the association from the uncertainty of the whims of the federation and total dependency on the agency's ability to generate income from year to year in order to stay afloat.[52] Hunter's goal for the agency was for them to become 80 percent self-supporting.[53] Solicitations for endowment were only moderately successful, probably in part because of a general lack of support for the effort on the part of the federation.[54]

In order to finance improvements and expansion of the building, the Phillis Wheatley asked the federation for permission to launch a capital funds drive. Permission from the planning and funding body for this kind of fund-raising effort was necessary because of a cooperation agreement between member agencies and the Community Chest. Included in the new plans for the association were a swimming pool, extra beauty parlors, and additional activities rooms. They also asked to add more residence space, including rooms with private baths.[55] Hunter believed that black working women were moving into jobs which would allow them to seek more private accommodations than the present building could afford. She also felt just as strongly, however, that the Phillis Wheatley offered safety and protection in a home-like atmosphere. Improvement of residence facilities would allow the association to take advantage of the needs of the modern woman.[56]

Much to Hunter's chagrin, the request for the fund drive was turned down by the federation. While the Budget and Policy Committee agreed that there was a need for beauty parlors and club rooms, they questioned the need for additional or more modern residence rooms. They also stated that since Negro girls could use the Outhwaite, Cedar YMCA, and Central YWCA pools, there was no need for another pool.[57] The attitude of the federation was perhaps best expressed by its financial secretary, C. F. Middleton (who also objected to the endowment fund effort). In a meeting of the Phillis

Wheatley Association board he told the group, "If Jane Hunter can get the money for her wishes, then she can find it for some necessities."[58]

Middleton's attitude probably reflected the federation's frustration with the endless fiscal management problems of the agency (no doubt compounded by the fact that they could never afford the services of an accountant and poorly trained bookkeepers could not handle the complicated budget responsibilities). Middleton also clearly reflected the federation's biases regarding the needs of agencies serving the black community. There was little support for the idea of first-class facilities for the agencies serving a predominately black clientele.[59] It seems no coincidence that the YWCA launched plans for a major capital funds campaign to upgrade their facility in the same year that the Phillis Wheatley was turned down, with the full blessings of the federation.[60] It was no longer fashionable to ask the community to contribute money to support separate facilities for housing women. Even though the YWCA still provided lodging for only an occasional black woman (with special arrangements made by a 'reliable' black person), the needs of the white group took precedence.[61]

The lesson was not lost on black Clevelanders. They were once again reminded that agencies serving the black community were still not considered of primary importance in the city. A national "Jane Hunter Appreciation Dinner" in 1946, and the sale of properties owned by the agency for some years, raised at least enough money to make minimal improvements to the building.[62] The leadership for planning the dinner reminded at least some of the prospective patrons that money for black institutions would become more and more the responsibility of the black community.[63]

Hunter's plans for the future of the Phillis Wheatley Association did not end with her efforts to secure endowment funds and to modernize the building. She also began to understand the necessity of changing the focus of training at the institution. As early as 1943, she wrote that "It is high time now for the Phillis Wheatley Association to offer young women of Cleveland the kind of training they want rather than the kind for which we have been equipped in the past."[64] However, she continued by stating that they must ". . . be prepared to take their rightful places and fill the needs of Negro business establishments here in Cleveland."[65] By 1945, she had changed her rationale for a new focus in training. Her ability to admit that she had misjudged the impact of the war was offered in a succinct statement in *The Open Door*:

It is regrettable that we here at the Phillis Wheatley Association must acknowledge that it has taken a horrible war to make this agency aware that there is a need for specialized training in a different kind of service for Negro girls. Yet such a thing is true.

The future holds a unique opportunity for thoroughly prepared colored girls, to not only serve their own group, but to serve in the general fields of industry and business.

It behooves the Phillis Wheatley Association to make some preparations to qualify our girls to meet the opportunities that will be waiting for adequately trained persons regardless of color.[66]

Hunter clearly did not intend to lose the opportunity to attract the funds, interest, or patronage of a growing number of black women in white collar jobs. While there is no doubt that this change of focus would put her in direct competition with the YWCA and other training agencies, she felt convinced that the black-oriented Phillis Wheatley could better serve the needs of black women.

Hunter's stubborn advocacy of the continuation of an association "for Negro women and girls" in many ways ran counter to the growing appeal of integration. Her philosophy, based on the early-century model of race uplift, was out of step with the post-war promise of integration. She held on to the idea of a separate institution at a time when few blacks comprehended that integration, as it would come to be defined in the next decade, could threaten the existence of institutions and traditions long held in high esteem among blacks. The growing appeal of the "melting pot" philosophy, popular during the fifties, favored minimizing cultural differences which had long separated races and nationalities within the country. "Liberal" national organizations would close their black outposts, embarrassed over the general inferiority of institutional facilities designated "for blacks." The more elusive loss of spirit and pride which all-black institutions had often generated was yet to be felt, as black Americans believed that they were finally on the threshold of acceptance into the mainstream. Not until well into the 1960s would blacks understand that integration was to mean for blacks that they would be expected to give up their own cultural identity in order to conform with the more acceptable standards and values of the white majority.

Jane Hunter did not anticipate future theories regarding the importance of cultural identity. She was old-fashioned. She simply believed that separate institutions did a better job of attending to the needs of black people. A black institution, for example, could tell young black mothers that they were "going to regret going to work and leaving your children to wander the streets . . . [and would] awaken from your money making only to find your children in the courts."[67] Hunter did not think that a white institution would know about that kind of black problem. Her insistence that the Phillis Wheatley offered a unique understanding of black women was based only on the belief that the race was still a long way from being completely acculturated and accepted into the majority white society of the United States.[68]

Hunter's unyielding loyalty to the old race ideology made her seem obsolete to many blacks. Her refusal to concede to more modern ideas and more modern relationships between black and white people made her seem obstructive to the process of integration for black women. Many thought that the YWCA would have moved faster in their plan to serve black women if Hunter had not held the loyalty of a few influential white YWCA/Phillis Wheatley board members.[69]

Jane Hunter never moved from her position regarding the purpose of the Phillis Wheatley. In a very poignant article published in *The Open Door*, she stated once again her beliefs and her philosophy about the association:

HOLDING FAST TO A PURPOSE

The Phillis Wheatley Association was founded in July, 1911, having for its purpose to maintain a home with wholesome surroundings; to afford colored girls and women an opportunity for fuller development; to promote growth in Christian character and service through physical, social, mental, and spiritual training; to create a social understanding which operates unceasingly for the extension of the Kingdom of God.

During these years, through vision and service, beginning with the small things of life, we have developed a great Institution. Through the help of a mixed board of trustees and their friends and the general public we have achieved a goal in character building. However, it is a good thing that we have the foresight and vision to change our program with a changing world, and to meet the demands from the girls that we keep pace with the improvement of facilities for training them and the girls who will follow.

We wish our readers to know and keep in mind that we have stuck to our purpose of meeting the spiritual and physical needs of Negro girls, and we have no desire to change our purpose. We do welcome interracial fellowship and the integration of the groups but we do not wish to lose sight of the purpose for which the Phillis Wheatley Association was founded. There are those who fought consistently the movement to establish the Phillis Wheatley Association on the basis that it was fostering segregation. Every step of the way, for thirty-four years, the Phillis Wheatley Association has kept in mind and fought to meet the needs of Negro girls and we hope that [we] will not lose sight of the purpose. We wish to continue building on that foundation stone of helping Negro girls.

Now that The Phillis Wheatley Association is established and is a going concern as a result of the service and suffering of a few friends, there is danger facing the Association of losing the very purpose for which it was founded. It will take a strong Board of Trustees to hold fast and to continue to improve upon the program and to create new activities which will meet the needs of all girls and we pray that God will continue to be with The Phillis Wheatley Association and let us not loose [sic] sight of the purpose for which it was founded.[70]

In October of 1947, the Phillis Wheatley Association Board of Trustees received a letter from the Welfare Federation informing them that Jane Hunter would reach the age of retirement in December.[71] According to the rules of the federation's retirement plan, she reluctantly submitted her resignation as director of the association in order to be eligible for benefits. However, she was by no means ready to give up the reins which she had carried for thirty-six years. In her letter to the board, she asked to name her own successor. She also made it clear that she did not consider her job with the association completed, pointing out to them that she had hoped to complete a swimming pool at the summer camp and other improvements.[72]

Despite much sentiment in favor of keeping Hunter at the helm, the reality was that keeping her on for more than a reasonable time would jeopardize the agency's position with the Welfare Federation.[73] The Personnel Committee recommended that Hunter's resignation be accepted with an extension of no longer than one year past her sixty-fifth birthday.[74] The following reasons were listed as justification for the recommendation:

1. When the pension falls due an employee should retire unless the Board has a good reason to extend the services.
2. For a number of years the budget has been unsatisfactory.
3. Constant argument from Miss Hunter.
4. The Welfare Federation is not in sympathy with the type of program carried on by Phillis Wheatley but thinks that emphasis should be placed on program rather than building.
5. There will be NO increase in budget as long as Miss Hunter is here.
6. Increased criticisms from papers were against Miss Hunter whether they should have been or not.[75]

After voting by secret ballot, the recommendation to retire Jane Hunter was passed. The list offered by the Personnel Committee revealed the problems of the association immediately after the boom experienced during war time, as well as Hunter's limitations as a modern-day administrator. For example, it is obvious that the Welfare Federation, long critical of Hunter and her administrative methods, had made it clear that they considered her an obstacle rather than a help to the association. Her lack of appropriate education credentials, despite her law degree, had been a criticism for years.[76] Hunter's failure to hire women from a pool of trained black social workers, many graduating from nearby Western Reserve School of Social Work, had spoiled the agency's opportunity to build a reputation of professionalism among social service organizations. The federation had also long criticized the agency's planning and management methods, especially as related to the budget.[77] Perhaps most harmful, in the opinion of the federation, was their perception that the Phillis Wheatley's program duplicated opportunities available to area citizens from other agencies.[78]

Hunter's continued description of the Phillis Wheatley as the black counterpart of the YWCA was no longer an acceptable rationale for its existence, especially in the face of an operating deficit at the end of 1946 which exceeded $5,000.[79] The agency's change in focus from a training program, their failure to define their mission in a way which expressed their unique role in the community, and their emphasis on the need for additional space in the building all had put the Phillis Wheatley in a position to be perceived by the community as a competitor to the YWCA. Hunter, as director of the association, was considered responsible for this untenable situation.

Perhaps to save face, Hunter tried to make her forced retirement into a racial issue, especially among her black supporters. She accused the white president and chairperson of the Personnel Committee of pressuring other white board members to vote to accept her resignation.[80] This charge was refuted when a black board member, Louise Evans, wrote a letter to the board to make her position in the matter clear. She wrote that although she went to the meeting to fight to retain Hunter as the agency's director, she had changed her mind after hearing the discussion.[81] Evans made it clear that the decision was not made along racial lines. Hunter later apologized to the board for making the allegations.[82]

Hunter was frustrated and confused by events surrounding her "forced" retirement. Although she understood very well the position of the association in relation to the federation's requirements for participation in the pension fund, and the agency's need for continued support from the planning and allocating body, she could not accept the board's action. Also, she had not, in the long run, been able to call upon the old dynamics between the races to protect her position. Race relations had changed dramatically over the years, and she no longer understood the people with whom she had to interact. The black women had become assertive and sophisticated in their participation as members of the board. They could not be manipulated as a group, and they seemed less willing than their predecessors to accept an accommodating or passive role in major decisions for the institution.[83] The white women had also changed. Hunter could no longer rely on the cadre of wealthy whites who felt obligated to give a small portion of their philanthropic dollars to take care of the black underclass. In their place were whites who had a broader view of interracial cooperation. They had come to understand the political and economic impracticality of segregation. They also were more sophisticated and aggressive regarding the management of the social agency. The era of paternalistic philanthropy was fast coming to an end.

Hunter expressed her confusion and frustration in a letter to a former white board president, Bertha Bailey (1927–29). Still clinging to the nostalgia of the old master/servant relationship, which for her seemed comfortable, she wrote in 1948:

My dear Miss Bailey:

It always gives me inspiration to get a letter from you in your own handwriting. It simply thrills me when I think of the years we have worked together. You have been such a friend to the work I have tried to do in Cleveland. Had you been here last night when we had OPEN HOUSE and seen the gymnasium packed to overflowing, including the balcony, largely with the poor people of this community, and some white people; you would have felt rewarded for the years of service you have given to us. It seemed like old times to see the parents coming with their children and the very fine program rendered. . . . The display by the students at Ford House of clothes, lamp shades and household articles would have made Booker T. Washington himself smile from the Heavens to see the work the graduates of his school are doing in the slum areas of Cleveland.

Phillis Wheatley Association has been unhappy since last August when the Welfare Federation put pressure on forcing me to retire upon reaching the retirement age. The majority of the colored women resented it and some of the white women also. Had Mrs. Morris and Mrs. Black not proven so unloyal there would not have been any feeling about it. However, the situation is clearing up and I am happy over it. It would be a shame after all these years of working to brake [sic] up our interracial fellowship. But the time will come when the colored women will demand that the majority of the Board members

141

be Negroes. The white women we are getting today are not as understanding and sympathetic as the women we had when you came on the Board. Some day I will come out and tell you all about it.

Many years ago when you were not so well you expressed the desire to stay on the Board and I have up to this time insisted on your name being carried. At every Board meeting when the roll is called I answer for you and I am asking that your name be carried at least until I retire. The nominating committee nominated you to remain on the Board until 1951. It may be possible that you would want to go on the Honorary Board when I leave. I shall want to feel that you have remained with me through the years.[84]

Retirement for Hunter was difficult at best. Removed from her lifelong work, she announced that she would work full time to establish a new organization to extend the work to which she had devoted her life. A new Phillis Wheatley Foundation was established for the purpose of providing scholarships to help worthy young working women to gain preparation for useful occupations. The scholarships were not to be restricted to college-bound women, but were to be extended to training in such fields as cosmetology, nursing, stenography, and domestic science. Another objective of the Foundation was a plan to give assistance to groups in other cities who wanted to give institutional assistance to working girls when no such service existed. Assistance would be available for founding, operating, and developing institutions which would provide shelter, guidance, and training for working girls.[85]

The Phillis Wheatley Foundation, an independent organization administered by a board of trustees, opened its national headquarters in a house directly across the street from the Phillis Wheatley Association. Hunter and her new board of prominent black citizens set about the task of raising money for the scholarships and to pay expenses for the new organization. Hunter launched a national speaking tour to outline her new plan and to recount her experiences as head of the Phillis Wheatley in Cleveland.[86] According to a report in 1952, the effort met with some success. The headquarters was fully paid for and the Foundation anticipated about $24,000 in stocks and bonds for the scholarship funds by the end of that year.[87] Hunter remained an active fund-raiser and speaker for her new cause until 1955, when she became ill.[88] There are indications that she had begun to suffer some mental deterioration by the time she decided to retire from active work for the Foundation.

It is sad to note that she grew increasingly hostile toward the Phillis Wheatley Association. She frequently harassed the board with complaints and accused them of abandoning her after she had given her life to the work.[89]

In 1960, Hunter was judged mentally incompetent by the Probation Court of the State of Ohio. At this time, her estate, worth $409,711, was placed into a trust and a lawyer, Charles Hadley, was appointed to be her legal guardian. Newspaper accounts at this time traced the origin of her wealth back to a few good investments in property in the Central Area. During the war years, her difficulties with the Office of Price Administration (OPA) labeled her a slum landlord. She was cited for violations of rent control regulations and of crowding more occupants than allowed into some of her properties.[90] Accounts also attributed her stock holdings (largely bank stocks) to the good advice she received from officers of the Cleveland Trust Bank.[91] Although her salary was said to have averaged little more than $3,000 per year during her time at the Phillis Wheatley Association, her frugal living habits and conservative investments had paid off extremely well.

Hunter was confined to a rest home in Cleveland in 1960, where she lived to the age of eighty-nine.[92] Thus came a tragic ending to a life full of energy and filled with service to the women of her race. Hunter's will, written in 1957, made it clear that she wanted the benefits of her labor to continue to aid young women. She stated that she felt no obligation to bequeath money to the Phillis Wheatley Association, since they had benefited from her many years of dedicated service.[93] She chose instead to set up a trust to provide scholarships for college-bound women, with special consideration for women from South Carolina and Ohio. In addition, she left money to five black colleges, including Claflin, Benedict, Fisk, Central State, and Houston-Tillitson colleges, and Harbison Presbyterian School (the school which replaced her old alma mater, Ferguson Academy).[94] To date, the fund is still awarding scholarships.

Throughout her life, Hunter had found her greatest inspiration in her deep religious beliefs and in her desire to change conditions for her race. In an interview in 1955, she revealed the pain which had driven her to work so hard for change, and at long last her ability to put into perspective the changes which she had so long resisted. The newspaper reported:

> Deeply religious, Miss Hunter said she underwent a profound spiritual experience last year in Switzerland at the International Conference on Moral Rearmament. "I always hated the Southern whites because I thought they deprived me of so many things, and made my life so hard as a child. Of course

143

I never told anyone how I carried this hate around for sixty years. Then, during my meditations, it dawned on me that they were all dead and times have changed and opportunities are fresh."[95]

Hunter's will best summarized her heartfelt sentiments for the work to which she had devoted her life. It provides a perfect farewell to the woman and her institution:

> For more than 50 years in Cleveland, Ohio, I have worked for and been associated with the Phillis Wheatley Association, a charitable corporation in the city of Cleveland, Ohio. I have seen that institution grow and develop from a mere idea to a living force in the community, which I have every faith it will continue to manifest. I feel as a proud mother with respect to her children, who gives them all she can during her lifetime, recognizing that there is a point at which the children, after nurturing and devotion, must become independent and live their own lives. I feel that with the devotion and thought I have given to the Phillis Wheatley Association and the success it has had and will continue to have because of the confidence in itself in the community, I can best say, "God, continue to bless it."[96]

Jane Edna Harris Hunter's life and work may be judged objectively in light of contemporary understandings of the intricate interrelationships between race, sex, and political, economic, and social systems. However, one cannot lose sight of her extraordinarily American accomplishments. In summary, she experienced a problem and found a solution. She acted on her personal beliefs and, in so doing, gave aid to thousands of women of her race. She was the ultimate patriot.

Hunter was not unique. Her belief that black Americans could eventually gain acceptance and equality in the American system is part of a long tradition of aspirations in the country's former slave population. Hunter came to Cleveland, Ohio, at a time when black Americans were faced with the necessity to find alternatives to the existing racially exclusive institutions. Her actions mirrored those of an impressive number of black women who also gave their lives to the building of institutions to serve the needs of the race. Mary McLeod Bethune, Charlotte Hawkins Brown, Nannie Burroughs, Lucy Laney, Lugenia Hope, Victoria Earle Matthews, Lucy Thurman, Eva Bowles, Josephine St. Pierre Ruffin, Daisy Lampkin, Janie Porter Barrett, and Elizabeth Lindsey Davis were only a few whose accomplishments were of equal or greater magnitude during the same era. These women represent a significant heritage which deserves to be noted in the annals of American history. The story of Jane Hunter's life and work is only a sample of the contributions to American life by black women which have been overlooked.

Notes

CHAPTER ONE

1. Rayford Logan, *The Betrayal of the Negro*, rev. ed. (London: Collier-Macmillan, 1970); originally published as *The Negro in American Life and Thought: The Nadir, 1877-1901* (New York: Macmillan, 1954).
2. Bishop Alexander Walter, *My Life and Work* (New York, 1917), p. 257, quoted in Logan, p. 341.
3. Logan, Chapter 8.
4. For a thorough discussion of population statistics in Cleveland, see Kenneth Kusmer, *A Ghetto Takes Shape: Black Cleveland, 1870-1930* (Urbana: University of Illinois Press, 1978), Chapter I.
5. Ibid., p. 10.
6. Ibid.
7. Ibid.
8. Ibid., p. 11.
9. Thomas J. Goliber, "Cuyahoga Blacks: A Social and Demographic study" (M.A. Thesis, Kent State University, 1972), pp. 22-34, quoted in Kusmer, Chapter I.
10. Ibid., p. 24.
11. Ibid., p. 41.
12. Russell H. Davis, *Black Americans in Cleveland: From George Peake to Carl B. Stokes, 1796-1969* (Washington, D.C.: Associated Publishers, 1972), p. 49.
13. Ibid., p. 88.
14. Charles T. Hickok, *The Negro in Ohio, 1802-70* (Cleveland, 1896). Also Helen M. Thurston, "The 1802 Constitutional Convention and the Status of the Negro," *Ohio History* 81 (Winter, 1972), pp. 15-37.
15. Ibid.
16. Wilbur Henry Siebert, *The Mysteries of Ohio's Underground Railroads* (Columbus, 1951), pp. 26-132. Also see Davis, pp. 52-53.
17. Kusmer, p. 143.
18. For a full examination of Myer's activities, see John Garraty, *The Barber and the Historian: The Correspondence of George A. Myers and James Ford Rhodes, 1910-1923* (Columbus, 1956). Also see the George A. Myers Papers, Ohio Historical Society, Columbus, Ohio.
19. Davis, pp. 104-105.
20. Ibid.
21. Ibid., p. 45. This organization was supported by subscription in order to pay a teacher for the city's black children. Three years later, John Malvin led a

similar state organization which helped to start schools in Columbus, Springfield, and Cincinnati.

22. Ibid., p. 46.
23. *Cleveland Herald and Gazette*, June 20, 1837.
24. Davis, pp. 45-47.
25. Kusmer, p. 97. Also see notices for meetings in the *Cleveland Gazette* (1883-1910) and *Cleveland Journal* (1903-1910). Also see Russell H. Davis, *Memorable Negroes in Cleveland's Past* (Cleveland: Western Reserve Historical Society, 1969). Notices also appeared in the *Cleveland Leader*, September 11, 1856, and June 19, 1868.
26. Davis, *Black Americans*, p. 74.
27. Kusmer, p. 10.
28. Wright held the position of secretary from about 1875 until he retired in 1922. Davis, *Black Americans*, pp. 98-99.
29. See issues of the *Cleveland Gazette* during the 1890s and the early twentieth century, especially editorials by Harry Smith. Also see minutes of black church organizations and lodges which give evidence of this theme.
30. Ibid.
31. David Gerber, *Ohio and the Color Line* (Urbana: University of Illinois Press, 1976), pp. 251-52.
32. An example of the *Plain Dealer*'s position can be found in a January 13, 1859, editorial. The role of the *Cleveland Plain Dealer* is discussed by Kusmer, Chapters 1-3, and Davis, *Black Americans*, pp. 71-2.
33. Gerber, p. 260.
34. For a thorough discussion of Washington's ideology and its impact and implications, see August Meier, *Negro Thought in America, 1880-1915* (Ann Arbor: University of Michigan Press, 1963).
35. Ibid., p. 117.
36. Kusmer, p. 40.
37. Ibid., p. 56.
38. *Cleveland Gazette*, April 18, 1905; March 11, 1911. Gerber, p. 260.
39. Kusmer, p. 41.
40. Ibid., Chapter 4.
41. Ibid.
42. Ibid., pp. 70-73.
43. Ibid., pp. 85-89.
44. Ibid., p. 161.
45. Ibid.
46. Ibid., Chapter 6, discusses the shift in ideology in Cleveland. Also see George A. Davis and O. Fred Donaldson, *Blacks in the United States: A Geographic Perspective* (Boston: Houghton Mifflin, 1975), and Gerber, Chapter 12.
47. Davis, *Black Americans*, p. 170.
48. The *Cleveland Journal* appeared in 1903 and was published until 1912. It was owned by three new Cleveland businessmen, Thomas Fleming, Welcome T. Blue, and Naham D. Brascher.

49. Lerone Bennet, Jr., "No Crystal Stair: The Black Woman in History," *Ebony* (August, 1977), pp. 164-170.
50. Alexander Crummell, *Africa and America: Addresses and Discourses* (Springfield, Massachusetts, 1891), p. 82, quoted in Bert James Loewenberg and Ruth Bogin, eds., *Black Women in Nineteenth Century American Life* (University Park, Pennsylvania: Pennsylvania State University Press, 1976), p. 33.
51. Davis, *Black Americans*, p. 56.
52. For detailed discussion on this topic, see Loewenberg and Bogin, pp. 20-24; Gerda Lerner, ed., *Black Women in White America: A Documentary History* (New York: Random House, Vintage Books, 1973), pp. 92-94; and Leon Litwack, *North of Slavery: The Negro in the Free States, 1790-1860* (Chicago: University of Chicago Press, 1961), pp. 113-152.
53. Davis, *Black Americans*, p. 124.
54. Kusmer, p. 25.
55. Gerber, p. 130. Also Helen K. Chesnutt, *Charles Wadell Chesnutt* (Chapel Hill: University of North Carolina Press, 1952), p. 61, and *Social Circle Journal*, XVIII (November, 1886).
56. Kusmer, p. 21.
57. Ibid., p. 19.
58. Ibid., p. 88.
59. Ibid.
60. David Thelen, *The New Citizenship* (Columbia: University of Missouri Press, 1972), pp. 60-65.
61. For discussion of the problems of black women in white women's clubs, see Alfreda Duster, ed., *Crusade for Freedom* (Chicago: University of Chicago Press, 1970); Lerner, pp. 440-458; and Mary Church Terrell, *Colored Woman in a White World* (Washington, D.C.: Associated Publishers, 1940).
62. Loewenberg and Bogin, p. 23.
63. Eleanor Flexnor, *Century of Struggle* (Cambridge: Harvard University Press, 1959), p. 187.
64. Ibid., p. 186.
65. News articles in the *Cleveland Gazette*, January 19, 1895 and March 6, 1897, reflect the attitudes of the community. Also see Kusmer, p. 148, and Davis, *Black Americans*, pp. 192-4.
66. Carrie Williams Clifford, "Cleveland and Its Colored People," *The Colored American*, Vols. 8-9 (1905), pp. 365-380.

CHAPTER TWO

1. August Meier and Elliott Rudwick, *From Plantation to Ghetto*, American Century Series, 3rd ed. (New York: Hill and Wang, 1966), pp. 171-72.
2. Ibid., p. 175.
3. George A. Davis and O. Fred Donaldson, *Blacks in the United States: A Geographic Perspective* (Boston: Houghton Mifflin, 1975), p. 30.

4. Ibid., p. 3.
5. Jane Edna Hunter, *A Nickel and a Prayer* (Cleveland: Elli Kani Publishing Company, 1940).
6. Ibid., p. 13.
7. Ibid., p. 11.
8. Eugene Genovese, *Roll, Jordan, Roll: The World the Slaves Made* (New York: Vintage Books, Random House, 1976), p. 414. Descriptions of the Piedmont area in South Carolina were taken from a taped interview with Richard Long, Ph, D., Atlanta University, for a radio program entitled "Women Themselves," Clemson University, 1981. Although only 5 percent to 9 percent of the slave population was officially listed as "mulatto" in South Carolina in 1860, the Piedmont section near Pendleton was dominated by small plantations and farms where interracial intimacy prevailed in sexual as well as other matters.
9. Hunter, p. 11.
10. According to James Blackwell, *The Black Community: Diversity and Unity* (New York: Dodd, Mead, and Co., 1975), p. 69: ". . . slavery produced a two-fold class system among black Americans: an upper class based almost exclusively upon color and a lower class that consisted primarily of the sons and daughters of field hands."
11. Hunter, p. 13.
12. Ibid., p. 12.
13. Ibid., p. 13.
14. Ibid., p. 15.
15. Ibid., p. 18.
16. For discussion of the slave work ethic, see Genovese, pp. 295-324.
17. John W. Blassingame, "Slave Personality Types," in *The Slave Community* (New York: Oxford University Press, 1972), pp. 184-216.
18. For further review of the historic role and prestige of the elder black woman in slavery and post-Civil War black society, see E. Franklin Frazier, *The Negro in the United States*, rev. and abridged ed. (Chicago: University of Chicago Press, 1948), pp. 114-126.
19. Andrew Billingsley, *Black Families in White America* (Englewood Cliffs, New Jersey: Prentice-Hall, 1968), p. 20.
20. Hunter, p. 24.
21. Ibid., pp. 36, 72. Religious expression, rooted in early family and school experiences, was an important source of strength to Hunter throughout her life. Although she admitted to "disobeying the church's rule" as a young adult, when she participated in card games and dancing, the family tradition of prayer and church attendance was never questioned. Hunter's choices of centers for her religious experiences were based first on family tradition (joining in wherever her family belonged) and later on satisfaction of personal social needs. As a young adult, she described herself as a "summertime revival jiner," who enjoyed the shouting and camaraderie of the summer revival meetings, not pretending to subscribe to any particular religious belief. As a young adult in Cleveland, she sought out the denomination which had supported her education in South Carolina. However, feeling uncomfortable in Cleveland's

all-white Bolton Presbyterian Church, she joined the all-black St. John's AME Church, where she could socialize with other blacks. The Presbyterian denomination finally reclaimed her when an all-black Presbyterian church was formed in Cleveland.

22. Ibid., p. 15.
23. Ibid.
24. Ibid., p. 21.
25. Ibid.
26. Ibid., p. 22.
27. Ibid., p. 28.
28. Ibid., p. 29. It is not clear to whom the neighbors complained about Jane's mistreatment.
29. Ibid.
30. Ibid., p. 30.
31. Ibid., p. 31.
32. Ibid.
33. Ibid., p. 32.
34. Ibid., p. 37.
35. Ibid. The Presbyterian church which controlled the school was pressured to rename the school from Ferguson Academy, named to honor a Northern white benefactor, to include the name of a black. The school was renamed Ferguson-Williams College in honor of the founder, Rev. Williams. Hunter's reference to the school as Ferguson-Williams reflects the change. Interview, May 21, 1982.
36. Booker T. Washington, *Up From Slavery* (New York: Lancer Books, 1968), p. 52.
37. Hunter, p. 39.
38. For discussion of the retrenchment of public funds for educating blacks in the South, see Henry Allen Bullock, *A History of Negro Education in the South* (New York: Praeger, 1970), pp. 60-88.
39. Hunter, p. 43.
40. Ibid.
41. Interview, May 21, 1982.
42. Bullock, p. 166.
43. Gerda Lerner, *Black Women in White America: A Documentary History* (New York: Vintage Books, 1973), pp. 226-228.
44. Hunter, pp. 48-49.
45. Ibid., p. 50.
46. Hunter always listed the academy as part of her educational experience, although she did not mention the school in her autobiography. The name of the institution also appears as Harlem Academy in some of Hunter's personal papers. Information about the school could not be verified.
47. Hunter, p. 50.
48. Ibid.
49. Ibid.
50. Ibid.

51. Ibid., pp. 50-51.
52. Ibid., p. 52.
53. Ibid., p. 53.
54. The school for nurses was organized by Dr. Alonzo C. McClennan in 1896. Lectures began in January, 1897, in a room in the Wallingford School Building. It was soon apparent that the trainees must have clinical experience, and in October, 1897, a hospital building was opened. The nurse's training consisted of instruction under the Squeers School method. Also, nurse trainees were obligated to do most of the maintenance work for the building, as well as menial chores for the patients. The school trained hundreds of nurses from all over the South. It was variously known as the Cannon Street Hospital and Training School and the McClennan-Banks Hospital and Training School, but no official name was ever given to the institution. Hunter, pp. 54-55; interview, May 20, 1982.
55. Hunter, p. 57.
56. Ibid., p. 64.
57. Bullock, p. 32.
58. Hunter, p. 11.
59. Hunter stated that she could recall only one incidence of racial conflict at Woodburn Farm, and the white owner of the plantation took an active role in its resolution. Hunter, pp. 35-36.

CHAPTER THREE

1. August Meier, *Negro Thought in America, 1880-1915* (Ann Arbor: University of Michigan Press, Ann Arbor Paperbacks, 1966), p. 124.
2. Ibid.
3. Ibid., pp. 178-183.
4. Hunter's migration pattern, from plantation to village to larger Southern towns and later to the urban North was very typical for blacks prior to World War I. For a detailed account of black migration, see George A. Davis and O. Fred Donaldson, *Blacks in the United States: A Geographic Perspective* (Boston: Houghton Mifflin, 1975).
5. Jane Edna Hunter, *A Nickel and a Prayer* (Cleveland: Elli Kani Publishing Co., 1940), p. 69.
6. Ibid.
7. Ibid., p. 85.
8. Although the YWCA and YMCA allowed membership and participation to a few among the black middle class, neither organization encouraged use of their downtown facilities. There was an unwritten policy at the Cleveland YWCA which prohibited black boarders. See chapter four and seven of this book.
9. Hunter, p. 86.
10. Ibid., p. 70.
11. Ibid.
12. Ibid.

13. Ibid., pp. 70-71.
14. Ibid., p. 74. Although training was available for black physicians at several area schools, there is only one reference to training for black nurses. Dr. C. L. Mottley established the Cleveland Training School for Colored Nurses in 1898 using his residence for classrooms. The school was incorporated in 1899 as the Bethesda Hospital and Training School for Nurses.
15. U.S. Census Reports, 1900-1920.
16. Kenneth Kusmer, *A Ghetto Takes Shape: Black Cleveland, 1870-1930* (Urbana: University of Illinois Press, 1978), pp. 41-42.
17. Ibid., p. 80. Also, see U.S. Census, 1900-1940; Lerone Bennett, "No Crystal Stair: The Black Woman in History," *Ebony* (August 1977), pp. 164-170; Thomas J. Jones, "Negro Population in the United States," in *The Negro's Progress in Fifty Years* (American Academy of Political and Social Science, 1913); Mary White Ovington, *Half a Man: The Status of the Negro in New York* (New York, 1911).
18. Hunter, p. 85.
19. Kusmer, p. 203.
20. Ibid., pp. 41-42.
21. Ibid., p. 47.
22. Hunter, p. 86.
23. Ibid., p. 87.
24. Ibid., p. 88.
25. Ibid.
26. Ibid.
27. Ibid.
28. Allan H. Spear, *Black Chicago: The Making of a Negro Ghetto, 1890-1920* (Chicago: University of Chicago Press, 1967), p. 102.
29. Gilbert Osofsky, *Harlem: The Making of a Ghetto, Negro New York, 1890-1930* (New York: Harper and Row, Harper Torchbooks, 1963), p. 57.
30. Ibid.
31. Ibid. Also Booker T. Washington Papers, Library of Congress, Box 1.
32. *Cleveland Plain Dealer*, December 31, 1905; *Cleveland Leader*, February 6, 1906. Also, see YWCA Papers, Western Reserve Historical Society, Cleveland, Ohio, hereafter abbreviated as WRHS.
33. Hunter, p. 81.
34. Ibid., p. 83.
35. Ibid.
36. *Cleveland Gazette*, January 12, 1912.
37. *Cleveland Gazette* editorials written by Harry Smith were consistent in this regard throughout his lengthy ownership of the paper.
38. *The Cleveland Journal*, 1903-12.
39. *The Cleveland Gazette*, January 21, 1911.
40. Ibid.
41. Hunter, pp. 90-91.
42. Ibid.
43. Ibid.

44. The most likely group that the author has been able to establish was a group of upper-class women called the Wisteria Club. These women were married to professional and small businessmen, well established in Cleveland. Although the women were not always as well-educated or accomplished as their husbands or fathers, their status was derived from family associations. According to sociologists who have studied stratification in the black community, until at least World War II, status was determined by the convergence of color, family background, and education. For a thorough discussion of class stratification, see James E. Blackwell, *The Black Community* (New York: Dodd, Mead & Co., 1975); David Gerber, *Black Ohio and the Color Line* (Urbana: University of Illinois Press, 1976); W. E. B. Du Bois, *The Philadelphia Negro* (Philadelphia, 1899) ; St. Clair Drake and Horace R. Cayton, *Black Metropolis* (New York: Harcourt, Brace and World, Harbinger Books, 1945). Also, Interview, December 1980.
45. Hunter, p. 91.
46. Ibid.
47. Interview, December 12, 1980.
48. Ibid.
49. *The Cleveland Advocate*, October 26, 1918.
50. Hunter, p. 93. Also, see *The Open Door* Vol. VI, No. 12 (February 1927).
51. Ibid.
52. Hunter, p. 97.
53. Ibid., p. 98.
54. Ibid.
55. Ibid., p. 99. Also, see *The Open Door*, Vol. VII, No. 1 (March 1927).
56. Traditionally, men served as treasurers for women's organizations. Wylie headed the Women's Division of Cleveland Trust Bank.
57. YWCA Papers, WRHS.
58. *The Open Door*, Vol. VII, No. 1.
59. Hunter, p. 99.
60. For a thorough discussion of Washington's philosophy, see Meier and also Rayford Logan, *The Betrayal of the Negro*, rev. ed. (London: Collier-Macmillan, 1970).
61. Hunter, p. 100.
62. YWCA Papers, WRHS.
63. Phillis Wheatley Association Papers, WRHS.
64. Hunter, p. 98. The rival home was named the Colored Working Girls' Christian Home, James Beason, president.
65. *The Open Door*, Vol. VII, No. 2 (April, 1927).
66. Kusmer, p. 151.
67. NAACP Papers, Library of Congress, Box G-157; also, see R. K. Moon Scrapbook, WRHS Manuscript Collection.
68. *Cleveland Gazette*, March 23, 1912.
69. Ibid., February 29, 1913.

CHAPTER FOUR

1. Kenneth Kusmer, *A Ghetto Takes Shape: Black Cleveland, 1870-1930* (Urbana: University of Illinois Press, 1978), p. 160.
2. *Cleveland Gazette*, April 3, 1915—April 10, 1915.
3. George Davis and O. Fred Donaldson, *Blacks in the United States: A Geographic Perspective* (Boston: Houghton Mifflin, 1975), Chapter 4.
4. John B. Abell, "The Negro in Industry," *Trade Winds* (March 22, 1924), pp. 17-20.
5. Kusmer, p. 68.
6. *Cleveland Gazette*, March 15, 1913.
7. Hunter, *A Nickel and a Prayer* (Cleveland: Elli Kani Publishing Co., 1940), p. 105.
8. Ibid.
9. Ibid., pp. 106-108.
10. *The Open Door* (July, 1927).
11. It seems important to note a movement to unionize domestic workers. According to William Ganson Rose, *Cleveland: The Making of a City* (Cleveland, 1950), p. 1913: "In Cleveland the Housemaids Union was growing in strength under leadership of Rose Charvat, its organizer. The union was preparing on June 27, to present a wage scale and a demand for a ten-hour work day, with a threat to blacklist housewives who hired non-union girls." Although no other references to the union could be found, there is a strong possibility that black workers may have been viewed as an alternative to union demands. In 1913, blacks were almost always excluded from unions. For a discussion of unions in Cleveland and their relationship with black workers, see Kusmer, Chapter 4.
12. *Cleveland Gazette*, March 29, 1913.
13. Hunter, p. 93.
14. Jane Olcott Walters, ed., "History of Colored Work," November/December, 1920, YWCA National Board Archives, New York.
15. Jane Edna Hunter, unpublished manuscript, Hunter Papers, Western Reserve Historical Society, Cleveland, Ohio, hereafter referred to as WRHS.
16. Russell Davis, *Black Americans in Cleveland* (Washington, D.C.: Associated Publishers, 1972), p. 260; *Cleveland Gazette*, January 16, 1895; October 30, 1897; January 13, 1900; January 16, 1903; February 28, 1908.
17. The YWCA and YMCA in Cleveland historically worked very closely together. There was no official relationship between the two Associations, but in the years prior to World War I, women's organizations looked to the men for leadership in race matters.
18. Minutes of the Meeting of the Joint Committee PWA/YWCA, March 6, 1922, Phillis Wheatley Association Papers (hereafter referred to as PWA Papers), WRHS.
19. Hunter Papers, WRHS.

20. Ibid. Also, see Minutes of the Meeting of the Board of Trustees, April 11, 1922; March 14, 1922; December 14, 1915; June 13, 1916; September 28, 1916; November 14, 1916; PWA Papers, WRHS.
21. "The YWCA Among Colored Women in Cities," 1915, YWCA National Board Archives.
22. Minutes of the Meeting of the Joint Committee PWA/YWCA, April 11, 1922 and March 14, 1922. PWA Papers, WRHS.
23. Hunter Papers, WRHS.
24. Minutes of the Meeting of the Board of Trustees, June 13, 1916; September 28, 1916; November 14, 1915; PWA Papers, WRHS.
25. The Cleveland YWCA Board of Trustees Minutes are missing from 1913 to 1915.
26. PWA Papers, WRHS.
27. Minutes of the Meeting of the Board of Directors, January 16, 1917, YWCA Papers, WRHS.
28. Hunter, *Nickel*, pp. 110-111.
29. Minutes of the Meeting of the Board of Directors, March 20, 1917, YWCA Papers, WRHS.
30. Minutes of the Meeting of the Board of Trustees, March 14, 1922; April 11, 1922; PWA Papers, WRHS.
31. Minutes of the Meeting of the Joint Committee PWA/YWCA, March 6, 1922, PWA Papers, WRHS.
32. For discussion of Southern black institutions, see Henry Allen Bullock, *A History of Negro Education in the South* (New York: Praeger, 1970), pp. 33, 96-100.
33. Beginning with the appointment of Edith Wright, a graduate of Western Reserve University, Hunter usually had college-trained assistants. However, they were always under her supervision. There was an impression on the part of some of her workers that Hunter was easily intimidated by people better educated than she, therefore requiring that she be in total control of such people. Interviews, December and March, 1980.
34. Walters.
35. Minutes of the Meeting of Membership Captains, September 6, 1921, PWA Papers, WRHS.
36. Minutes of the Meeting of the Board of Trustees, August 26, 1921; November 8, 1921; December 8, 1921; November 19, 1920; PWA Papers, WHRS.
37. *The Open Door* (October 1927); WA Annual Report, 1915, WRHS.
38. Minutes of the Meeting of the Board of Trustees, December 9, 1919, PWA Papers, WRHS.
39. Ibid., February 13, 1917.
40. PWA Annual Report, 1923, PWA Papers, WRHS.
41. *The Open Door* (October 1927); Minutes of the Meeting of the Board of Trustees, March 13, 1917, PWA Papers, WRHS.
42. Hunter, *Nickel*, p. 110.
43. *The Open Door* (September 1927).
44. Hunter Papers, WRHS.

45. Minutes of the Meeting of the Board of Trustees, April 11, 1922; March 14, 1922, PWA Papers, WRHS. Also, see Hunter Papers, WRHS.
46. Minutes of the Meeting of the Joint Committee PWA/YWCA, April 4, 1922, PWA Papers, WRHS.
47. Although an all-black statewide organization, the Ohio Federation for Uplift Among Colored People, Alpha Chapter, was organized six months earlier in July, 1917, it produced little more than discussion and soon became moribund. The local delegate and one of the founders, Nahum Brascher, represented the Cleveland Association of Colored Men, which had begun to sponsor discussions on the Southern influx and its problems. Kusmer, p. 254; *Cleveland Gazette*, March 10 and 17, 1917; July 21, 1917; November 17 and 24, 1917; May 25, 1918.
48. "Accomplishments of the Negro Welfare Association, 1919-1920," Negro Welfare Association Annual Report, 1922, Urban League Papers, WRHS.
49. In 1919, when the Negro Welfare Association board first proposed to turn over the Community House to the YMCA, the board decided to "put off the change until the question of segregation would not loom so large as to prevent success to the movement." Minutes of the Meeting of the Board of Trustees, 1919-21, Urban League Papers, WRHS. Also, see Kusmer, p. 265.
50. Ibid.
51. Hunter, *Nickel*, pp. 68, 123.
52. Ibid., p. 125.
53. Ibid.
54. Kusmer, p. 147.
55. Hunter, *Nickel*, p. 69.
56. Davis, p. 144.
57. Ibid. Carrol Scott, a native Clevelander and a prominent member of St. John's Church ran against Fleming in 1919. He received endorsement of the Cleveland Civic League, which stated that he was "Intelligent and honest and industrious."
58. Hunter, p. 126.
59. Ibid., p. 127.
60. Ibid., p. 129.
61. Ibid., p. 127.
62. Hunter resigned from the Executive Committee in 1937.

CHAPTER FIVE

1. Jane Edna Hunter, *A Nickel and a Prayer* (Cleveland: Elli Kani Publishing Co., 1940), p. 114.
2. Minutes of the Meeting of the Board of Trustees, December 12, 1924, Phillis Wheatley Association Papers (hereafter referred to as PWA Papers), Western Reserve Historical Society, Cleveland, Ohio (hereafter referred to as WRHS).
3. Phillis Wheatley Association Annual Report, 1922, PWA Papers, WRHS. Trustees, April 27, 1920, WHRS.

4. Minutes of the Meeting of the Board of Trustees, April 27, 1920, WRHS.
5. Ibid., December 14, 1920.
6. Ibid., July 10, 1924.
7. Phillis Wheatley Association Internal Report, undated, PWA Papers, Phillis Wheatley Association, Cleveland, Ohio (hereafter referred to as PWA).
8. Ibid.
9. Ibid.
10. *Gazette*, April 27, 1917.
11. Ibid., May 5, 1917.
12. Ibid., February 3, 1917.
13. Kenneth Kusmer, *A Ghetto Takes Shape: Black Cleveland, 1870-1930* (Urbana: University of Illinois Press, 1978), p. 178.
14. Ibid., p. 179.
15. Minutes of the Meeting of the Board of Trustees, February 18, 1924, PWA Papers, WHRS.
16. Ibid., April 5, 1923.
17. Speech by Fannie Pitcairn Frackelton, PWA Papers, PWA.
18. Ibid.
19. Minutes of the Meeting of the Board of Trustees, July 14, 1923, PWA Papers, WRHS.
20. Ibid.
21. Minutes of the Meeting of the Preliminary Gifts Committee, August 1, 1924, PWA Papers, WRHS.
22. PWA Internal Report, undated, PWA Papers, PWA.
23. Ibid.
24. This was evidenced by the opening of a segregated YMCA in 1922, as well as the segregation of most public and semi-public facilities.
25. "Request of Phillis Wheatley Association of Cleveland to the Laura Spellman Rockefeller Foundation," PWA Papers, PWA.
26. Ibid.
27. Ibid.
28. Hunter, p. 116.
29. Ibid.
30. Phillis Wheatley Association Internal Report, undated, PWA Papers, PWA.
31. *The Open Door* (July, 1924).
32. Olson to Robert H. Bishop, Jr., February 4, 1925, PWA Papers, PWA.
33. Ibid.
34. Ibid.
35. Robert H. Bishop, Jr., to Fannie P. Frackelton, January 7, 1925, PWA Papers, PWA.
36. *Cleveland Plain Dealer*, January 29, 1925.
37. NAACP Resolution, January 29, 1925, PWA Papers, PWA.
38. Hunter, p. 116.
39. Ibid., p. 117.
40. Minutes of the Meeting of the Board of Trustees, March 10, 1925, PWA Papers, WRHS.

41. *Cleveland Plain Dealer*, May 1, 1925.
42. Ibid., May 29, 1925.
43. Ibid., September 13, 1925.
44. Ibid.
45. *The Open Door* (February, 1927).
46. Minutes of the Meeting of the Building Committee, May 19, 1925, PWA Papers, WRHS.
47. Ibid.
48. Ibid.
49. Minutes of the Meeting of the Board of Trustees, April 13, 1926, PWA Papers, WRHS.
50. *The Open Door* (July, 1927).
51. Ibid.
52. Ibid., February, 1927.
53. Hunter, p. 118.
54. Ibid., p. 119.
55. Ibid.
56. Hunter, unpublished manuscript, Hunter Papers, WRHS.
57. Mercy Hospital Association, "Does Cleveland Need a Negro Manned Hospital," May, 1927, NAACP Papers, Library of Congress, Washington, D.C. (hereafter referred to as LC).
58. Ibid.
59. Ibid.
60. Ibid.
61. Russell Jelliff to Robert W. Bagnall, May 7, 1926, NAACP Papers, LC.
62. Russell Jelliff to Robert W. Bagnall, May 12, 1926, NAACP Papers, LC.
63. Charles White to Robert W. Bagnall, March 28, 1927, NAACP Papers, LC.
64. Hunter, *Nickel*, p. 72.
65. *Gazette*, September 15, 1917.
66. Minutes of the Meeting of November 13, 1924, the Union Realty Company, PWA Papers, PWA. Members of the Union Realty Company were President J. F. Meeks, Frances Meeks, John S. Hall, Hooker Pages, E. E. Griggs, H. Skinner, Frank Boozer, Anna Towes, and Jane Hunter.
67. *Cleveland Plain Dealer*, January 19, 1971.
68. Although her salary averaged only $3,000 per year for most of her term at the Phillis Wheatley, Hunter left an estate valued at over $400,000 at her death.
69. *The Open Door* (April, 1934).
70. Estella R. Davis to Jane E. Hunter, September 18, 1925, PWA Papers, WRHS.
71. *Cleveland Plain Dealer*, June 19, 1927.
72. Ibid., April 10, 1928.
73. John Hope Franklin, *From Slavery to Freedom: A History of Negro Americans*, 5th ed. (New York: Alfred A. Knopf, Borzoi Books, 1980), p. 381.

CHAPTER SIX

1. Christopher Wye, "Midwest Ghetto: Patterns of Negro Life and Thought in Cleveland, Ohio, 1929-1945" (Ph.D. Dissertation, Kent State University, 1973), p. 30.
2. Ibid., pp. 30-40.
3. Ibid., p. 32.
4. Ibid., p. 43. Such practices as blacks being admitted into movie theaters and then being segregated into a specified area for seating or admitting them into nightclubs and taverns and refusing to serve them were not uncommon, according to Wye.
5. Ibid., p. 44.
6. Charles Chesnutt, "The Negro in Cleveland," *The Clevelander* 5 (November, 1930), p. 24.
7. Wye, p. 49.
8. Ibid.
9. Ibid., pp. 54-55.
10. *Cleveland Gazette*, February 27, 1936; *Cleveland Eagle*, April 17, 1936; and *Cleveland Call and Post*, September 1, 1938.
11. William Franklin Moore, "The Status of the Negro in Cleveland" (Ph.D. Dissertation, Ohio State University, 1953), p. 78.
12. David Gerber, *Ohio and the Color Line* (Urbana: University of Illinois Press, 1976), p. 462; *Gazette*, January 30, and May 15, 1909.
13. The city's Portland Outhwaite Pool and Central Avenue Pool were generally regarded as Negro pools. The Woodland Hills Pool, situated on the fringe of a black neighborhood, was the scene of constant racial strife which, when it opened, erupted into a race riot in 1927. From then until the forties, it was a source of constant concern for black citizens. See Wye, p. 63; Charles White, "Statement of the Activities of the Cleveland Branch for the Year Ending January 6, 1928," NAACP Branch Files, Library of Congress, Washington, D.C. (hereafter referred to as LC).
14. Wye, pp. 50-51.
15. "Central Area Social Study," unpublished report of the Research Committee of the Welfare Federation of Cleveland, Cleveland Public Library, 1944, p. 82; Wye, p. 51; Cleveland Branch Quarterly, October, 1935, NAACP Branch Files, LC.
16. Interview, February 19, 1982.
17. Wye, pp. 110-111.
18. Ibid., p. 114.
19. Ibid.
20. Ibid.
21. Ibid., p. 119.
22. Ibid.
23. Annual Report of the Negro Welfare Association, 1933, Cleveland Urban League Papers, Western Reserve Historical Society, Cleveland, Ohio (hereafter referred to as WRHS).

24. Lucia Johnson Bing, *Social Work in Greater Cleveland* (Cleveland: The Welfare Federation, 1938).
25. Ibid.
26. Wye, p. 127.
27. Ibid., p. 67.
28. Ibid.
29. This list was derived from the NAACP Branch Quarterly, 1935; "Central Area Social Study," Phillis Wheatley Board of Trustees Minutes; and Chesnutt, "The Negro in Cleveland."
30. *The Open Door* (January, 1939).
31. Jane Edna Hunter, unpublished manuscript, Jane E. Hunter Papers, WRHS.
32. Ibid.
33. Ibid.
34. Ibid.
35. Ibid.
36. Ibid.
37. "Reasons Why We Should Vote Against City 5.5 Mills Levy," flier attached to the Minutes of the Meeting of the Board of Trustees, December 15, 1936, Phillis Wheatley Association Papers (hereafter referred to as PWA Papers), WRHS.
38. Ibid., meetings between 1932-1946.
39. Ibid., December 8, 1936.
40. Ibid.
41. Ibid., dated February 9, 1937. This date is apparently incorrect, as the body of the minutes indicates that the meeting was held before December 15, 1936. Also, see Wye, pp. 364-366.
42. Minutes of the Meeting of the Board of Trustees, February 9, 1937, PWA Papers, WRHS.
43. Ibid., May 11, 1937 and June 8, 1937.
44. Ibid., December 8, 1936.
45. Ibid.
46. *Gazette*, October 19, 1926.
47. Ibid., February 10, 1934.
48. Minutes of the Meeting of the Board of Trustees, February 13, 1934, PWA Papers, WRHS.
49. Chairman of Fiscal Advisors to Mrs. Mary T. Gates, March 30, 1934, PWA Papers, WRHS.
50. *The Open Door* (February, 1925).
51. Ibid., July, 1937.
52. Kenneth Kusmer, *A Ghetto Takes Shape: Black Cleveland, 1870-1930* (Urbana: University of Illinois Press, 1978) p. 203.
53. "Story of the Phillis Wheatley," *The Open Door* (July, 1927).
54. Phillis Wheatley Association Annual Report, 1923, PWA Papers, WRHS.
55. *The Open Door* (February, 1925).
56. Jane Edna Hunter, *A Nickel and a Prayer* (Cleveland: Elli Kani Press, 1940), p. 154.

57. Ibid., pp. 135-149.
58. Hunter, unpublished manuscript. In *The Open Door* (February, 1938), Hunter quoted the presumed originator of the "same nationality or race thesis," Dr. Richard Cabot, who said, "a nationality can best be served by a physician of its own race."
59. *The Open Door* (June, 1937). This observation was based on a study made by a committee from the Phillis Wheatley on Unemployed Negro Girls, 1935. Julia Johnson, a Phillis Wheatley staff member, wrote the report.
60. Ibid., January, 1940.
61. Wye, pp. 60-61; *Gazette*, September, 1936 and February 25, 1939.
62. Charles H. Loeb, *The Future Is Yours: The History of the Future Outlook League* (Cleveland: Future Outlook League, 1947). Hunter supported some of the boycott activities of the Future Outlook League in their "Don't Buy Where You Can't Work" campaigns. However, she seemed to emphasize that companies that did not contribute to black charities were the greater offenders. See *The Open Door* (June, 1936).
63. Caroline Bird, *The Invisible Scar* (New York: David McKay, 1966), pp. 278-279.
64. *The Open Door* (April, 1939).
65. According to Wye, p. 124, the actual loss of jobs by blacks to whites was minimal during the depression, especially among the women: "The most expendable item on the budget of middle class white families whose incomes were reduced by the depression was the domestic servant."
66. *The Open Door* (July, 1938).
67. Hunter to Mary McLeod Bethune, April 5, 1933, PWA Papers, Phillis Wheatley Association, Cleveland, Ohio (hereafter referred to as PWA).
68. Minutes of the Meeting of the Board of Trustees, February 16, 1934, PWA Papers, WRHS.
69. PWA Papers, PWA. Also, see Hunter, *Nickel*, p. 119.
70. "Accomplishments of the Phillis Wheatley Association," 1932, PWA Papers, PWA.
71. Hunter, *Nickel*, p. 119.
72. Hunter to Walter McCornack, June 16, 1934, PWA Papers, PWA.
73. Hunter to Maurice Masche, January 8, 1935, PWA Papers, PWA.
74. Hunter to W. E. Carter, April 27, 1934, May 3, 1934, and May 10, 1934, PWA Papers, PWA.
75. There is no further documentation to determine completion of the deal between Hunter and Carter.
76. Announcement of an Open House, December 9, 1934, PWA Papers, PWA.
77. *The Open Door* (January, 1931).
78. Ibid., March, 1940.
79. Ibid., March, 1937.
80. Interview, June, 1980.
81. "Phillis Wheatley Department of National Association of Colored Women," pamphlet, July, 1939, PWA.
82. Ibid.

83. Eugene T. Lies, "The Cleveland Group Work Study," Welfare Federation, 1935, WRHS.
84. Minutes of the Meeting of the Board of Trustees, September 24, 1935, PWA Papers, WRHS.
85. Ibid., October 29, 1935.
86. Hunter was made an honorary member of the organization in 1928.
87. Bethune to Hunter, March 10, 1938, PWA Papers, PWA.
88. Minutes of the Meeting of the Board of Trustees, September 10, 1935, PWA Papers, WRHS. Hunter did not accept the invitation because of pressures from local authorities and possibly board members to concentrate on local problems.
89. Hunter was a member of the Cuyahoga County Republican Executive Committee from 1935 to 1937. She also was an active member of the state Republican Women's Committee and campaigned in Michigan and Ohio for Alf Landon's candidacy for president.
90. Hunter, *Nickel*, p. 178.

CHAPTER SEVEN

1. Richard Kluger, *Simple Justice* (New York: Alfred A. Knopf, 1975), Vol. I, p. 240.
2. Dorothy K. Newman, et. al., *Protest, Politics, and Prosperity: Black Americans and White Institutions, 1940-1975* (New York: Pantheon Books, 1978), p. 45.
3. Ibid.
4. Ibid., p. 14.
5. Ibid., p. 11.
6. Ibid., p. 12.
7. Negro Welfare Association, Minutes of the Meetings of the Board of Trustees, June 7, 1940, Cleveland Urban League Papers, Western Reserve Historical Society (hereafter WRHS), Cleveland, Ohio.
8. Charles Loeb, *The Future Is Yours: The History of the Future Outlook League* (Cleveland: FOL, 1947).
9. Christopher Wye, "Midwest Ghetto: Patterns of Negro Life and Thought in Cleveland, Ohio, 1929-1945" (Ph.D. Dissertation, Kent State University, 1973), p. 95.
10. "Cleveland Branch Quarterly," October, 1935. NAACP Branch Files, Library of Congress (hereafter LC), Washington, D.C.
11. Even though blacks protested segregation in the housing estates, the Outhwaite Extension and Carver Park projects were designated for black families. Pressure from local black politicians resulted in some relocation efforts for displaced families, but limited housing available to blacks simply added to their concentration in already crowded areas.
12. Wye, p. 96.
13. "Central Area Social Study," Welfare Federation, March, 1942—July, 1944, Cleveland Public Library.
14. Wye, p. 104.

15. Interview, July 20, 1982.
16. Ibid.
17. Minutes of the Meeting of the Staff, January 28, 1944, and December 17, 1943, Phillis Wheatley Association Papers (hereafter PWA Papers), Phillis Wheatley Association (hereafter PWA), Cleveland, Ohio.
18. "Annual Report of the Cleveland Urban League, 1942," Cleveland Urban League Papers, WRHS.
19. Ibid.
20. *The Call and Post*, January 3, 1942.
21. *The Open Door* (October, 1941).
22. Ibid.
23. "NYA and OSY Defense Training Supplementary Report, July 1, 1941-June 30, 1942," Department of Vocational Education, 1942, Cleveland Public Schools, pp. 9 and 14.
24. *Call and Post*, January 9, 1943.
25. Ibid.
26. "Annual Report of the Urban League of Cleveland, 1944," Cleveland Urban League Papers, WRHS.
27. Wye, p. 161.
28. Ibid., p. 162.
29. "The Negro in Cleveland: 1950-1963," Cleveland Urban League, June, 1964, p. 5.
30. Wye, p. 273.
31. Ibid., p. 222.
32. *Call and Post*, September 28, 1940.
33. Ibid., May 16, 1942.
34. *Cleveland Press*, June 24, 1942.
35. Virginia Esch to Mrs. Judson L. Stewart, July 26, 1940, YWCA Papers, WRHS. The YWCA National Convention voted a statement of resolution in 1938 which encouraged associations to serve women and girls without regard to race or creed or national origin.
36. Mrs. Judson L. Stewart to Virginia Esch, August 1, 1940, YWCA Papers, WRHS.
37. Minutes of the Meeting of the Board of Trustees, September 17, 1940, YWCA Papers, WRHS.
38. Ibid.
39. Minutes of the Meeting of the Interracial Committee, September 25, 1946, YWCA Papers, WRHS.
40. Minutes of the Meeting of the Board of Trustees, October 15, 1940, YWCA Papers, WRHS.
41. Ibid., June 16, 1942.
42. Minutes of the Meeting of the Board of Trustees, Attendance Sheet for 1944, YWCA Papers, WRHS.
43. Ibid., attendance sheet for 1945; *The Open Door* (February, 1945).
44. *The Open Door* (June, 1944).
45. Ibid., September, 1944.

46. Ibid., November, 1943.
47. For example, the Music School always had male students enrolled. The Association also held adult education classes for men as well as women. The Phillis Wheatley Building also allowed the use of designated residence space for men and women attending conventions, because of the discrimination in Cleveland hotels.
48. Hunter to Mr. F. C. Fulton, December 12, 1945, PWA Papers, WRHS.
49. *The Open Door* (June, 1944).
50. Hunter to Nannie Burroughs, December 22, 1942, Nannie Burroughs Papers, LC, MSS Department.
51. *The Open Door* (January, 1944 and July, 1943).
52. Ibid.
53. Ibid., January, 1945.
54. Minutes of the Meeting of the Board of Trustees, October 8, 1946, PWA Papers, WRHS.
55. Ibid.
56. *The Open Door* (January, 1945).
57. Mrs. Frank M. Barry to Mr. Herman Neff, December 11, 1945, PWA Papers, WRHS.
58. Minutes of the Meeting of the Board of Trustees, October 8, 1946, PWA Papers, WRHS.
59. Perhaps the best indication of the kinds of buildings which were considered adequate for the Central Area would be the school buildings in the area. With the exception of the newly built Central High School, schools were of turn of the century vintage and citizens often complained that they were poorly maintained. Interviews, July 20, 1982, and December, 1980.
60. Minutes of the Meeting of the Board of Trustees, December 17, 1946, YWCA Papers, WRHS.
61. Interview, July 12, 1982.
62. Minutes of the Meeting of the Board of Trustees, October 14, 1947, PWA Papers, WRHS.
63. Jane Edna Hunter Papers, WRHS.
64. *The Open Door* (December, 1943).
65. Ibid.
66. Ibid., July, 1945.
67. Ibid., June, 1944.
68. For examples of Hunter's continuing emphasis on "uplift," see *The Open Door* (December, 1943) and Hunter to Nathaniel Howard, December 26, 1945, PWA Papers, WRHS.
69. Interview, May, 1980.
70. *The Open Door* (November, 1945).
71. Minutes of the Meeting of the Board of Trustees, October 14, 1947, PWA Papers, WRHS.
72. Ibid. The letter of resignation is not on file, but board discussions revealed Hunter's requests.
73. Ibid.

74. Ibid.
75. Ibid.
76. Eugene T. Lies, "The Cleveland Group Work Study," Welfare Federation, 1935, WRHS.
77. Ibid.
78. For examples, see Mrs. Frank M. Barry to Herman Neff, December 11, 1945, and Minutes of the Meeting of the Board of Trustees, October 9, 1945, PWA Papers, WRHS. The Welfare Federation adopted a statement for Interracial and Intercultural Relations in 1946 which recommended board appointments and services in all social agencies which would encourage participation by all racial and cultural groups.
79. *The Open Door* (March, 1946); Hunter to Dr. William Edward Stevenson, November 21, 1947, PWA Papers, WRHS.
80. Minutes of the Meeting of the Board of Trustees, March 9, 1948, PWA Papers, WRHS.
81. Louis Evans to Phillis Wheatley Association Board of Trustees, November 18, 1947, PWA Papers, WRHS.
82. Minutes of the Meeting of the Board of Trustees, December 14, 1948, PWA Papers, WRHS.
83. For example, see Minutes of the PWA Board of Trustees, February 12, 1946, PWA papers, WRHS. At the meeting, a white nominee for board presidency was challenged from the floor by the nomination of a black.
84. Hunter to Bertha Bailey, February 14, 1948, PWA Papers, WRHS.
85. *Call and Post*, May 7, 1949.
86. Ibid.
87. Hunter to Nannie Burroughs, July 14, 1952, Nannie Burroughs Papers, LC, MSS Department.
88. Ibid., July 7, 1955
89. Hunter to Henrietta Wright, May 7, 1955; Wright to Hunter, May 15, 1955; PWA Papers, WRHS.
90. *Cleveland Plain Dealer*, August 10, 1960.
91. Ibid., January 19, 1971.
92. Ibid.
93. "Last Will and Testament of Jane Edna Hunter," Hunter Papers, WRHS.
94. Ibid.
95. *Cleveland News*, May 10, 1955.
96. Hunter Papers, WRHS.

Bibliography

BOOKS

Baker, Ray Stannard. *Following the Color Line: American Negro Citizenship in the Progressive Era*, reprint ed. New York: Doubleday, Page and Company, 1964.

Bardolph, Richard. *The Negro Vanguard*. New York: Rinehart and Company, 1959.

Berry, Mary Frances, and John W. Blassingame. *Long Memory: The Black Experience in America*. New York: Oxford University Press, 1982.

Billingsley, Andrew. *Black Families in White America*. Englewood Cliffs, New Jersey: Prentice-Hall, 1968.

Bing, Lucia Johnson. *Social Work in Greater Cleveland*. Cleveland: Welfare Federation of Cleveland, 1938.

Bird, Caroline. *The Invisible Scar*. New York: David McKay Company, 1966.

Blackwell, James. *The Black Community: Diversity and Unity*. New York: Dodd, Mead and Company, 1975.

Blassingame, John W. *The Slave Community: Plantation Life in the Antebellum South*. New York: Oxford University Press, 1972.

Bond, Horace Mann. *Education of the Negro in the American Social Order*. New York: Prentice Hall, 1934.

Boorstin, Daniel. *The Americans: The National Experience*. New York: Random House, 1965.

Brisbane, Robert. *Black Activism: Racial Revolution in the United States, 1954-1970*. Valley Forge: Judson Press, 1974.

———. *The Black Vanguard: Origins of the Negro Social Revolution, 1900-1960*. Valley Forge: Judson Press, 1970.

Brown, Hallie Q. *Homespun Heroines and Other Women of Distinction*. Xenia, Ohio: Aldine Press, 1892.

Bullock, Henry Allen. *A History of Negro Education in the South: From 1619 to the Present*. New York: Praeger Publishers, 1967.

Campbell, Thomas F. *Daniel E. Morgan, 1877-1949: The Good Citizen in Politics*. Cleveland: Case Western Reserve University Press, 1975.

Chatterjee, Pranab. *Local Leadership in Black Communities: Organizational and Electoral Developments in Cleveland in the Nineteen Sixties*. Cleveland: Case Western Reserve University Press, 1975.

Chesnutt, Helen K. *Charles Waddell Chesnutt*. Chapel Hill: University of North Carolina Press, 1952.

Clark, Kenneth. *Dark Ghetto: Dilemmas of Social Power*. New York: Harper and Row, 1965.

Condon, George E. *Cleveland: Prodigy of the Western Reserve*. Tulsa, Oklahoma: Continental Heritage Press, 1979.

Cone, James. *God of the Oppressed*. New York: The Seabury Press, 1975.

Cooper, Anna Julia. *A Voice from the South, By a Black Woman of the South*. Xenia, Ohio: Aldine Press, 1892.

Cott, Nancy F., ed. *Root of Bitterness: Documents of the Social History of American Women*. New York: E. P. Dutton & Company, 1972.

Cox, Oliver C. *Caste, Class and Race: A Study in Social Dynamics*. New York: Doubleday, 1947.

Cruse, Harold. *The Crisis of the Negro Intellectual*. New York: William Morrow & Company, 1967.

Daniel, Sadie Iola. *Women Builders*. Washington, D.C.: Associated Publishers, 1931.

Davis, Allen F. *Spearheads for Reform: The Social Settlements and the Progressive Movement, 1890-1914*. New York: Oxford University Press, 1967.

Davis, Allison and John Dollard. *Children of Bondage: The Personality Development of Negro Youth in the Urban South*. Washington: American Council on Education, 1940.

———, Burleigh Gardner, and Mary B. Gardner. *Deep South: A Social Anthropological Study of Caste and Class*. Chicago: University of Chicago Press, 1941.

Davis, David Brion. *The Problem of Slavery in Western Culture*. Ithaca: Cornell University Press, 1966.

Davis, George A, and O. Fred Donaldson. *Blacks in the United States: A Geographic Perspective*. Boston: Houghton Mifflin, 1975.

Davis, Russell A. *Black Americans in Cleveland: From George Peake to Carl B. Stokes, 1796-1969*. Washington, D.C: Associated Publishers, 1972.

DeNevi, Donald P., and Doris A. Holmes. *Racism at the Turn of the Century: Documentary Perspectives, 1870-1910*. San Rafael, California: Leswing Press, 1973.

Dollard, John. *Caste and Class in a Southern Town*. New York: Doubleday, 1937.

Drake, St. Clair, and Horace Cayton. *Black Metropolis: A Study of Negro Life in a Northern City*, Vols. I and II. New York: Harcourt, Brace and World, 1945.

Du Bois, William E. B. *Dusk of Dawn: An Essay Toward an Autobiography of a Race Concept*. New York: Harcourt, Brace and Company, 1940.

———. *The Philadelphia Negro: A Social Study*. New York: Schocken Books, 1967.

———. *The Souls of Black Folk*. Greenwich, Connecticut: Fawcett Publications, 1961.

Duster, Alfrea M. *Crusade for Justice: The Autobiography of Ida B. Wells*. Chicago: University of Chicago Press, 1970.

Flexner, Eleanor. *Century of Struggle: The Woman's Rights Movement in the United States*. New York: Atheneum, 1959.

Foner, Phillip, ed. *The Voice of Black America*, Vols. I and II. New York: Capricorn Books, 1972.

Franklin, John Hope. *From Slavery to Freedom: A History of Negro Americans*, 5th ed. New York: Alfred A. Knopf, Borzoi Books, 1980.

———. *Reconstruction After the Civil War*. Chicago: University of Chicago Press, 1961.

——— and Isidore Starr. *The Negro in the 20th Century America: A Reader on the Struggle for Civil Rights*. New York: Random House, 1967.

Frazier, E. Franklin. *Black Bourgeoisie: The Rise of a New Middle Class In the United States*. New York: The Free Press, 1957.

———. *The Negro Church in America*. New York: The Free Press, 1964.

———. *The Negro Family in the United States*. Chicago: University of Chicago Press, 1939.

Fredrickson, George M. *The Black Image in the White Mind: Debate on Afro-American Character and Destiny, 1817-1914*. New York: Harper & Row, 1971.

Garraty, John. *The Barber and the Historian: The Correspondence of George A. Myers and James Ford Rhodes, 1910-1923*. Columbus: Ohio Historical Society, 1956.

Genovese, Eugene. *Roll Jordan Roll: The World the Slaves Made*. New York: Random House, 1972.

Gerber, David A. *Black Ohio and the Color Line, 1860-1915*. Urbana: University of Illinois Press, 1976.

Graham, Otis L. *An Encore for Reform: The Old Progressives and the New Deal*. New York: Oxford University Press, 1967.

Green, John P. *Fact Stranger Than Fiction: Seventy-Five Years of a Busy Life With Remembrances of Many Great and Good Men and Women*. Cleveland: Riehl Printing Company, 1920.

Gutman, Herbert. *The Black Family in Slavery and Freedom, 1750-1925*. New York: Pantheon Books, 1976.

Hackley, Mrs. E. Azalia. *The Colored Girl Beautiful*. Hicksville, New York: Exposition Press, 1916.

Harlan, Louis. *Booker T. Washington: The Making of a Black Leader, 1856-1901*. London: Oxford University Press, 1972.

Harris, William. *Keeping the Faith: A. Phillip Randolph and the Brotherhood of Sleeping Car Porters, 1925-1937*. Urbana: University of Illinois Press, 1977.

Herskovits, Melville J. *The Myth of the Negro Past*. Boston: Beacon Press, 1941.

Hickok, Charles T. *The Negro in Ohio, 1802-1870*. Cleveland: Francis G. Butler Publication Fund, 1896.

Hill, Robert B. *The Strength of Black Families*. New York: Emerson Hall Publishing, 1971.

The History of Women's Suffrage and the League of Women Voters in Cuyahoga County, 1911-1945. Cleveland: William Feather Company, 1949.

Huggins, Nathan. *Harlem Renaissance*. London: Oxford University Press, 1971.

Hughes, Langston. *The Big Sea: An Autobiography*. New York: Hill & Wang, 1940.

Hunter, Jane Edna. *A Nickel and a Prayer: An Autobiography*. Cleveland: Elli Kani Press, 1940.

Jenners, Mary. *Twelve Negro Americans*. New York: Friendship Press, 1936.

Johnson, Charles S. *Backgrounds to Patterns of Negro Segregation*. New York: Thomas Y. Crowell Company, 1943.

———. *Shadows of the Plantation*. Chicago: University of Chicago Press, 1934.

Johnson, James Weldon. *Black Manhattan*. New York: Alfred A. Knopf, 1930.

———. *Negro Americans: What Now?* New York: Viking Press, 1934.

Kennedy, Louise Venable. *The Negro Peasant Turns Cityward: Effects of Recent Migrations to Northern Centers*. New York: Columbia University Press, 1930.

Kletzing, H. F., and W. H. Crogman. *Progress of a Race, or the Remarkable Advancement of the Afro-American*. Atlanta: J. L. Nichols, 1897.

Kluger, Richard. *Simple Justice*, Vols. I and II. New York: Alfred A. Knopf, 1975.

Kolko, Gabriel. *The Triumph of Conservatism: A Reinterpretation of American History, 1900-1916*. New York: The Free Press, 1977.

Kusmer, Kenneth L. *A Ghetto Takes Shape: Black Cleveland, 1870-1930*. Urbana: University of Illinois Press, 1978.

Lasch, Christopher, ed. *The Social Thought of Jane Addams*. Indianapolis: Bobbs-Merrill Company, 1965.

Leech, Margaret. *In the Days of McKinley*. New York: Harper Brothers, 1959.

Lerner, Gerda, ed. *Black Women in White America: A Documentary History*. New York: Random House, 1972.

———. *The Majority Finds Its Past: Placing Women in History*. New York: Oxford University Press, 1979.

Levine, Lawrence W. *Black Culture and Black Consciousness*. Oxford: Oxford University Press, 1977.

Lincoln, C. Eric. *The Black Experience in Religion*. Garden City, New York: Doubleday, 1974.

Litwack, Leon. *North of Slavery: The Negro in the Free States, 1790-1860*. Chicago: University of Chicago Press, 1961.

Locke, Alain. *The New Negro: An Interpretation*. New York: Albert and Charles Boni, 1925.

Loeb, Charles H. *The Future Is Yours: The History of the Future Outlook League, 1935-1946*. Cleveland: Future Outlook League, 1947.

Loewenberg, Bert James, and Ruth Bogin. *Black Women in Nineteenth-Century American Life: Their Words, Their Thoughts, Their Feelings*. University Park: Pennsylvania State University Press, 1976.

Logan, Rayford. *The Betrayal of the Negro*, rev. ed. (London: Collier-Macmillan, 1970); originally published as *The Negro in American Life and Thought: The Nadir, 1877-1901* (New York: Macmillan, 1954).

———. *The Negro in the United States*. Princeton: C. Van Nostrand Company, 1957.

Lubove, Roy. *The Progressives and the Slums: Tenement House Reform in New York City, 1890-1917*. Pittsburgh: University of Pittsburgh Press, 1963.

Marx, Gary T. *Protest and Prejudice*. New York: Harper & Row, 1969.

Mays, Benjamin E. and Joseph W. Nicholson. *The Negro's Church*. New York: n.p., 1933.

Meier, August. *Black Protest Thought in the Twentieth Century*. Indianapolis: Bobbs-Merrill Company, 1965.

———. *Negro Thought in America, 1880-1915: Racial Ideologies in the Age of Booker T. Washington*. Ann Arbor: University of Michigan Press, 1966.

———, and Elliott Rudwick. *From Plantation to Ghetto*. New York: Hill & Wang, 1966.

Meltzer, Milton. *In Their Own Words: A History of the American Negro, 1865-1916*. Englewood Cliffs, New Jersey: Prentice-Hall, 1970.

Muraskin, William Alan. *Middle-Class Blacks in a White Society: Prince Hall Freemasonry in America*. Berkeley: University of California Press, 1975.

Myrdal, Gunnar, et. al. *An American Dilemma: The Negro Problem and Modern Democracy*, Vols. I and II. New York: Random House, 1941.

National Association of Colored Women. *Book of Honor*. n.p., n.d.

Newman, Dorothy, et. al. *Protest, Politics, and Prosperity: Black Americans and White Institutions, 1940-1975*. New York: Pantheon Books, 1978.

Nye, Russell Blaine. *Midwestern Progressive Politics: A Historical Study of Its Origins and Development, 1870-1950*. East Lansing: Michigan State College Press, 1951.

Osofsky, Gilbert. *Harlem: The Making of a Ghetto: Negro New York, 1890-1930*, 2nd ed. New York: Harper & Row, 1963.

———. ed. *Puttin On Ole Massa: The Slave Narratives of Henry Bibb, William Wells Brown, and Solomon Northup*. New York: Harper & Row, 1969.

Ottley, Roi. *New World A-Comin'*. Boston: Houghton Mifflin, 1943.

Ovington, Mary White. *Half a Man: The Status of the Negro in New York*. New York: Negro Universities Press, 1969. Reprint from 1911 edition.

Petry, Ann. *The Street*. New York: Houghton Mifflin, 1946.

Quillin, Frank U. *The Color Line in Ohio: A History of Race Prejudice In a Typical Northern State*. Ann Arbor: George Wahr, 1913.

Rawick, George. *The American Slave: A Composite Autobiography*, Vol. 1 of *From Sunup to Sundown: The Making of the Black Community*. Westport, Connecticut: Greenwood Publishing Company, 1972.

Reid, Ira DeA. *The Negro Immigrant: His Background, Characteristics and Social Adjustment, 1899-1937*. New York: Oxford University Press, 1939.

Reimers, David M. *White Protestantism and the Negro*. New York: Oxford University Press, 1965.

Richings, G. F. *Evidence of Progress Among Colored People*. Philadelphia: Ferguson, 1909.

Rose, William Ganson. *Cleveland: The Making of a City*. Cleveland: The World Publishing Company, 1950.

Selby, John. *Beyond Civil Rights*. Cleveland: The World Publishing Company, 1966.

Sheppard, Gladys Byrum. *Mary Church Terrell: Respectable Person*. Baltimore: Human Relations Press, 1959.

Siebert, Wilbur Henry. *The Mysteries of Ohio's Underground Railroads*. Columbus: Long's College Book Company, 1951.

Sitkoff, Harvard. *The Depression Decade*, Vol. I in *A New Deal for Blacks: The Emergence of Civil Rights as a National Issue*. Oxford: Oxford University Press, 1978.

Sochen, June, ed. *The Black Man and the American Dream: Negro Aspirations in America, 1900-1930*. Chicago: Quadrangle Books, 1971.

Stampp, Kenneth. *The Era of Reconstruction, 1865-1877*. New York: Random House, 1965.

Staples, Robert, ed. *The Black Family: Essays and Studies*. Belmont, California: Wadsworth Publishing Company, 1971.

———. *The Black Woman: Sex, Marriage, and the Family*. Chicago: Nelson-Hall, 1973.

Steinfield, Melvin. *Our Racist Presidents: From Washington to Nixon*. San Ramon, California: Consensus Publishing Company, 1972.

Sternsher, Bernard, ed. *The Negro in Depression and War: Prelude to Revolution, 1930-1945*. Chicago: Quadrangle Books, 1969.

Sussman, Marvin B., and R. Clyde White. *Hough: A Study of Cleveland's Social Life and Change*. Cleveland: Case Western Reserve University Press, 1959.

Terrell, Mary Church. *Colored Woman in a White World*. Washington, D.C.: Associated Publishing Company, 1940.

Thelen, David. *The New Citizenship*. Columbia: University of Missouri Press, 1972.

Thompson, Daniel C. *The Negro Leadership Class*. Englewood Cliffs, New Jersey: Prentice-Hall, 1963.

Thornborough, Emma Lou. *T. Thomas Fortune*. Chicago: University of Chicago Press, 1972.

Twombly, Robert C., ed. *Blacks in White America Since 1865: Issues and Interpretations*. New York: David McKay Company, 1971.

Walker, Margaret. *Jubilee*. Boston: Houghton Mifflin, 1966.

Warner, Hoyt Landon. *Progressivism in Ohio, 1897-1917*. Columbus: Ohio State University Press, 1964.

Washington, Booker T. *The Future of the American Negro*. New York: Negro University Press, 1969.

———. *The Story of the Negro*. New York: n.p., 1909.

———. *Up From Slavery*. New York: Lancer Books, 1968.

———. et. al. *The Negro Problem*. New York: Arno Press, 1969.

Washington, Joseph. *Black Religion: The Negro and Christianity in the United States*. Boston: Beacon Press, 1964.

Wiebe, Robert. *The Search for Order: 1877-1920*. New York: Hill & Wang, 1967.

Wolseley, Roland E. *The Black Press, U.S.A.: A Detailed and Understanding Report on What the Black Press Is and How It Came to Be*. Iowa State University Press, 1971.

Woodson, Carter. *A Century of Negro Migration*. Washington, D.C.: Associated Publishing Company, 1918.

———. *The History of the Negro Church*. Washington, D.C.: Associated Publishing Company, 1945.

———. *The Mis-Education of the Negro*. Washington, D.C.: Associated Publishing Company, 1933.

———. *The Negro Professional Man and His Community*. Washington: Associated Publishing Company, 1934.

Woodward, C. Vann, *The Strange Career of Jim Crow*. Oxford: Oxford University Press, 1955.

BIBLIOGRAPHIES

Dannett, Sylvia G. L. *Profiles of Negro Womanhood*, Vol. I, *1619-1900*; Vol. II, *Twentieth Century*. New York: Educational Heritage, Inc., 1966.

Davis, Lenwood. *Black Women in the Cities, 1872-1972: Bibliography of Published Works on the Life and Achievements of Black Women in the Cities of the United States*. Monticello, Illinois: Council of Planning Librarians, 1972.

————. *The Black Woman in American Society: A Selected Annotated Bibliography*. Boston: G. K. Hall, 1975.

Fisher, Edith Maureen. *Focusing on Afro-American Research*, Ethnic Studies Publication #1. San Diego: University of California Press, 1975.

Indiana University. *The Black Family and the Black Woman: A Bibliography*. Bloomington: Indiana University Press, 1972.

McPherson, James, et. al. *Blacks in America: Bibliographical Essays*. Garden City, New York: Doubleday, 1971.

Miller, Elizabeth W. *The Negro in America: A Bibliography*. Cambridge: Harvard University Press, 1966.

Williams, Ora. *American Black Women in the Arts and Social Sciences: A Bibliographical Survey*. Metuchen, New Jersey: Scarecrow Press, 1978.

ARTICLES

Abell, John B. "The Negro in Industry." *Trade Winds*, March 22, 1924, pp. 17-20.

Anderson, Mary. "The Plight of Negro Domestic Labor." *Journal of Negro Education* 5 (January 1936) : 66-72.

Aptheker, Bettina. "W. E. B. Du Bois and the Struggle for Women's Rights: 1910-1920." *San Jose Studies* 1 (May 1975) : 7-16.

Aptheker, Herbert. "The Negro College Student in the 1920s—Years of Preparation and Protest: An Introduction." *Science and Society* 33 (1969): 150-167.

Bennett, Lerone. "No Crystal Stair: The Black Woman in History." *Ebony*, August 1977, pp. 164-170.

Blauvelt, Mary Taylor. "The Race Problem as Described by Negro Women." *American Journal of Sociology* 6 (March 1901) : 662-672.

Bloom, R., et al. "Race and Social Class as Separate Factors Related to Social Environment." *American Journal of Sociology* 70 (January 1965): 471-476.

Blue, John J. "Patterns of Racial Stratification, A Categoric Typology." *Phylon* 20 (Winter 1959): 364-371.

Bowles, Eva D. "Opportunities for Educated Colored Women." *Opportunity* 1 (March 1923) : 15-19.

Boyer, Sallie C. "Visit with Ethel Hedgeman Lyle: Founder of AKA." *The Brown American*, November 1941, pp. 18-19.

Bunche, Ralph. "A Critical Analysis of the Tactics and Programs of Minority Groups." *Journal of Negro Education* 4 (July 1935): 308-320.

Burroughs, Nannie. "Not Color But Character." *Voice of the Negro*, July 1904, p. 277.

Chaffee, Mary Law. "W. E. B. Du Bois' Concept of the Racial Problem in the United States." *Journal of Negro History* 41 (1956) : 241-258.

Chesnutt, Charles. "The Negro in Cleveland." *The Clevelander*, November 1930, pp. 24-27.

Clark, Kenneth. "Morale of the Negro on the Homefront: WWI and WWII." *Journal of Negro Education* 12 (Summer 1943) : 417-428.

Clifford, Carrie Williams. "Cleveland and Its Colored People." *Colored American*, Vols. 8-9, 1905, pp. 365-380.

Conway, Jill. "Women Reformers and American Culture, 1870-1930." *Journal of Social History* 5 (Winter 1971-72): 164-177.

Cuban, Larry. "A Strategy for Racial Peace: Negro Leadership in Cleveland, 1900-1919." *Phylon* 28 (Fall 1967): 300-311.

Dalfuime, Richard M. "The Forgotten Years of the Negro Revolution." *Journal of American History* 55 (1968): 90-106.

Davidson, William. "Our Negro Aristocracy." *Saturday Evening Post*, January 13, 1962, pp. 9-16.

Davis, Ralph N. "The Negro Newspapers and the War." *Sociology and Social Research* 27 (May-June 1943): 373-380.

Du Bois, W. E. B. "Jim Crow." *Crisis* 17 (January 1919): 112-113.

Frazier, E. Franklin. "Occupational Classes Among Negroes in Cities." *American Journal of Sociology* 35 (March 1930) : 718-738.

Fuller, Hoyt W. "The Myth of the New Negro." *Southwest Review* 48 (1963) : 353-357.

Glenn, Norval D. "Negro Prestige Criteria: A Case Study in the Basis of Prestige." *American Journal of Sociology* 68 (November 1963): 645-657.

——. "The Role of White Resistance and Facilitation in the Negro Struggle for Equality." *Phylon* 26 (1965): 105-116.

Goldin, Claudia. "Female Labor Force Participation: The Origins of Black and White Differences, 1870-1880." *Journal of Economic History* 37 (March 1977): 87-112.

Graham, Edward K. "The Hampton Institute Strike of 1927: A Case Study in Student Protest." *American Scholar* 38 (1969) : 668-684.

Graham, Jones D. "Negro Protest in America, 1900-1955: A Bibliographical Guide." *South Atlantic Quarterly* 67 (1968): 94-107.

Gregor, A. James. "Black Nationalism." *Science and Society* 27 (Fall 1963): 415-432.

Gullattee, Alyce C. "Psychiatric Factors to Consider in Research on the Black Woman." *Journal of Afro-American Issues* 2 (Summer 1974): 199-203.

Haynes, Elizabeth Ross. "Negroes in Domestic Service in the U.S." *Journal of Negro History* 8 (October 1923): 384-389.

——. "Two Million Negro Women at Work." *Southern Workman* 51 (February 1922) : 64-72.

Haynes, George Edmond. "Negro Migration: Its Effect on Family and Community Life in the North." *Opportunity* 2 (September-October 1924): 271-274.

Hill, M. C., and T. D. Ackiss. "Social Classes, a Frame of Reference for the Study of Negro Society." *Social Forces* 22 (October 1943): 92-93.

Hill, Ruth Edmonds. "This Little Light of Mine." *Radcliffe Quarterly* (December 1980): 15-18.

Hundley, Mary S. "The National Association of Colored Women." *Opportunity* 3 (June 1925) : 185.

Hunton, Addie. "Negro Womanhood Defended." *Voice of the Negro*, July 1904, pp. 180-182.

Irele, Abiola. "Negritude or Black Cultural Nationalism." *Journal of Modern African Studies* 3 (1965): 321-348.

Jackson, J. "A Partial Bibliography on or Related to Black Women." *Journal of Social and Behavioral Sciences* 21 (1975): 90-135.

Johnson, Charles S. "Social Philosophy of Booker T. Washington." *Opportunity* 6 (April 1928): 102.

Johnson, Guy B. "Some Factors in the Development of Negro Social Institutions in the U.S." *American Journal of Sociology* 30 (November 1934): 329-337.

Jones, Anna H. "A Century's Progress of the American Colored Woman." *Voice of the Negro*, September 1905, pp. 631-633.

———. "The American Colored Woman." *Voice of the Negro*, October 1905, pp. 692-694.

Jones, Thomas J. "Negro Population in the United States." *American Academy of Political and Social Sciences*, 1913.

Kellor, Frances A. "Opportunities for Southern Negro Women in Northern Cities." *Voice of the Negro*, July 1905, pp. 470-473.

———. "Southern Colored Girls in the North." *Charities* 18 (March 1905).

Kilson, Marion. "Black Women in the Professions, 1890-1970." *Monthly Labor Review* 100 (May 1977): 38-41.

King, Charles E. "The Process of Social Stratification Among Urban Southern Minority Populations." *Social Forces* 31 (May 1953) : 352-355.

Lasch, Christopher. "Selfish Women: The Campaign to Save the American Family, 1890-1920." *Columbia Forum* 4 (September 1975) : 24-31.

Lefall, Delores, and Janet L. Sims. "Mary M. Bethune: The Educator—Also Including a Selected Annotated Bibliography," *Journal of Negro Education* 45 (Summer 1976): 342-359.

Leonard, Edward A. "Nonviolence and Violence in American Racial Protests, 1942-1967." *Rocky Mountain Social Science Journal* 6 (1969): 10-22.

Lerner, Gerda. "Early Community Work of Black Club Women." *Journal of Negro History* 59 (April 1974): 158-167.

McCoy, Donald R., and Richard T. Ruetten. "The Civil Rights Movement: 1940-1954." *Midwest Quarterly* 11 (1967): 11-34.

Matthews, Victoria E. "Dangers Encountered by Southern Girls in Northern Cities." *Hampton Negro Conference Proceedings*, July 1898.

Meier, August. "Class Structure and Ideology in the Age of Booker T. Washington." *Phylon* 23 (Fall 1962): 258.

———. "Negro Protest Movements and Organizations." *Journal of Negro Education* 32 (1963): 437-450.

———, and Elliott Rudwick. "How CORE Began." *Social Science Quarterly* 49 (1969): 789-799.

Morsell, John A. "Black Nationalism." *Journal of Intergroup Relations* 3 (Winter 1961-62): 5-11.

Murray, Anne E. "The Negro Woman." *Southern Workman* 33 (April 1904): 232-234.

Palmer, R. Roderick. "The Negro's Quest for Freedom and the Good Life." *Journal of Negro Education* 34 (1965): 11-16.

Peiser, Andrew. "The Education of Women: A Historical View." *Social Studies* 67 (March-April 1976) : 69-72.

Porter, Dorothy. "The Organized Educational Activities of Negro Literary Societies, 1826-1846." *Journal of Negro Education* 5 (October 1936): 555-576.

Record, Wilson. "American Racial Ideologies and Organizations in Transition." *Phylon* 26 (1965): 315-329.

———. "Negro Intellectual Leadership in the NAACP: 1910-1940." *Phylon* 17 (1956): 375-389.

———."Negro Intellectuals and Negro Movements in Historical Perspective." *American Quarterly* 8 (Spring 1956): 3-20.

Rudwick, Elliott M. "The Niagara Movement." *Journal of Negro History* 42 (1957): 177-200.

———. "W. E. B. Du Bois and the Universal Races Congress of 1911." *Phylon* 20 (1959) : 372-378.

Sayre, Helen B. "Negro Women in Industry." *Opportunity* 2 (August 1924): 242-244.

Schmelz, Annie M. "A Presbyterian Conference for Colored Women." *Southern Workman* 54 (September 1925): 416.

Shover, Michele. "Roles and Images of Women in WWI Propaganda." *Politics and Society* 5 (1975): 469-486.

Silone-Yates, Josephine. "The National Association of Colored Women." *Voice of the Negro*, July 1904, pp. 283-287.

Silverstone, Rosalie. "Office Work for Women: An Historical Review." *Business History* 18 (January 1976): 98-110.

Slowe, Lucy D. "Higher Education for Negro Women." *Journal of Negro Education* 2 (July 1933) : 352-358.

Sorkin, Alan L. "On the Occupational Status of Women, 1870-1970." *American Journal of Economics and Sociology* 32 (July 1973) : 235-244.

Terrell, Mary Church. "The Progress of Colored Women." *Voice of the Negro*, July 1904, pp. 291-294.

Thurston, Helen M. "The 1802 Constitutional Convention and the Status of the Negro." *Ohio History* 81 (Winter 1972): 15-37.

Tillman, Katherine D. "Paying Professions for Colored Girls." *Voice of the Negro*, January/February, 1907.

Tinker, Irene. "Nationalism in a Plural Society: The Case of the American Negro." *Western Political Quarterly* 19 (1966): 112-122.

179

Tuttle, William M. "Views of a Negro During the Red Summer of 1919, A Document." *Journal of Negro History* 51 (1966): 209-218.

Washington, Margaret M. "Social Improvement of the Plantation Woman." *Voice of the Negro*, July 1904, pp. 288-290.

Welden, Daniel, ed. "The Problem of Color in the Twentieth Century: A Memorial to W. E. B. Du Bois." *Journal of Human Relations* 14 (1966): 2-179.

Williams, Fannie B. "Colored Women of Chicago." *Southern Workman* 43 (October 1914) : 564-566.

———. "The Woman's Part in a Man's Business." *Voice of the Negro*, December 1904, p. 544.

Wolfe, Alles R. "Women, Consumerism, and the National Consumer's League in the Progressive Era, 1900-1923." *Labor History* 16 (Summer 1975): 378-392.

Yellin, Jean F. "Du Bois Crisis and Woman's Suffrage." *The Massachusetts Review* 13 (Spring 1973) : 365-375.

NEWSPAPERS

Cleveland Advocate, 1914-1923.

Cleveland Call and Post, 1928-1971.

Cleveland Eagle, 1935-1936.

Cleveland Gazette, 1892-1941.

Cleveland Journal, 1903-1910.

Cleveland Plain Dealer, 1850-1971.

Cleveland Press, 1930-1971.

Cleveland News, 1915-1950.

UNPUBLISHED SOURCES

General

Caplan, Eleanor K. "Non-White Residential Patterns: An Analysis of Changes in the Non-White Residential Pattern in Cleveland, Ohio, from 1910 to 1959." Cleveland Community Relations Board.

Esgar, Mildred. "A History of the Cleveland YWCA." Young Women's Christian Association, Cleveland Metropolitan Board.

Fleming, Thomas Wallace. "My Rise and Persecution." Western Reserve Historical Society, circa 1930. (Typewritten.)

Lies, Eugene T. "The Cleveland Group Work Study." Welfare Federation, Western Reserve Historical Society, July 1935.

Lowry, H. J. "Vocational Opportunities for Negroes in Cleveland." National Youth Administration, Cleveland Department of Vocational Education, 1938.

Mercy Hospital Association. "Does Cleveland Need a Negro Manned Hospital?" NAACP Branch Files, Library of Congress, Washington, D.C., May 1927.

National Youth Administration. "N.Y.A. and O.S.Y. Defense Training Supplementary Report, July 1, 1941-June 30, 1942." Department of Vocational Education, Cleveland Public Schools.

Ohio Federation of Colored Women. "The Queen's Garden." Monthly newsletter.

Phillis Wheatley Association. *The Open Door.* Monthly newsletter. Phillis Wheatley Association, Cleveland, Ohio.

The Social Circle. *The Social Circle Journal.* Western Reserve Historical Society, November, 1886.

Urban League. "The Negro in Cleveland: 1950-1963." Western Reserve Historical Society.

Walters, Jane Olcott. "The Work of Colored Women." Young Women's Christian Association, National Board, 1919.

Welfare Federation. "Central Area Social Study." Cleveland Public Library, 1944.

White Rose Industrial Association. "The Annual Report." Schomburg Collection. New York Public Library.

Young Women's Christian Association. "The YWCA Work Among Colored Women in Cities." YWCA National Board, 1915.

Theses and Dissertations

Fishel, Leslie H. "The North and the Negro, 1865-1900." Unpublished Ph.D. Dissertation, Harvard University, 1954.

Giffin, William Wayne. "The Negro in Ohio, 1914-1939." Unpublished Ph.D. Dissertation, Ohio State University, 1968.

Goliber, Thomas J. "Cuyahoga Blacks: A Social and Demographic Study." Unpublished Master's Thesis, Kent State University, 1972.

Hamilton, Tulia. "The National Association of Colored Women, 1896-1920." Unpublished Ph.D. Dissertation, Emery University, 1978.

Moore, William F. "Status of the Negro in Cleveland." Unpublished Ph.D. Dissertation, Ohio State University, 1953.

Wye, Christopher G. "Midwest Ghetto: Patterns of Negro Life and Thought in Cleveland, Ohio, 1929-1945." Unpublished Ph.D. Dissertation, Kent State University, 1973.

Manuscript Collections

Myrtle Johnson Bell Papers. Western Reserve Historical Society, Cleveland, Ohio.

Nannie Burroughs Papers. Library of Congress, Washington, D.C.

Charles Waddell Chesnutt Papers. Western Reserve Historical Society, Cleveland, Ohio.

Cleveland Urban League Papers. Western Reserve Historical Society, Cleveland, Ohio.

Federation for Community Planning Papers. Western Reserve Historical Society, Cleveland, Ohio.

Lethia Fleming Papers. Western Reserve Historical Society, Cleveland, Ohio.

Thomas Fleming Papers. Western Reserve Historical Society, Cleveland, Ohio.

Charles H. Garvin Papers. Western Reserve Historical Society, Cleveland, Ohio.

John P. Green Papers. Western Reserve Historical Society, Cleveland, Ohio.

Jane Edna Hunter Papers. Western Reserve Historical Society, Cleveland, Ohio.

Wade O. McKinney Papers. Western Reserve Historical Society, Cleveland, Ohio.

L. Pearl Mitchell Papers. Western Reserve Historical Society, Cleveland, Ohio.

Rodney K. Moon Family Papers. Western Reserve Historical Society, Cleveland, Ohio.

George Myers Papers. Ohio Historical Society, Columbus, Ohio.

National Association for the Advancement of Colored People Branch Files. Library of Congress, Washington, D.C.

Booker T. Washington Papers. Library of Congress, Washington, D.C.

Phillis Wheatley Association Papers. Western Reserve Historical Society, Cleveland, Ohio.

Phillis Wheatley Association Papers. Phillis Wheatley Association, Cleveland, Ohio.

Young Women's Christian Association of Cleveland Papers. Western Reserve Historical Society, Cleveland, Ohio.

Young Women's Christian Association. National Board Archives, New York, New York.

Miscellaneous

Clemson University Tape, Radio Program, "Women Themselves." Clemson, South Carolina, 1981.

Interviews

Louise Evans
Bea Wright Fox
Zelma George
Olive Hackney
Lolette Hanserd
Rowena Jelliffe
Mrs. T. B. Jones
Tommie Patty
Ella Mae Sharpe
Janet Smith
Lockwood Thompson
Carrie Turner

The interviews are in the possession of the author and are referred to by date only in the footnotes to maintain confidentiality.

Index

Black Women in United States History: A Guide to the Series

PUBLISHER'S NOTE

The sixteen volumes in this set contain 248 articles, in addition to five monographs. This *Guide to the Series* is designed to help the reader find *every* substantive discussion of a topic of interest in the articles. Included in the subject index are general topics such as education and family life, as well as individuals to whom articles are devoted. Geographical locations are included when they are an important part of the article. Professions are also included. Thus, one can look up Fannie Lou Hamer (three articles), Kansas (two articles), or nursing (four articles). The more than 200 authors represented in the index to authors are a who's who of contemporary scholarship.

For topics in the five monographs and for specific discussions in the articles, please see the comprehensive indexes for every title. The more than 10,000 entries in these indexes make this series a virtual encyclopedia of black women's history.

Contents of the Series

Volumes 1-4, continued

Volumes 1-4, continued

Vols. 5-8. **BLACK WOMEN IN AMERICAN HISTORY: THE TWENTIETH CENTURY**, Edited with a Preface by Darlene Clark Hine

Volumes 5-8, continued

5. Blackwelder, Julia Kirk. *Women in the Work Force: Atlanta, New Orleans, and San Antonio, 1930 to 1940.*
6. Brady, Marilyn Dell. *Kansas Federation of Colored Women's Clubs, 1900-1930.*
7. Brady, Marilyn Dell. *Organizing Afro-American Girls' Clubs in Kansas in the 1920's.*
8. Breen, William J. *Black Women and the Great War: Mobilization and Reform in the South.*
9. Brooks, Evelyn. *Religion, Politics, and Gender: The Leadership of Nannie Helen Burroughs.*
10. Brown, Elsa Barkley. *Womanist Consciousness: Maggie Lena Walker and the Independent Order of Saint Luke.*
11. Bryan, Violet H. *Frances Joseph-Gaudet: Black Philanthropist.*
12. Cantarow, Ellen and Susan Gushee O'Malley. *Ella Baker: Organizing for Civil Rights.*
13. Carby, Hazel V. *It Jus Be's Dat Way Sometime: The Sexual Politics of Women's Blues.*
14. Chateauvert, Melinda. *The Third Step: Anna Julia Cooper and Black Education in the District of Columbia, 1910-1960.*
15. Clark-Lewis, Elizabeth. *'This Work Had a End:' African-American Domestic Workers in Washington, D.C., 1910-1940.*
16. Coleman, Willi. *Black Women and Segregated Public Transportation: Ninety Years of Resistance.*
17. Ergood, Bruce. *The Female Protection and the Sun Light: Two Contemporary Negro Mutual Aid Societies.*
18. Farley, Ena L. *Caring and Sharing Since World War I: The League of Women for Community Service—A Black Volunteer Organization in Boston.*
19. Feinman, Clarice. *An Afro-American Experience: The Women in New York City's Jail.*
20. Ferguson, Earline Rae. *The Women's Improvement Club of Indianapolis: Black Women Pioneers in Tuberculosis Work, 1903-1938.*
21. Ford, Beverly O. *Case Studies of Black Female Heads of Households in the Welfare System: Socialization and Survival.*
22. Gilkes, Cheryl Townsend. *'Together and in Harness': Women's Traditions in the Sanctified Church.*
23. Gilkes, Cheryl Townsend. *Going Up for the Oppressed: The Career Mobility of Black Women Community Workers.*
24. Gilkes, Cheryl Townsend. *Successful Rebellious Professionals: The Black Woman's Professional Identity and Community Commitment.*
25. Gunn, Arthur C. *The Struggle of Virginia Proctor Powell Florence.*
26. Guzman, Jessie P. *The Social Contributions of the Negro Woman Since 1940.*
27. Harley, Sharon. *Beyond the Classroom: Organizational Lives of Black Female Educators in the District of Columbia, 1890-1930.*
28. Harley, Sharon. *Black Women in a Southern City: Washington, D.C., 1890-1920.*
29. Haynes, Elizabeth Ross. *Negroes in Domestic Service in the United States.*
30. Helmbold, Lois Rita. *Beyond the Family Economy: Black and White Working-Class Women during the Great Depression.*
31. Hine, Darlene Clark. *The Ethel Johns Report: Black Women in the Nursing Profession, 1925.*
32. Hine, Darlene Clark. *From Hospital to College: Black Nurse Leaders and the Rise of Collegiate Nursing Schools.*
33. Hine, Darlene Clark. *Mabel K. Staupers and the Integration of Black Nurses into the Armed Forces.*
34. Hine, Darlene Clark. *The Call That Never Came: Black Women Nurses and World War I, An Historical Note.*

Volumes 5-8, continued

Vol. 11. Daughters of Sorrow: Attitudes Toward Black Women, 1880-1920, by Beverly Guy-Sheftall

Vol. 12. Jane Edna Hunter: A Case Study of Black Leadership, 1910-1950, by Adrienne Lash Jones; Preface by Darlene Clark Hine

Vol. 13. Quest for Equality: The Life and Writings of Mary Eliza Church Terrell, 1863-1954, by Beverly Washington Jones
including Mary Church Terrell's selected essays:

1. *Announcement* [of NACW].
2. *First Presidential Address to the National Association of Colored Women.*
3. *The Duty of the National Association of Colored Women to the Race.*
4. *What Role is the Educated Negro Woman to Play in the Uplifting of Her Race?*
5. *Graduates and Former Students of Washington Colored High School.*
6. *Lynching from a Negro's Point of View.*
7. *The Progress of Colored Women.*
8. *The International Congress of Women.*
9. *Samuel Coleridge-Taylor.*
10. *Service Which Should Be Rendered The South.*
11. *The Mission of Meddlers.*
12. *Paul Laurence Dunbar.*
13. *Susan B. Anthony.*
14. *A Plea for the White South By A Colored Woman.*
15. *Peonage in United States: The Convict Lease System and Chain Gangs.*
16. *The Disbanding of the Colored Soldier.*
17. *What it Means to be Colored in the Capital of the United States.*
18. *A Sketch of Mingo Saunders.*
19. *An Interview with W.T. Stead on the Race Problem.*
20. *The Justice of Woman Suffrage.*
21. *Phyllis Wheatley, An African Genius.*
22. *The History of the Club Women's Movement.*
23. *Needed: Women Lawyers.*
24. *Sara W. Brown.*
25. *I Remember Frederick Douglass.*

Vol. 14. **To Better Our World: Black Women in Organized Reform, 1890-1920,** by Dorothy Salem

Vol. 15. **Ida B. Wells-Barnett: An Exploratory Study of an American Black Woman, 1893-1930,** by Mildred Thompson

including Ida B. Wells-Barnett's Selected Essays

1. *Afro-Americans and Africa.*
2. *Lynch Law in All Its Phases.*
3. *The Reason Why the Colored American is not in the World's Columbian Exposition.* Chapter IV. *Lynch Law,* by Ida B. Wells Chapter VI. *The Reason Why,* by F.L. Barnett
4. *Two Christmas Days: A Holiday Story.*
5. *Lynch Law in America.*
6. *The Negro's Case in Equity.*
7. *Lynching and the Excuse for It.*
8. *Booker T. Washington and His Critics.*
9. *Lynching, Our National Crime.*
10. *How Enfranchisement Stops Lynchings.*
11. *Our Country's Lynching Record.*

Vol. 16. **Women in the Civil Rights Movement: Trailblazers and Torchbearers, 1941-1965**

Edited by Vicki Crawford, Jacqueline A. Rouse, Barbara Woods; Associate Editors: Broadus Butler, Marymal Dryden, and Melissa Walker

1. Black, Allida. *A Reluctant but Persistent Warrior: Eleanor Roosevelt and the Early Civil Rights Movement*
2. Brock, Annette K. *Gloria Richardson and the Cambridge Movement*
3. Burks, Mary Fair. *Trailblazers: Women in the Montgomery Bus Boycott.*
4. Cochrane, Sharlene Voogd. *'And the Pressure Never Let Up': Black Women, White Women, and the Boston YWCA, 1918-1948.*
5. Crawford, Vicki. *Beyond the Human Self: Grassroots Activists in the Mississippi Civil Rights Movement.*
6. Grant, Jacquelyn. *Civil Rights Women: A Source for Doing Womanist Theology.*
7. Knotts, Alice G. *Methodist Women Integrate Schools and Housing, 1952-1959.*
8. Langston, Donna. *The Women of Highlander.*
9. Locke, Mamie E. *Is This America: Fannie Lou Hamer and the Mississippi Freedom Democratic Party.*
10. McFadden, Grace Jordan. *Septima Clark.*
11. Mueller, Carol. *Ella Baker and the Origins of 'Participatory Democracy.'*
12. Myrick-Harris, Clarissa. *Behind the Scenes: Doris Derby, Denise Nicholas, and the Free Southern Theater.*
13. Oldendorf, Sandra. *The South Carolina Sea Island Citizenship Schools.*
14. Payne, Charles. *Men Led, But Women Organized: Movement Participation of Women in the Mississippi Delta.*
15. Reagon, Bernice Johnson. *Women as Culture Carriers in the Civil Rights Movement: Fannie Lou Hamer.*
16. Standley, Anne. *The Role of Black Women in the Civil Rights Movement.*
17. Woods, Barbara. Modjeska Simkins and the South Carolina Conference of the NAACP.

Author Index

Boldface indicates volume numbers and roman
indicates article numbers within volumes.

Subject Index

Boldface indicates volume numbers and roman indicates article numbers within volumes.